ASPEN P

EVIDENCE

5TH EDITION

NEIL C. BLOND

Fourth Edition Revised by

Professor Joel Wm. Friedman

Jack M. Gordon Professor of Procedural
Law & Jurisdiction
Tulane University Law School

Law & Business

AUSTIN   BOSTON   CHICAGO   NEW YORK   THE NETHERLANDS

To contact Customer Care, e-mail customer.care@aspenpublishers.com, call 1-800-234-1660, fax 1-800-901-9075, or mail correspondence to:

Aspen Publishers
Attn: Order Department
PO Box 990
Frederick, MD 21705

Printed in the United States of America.
1 2 3 4 5 6 7 8 9 0

ISBN 978-0-7355-8616-1

About Wolters Kluwer Law & Business

Wolters Kluwer Law & Business is a leading provider of research information and workflow solutions in key specialty areas. The strengths of the individual brands of Aspen Publishers, CCH, Kluwer Law International and Loislaw are aligned within Wolters Kluwer Law & Business to provide comprehensive, in-depth solutions and expert-authored content for the legal, professional and education markets.

CCH was founded in 1913 and has served more than four generations of business professionals and their clients. The CCH products in the Wolters Kluwer Law & Business group are highly regarded electronic and print resources for legal, securities, antitrust and trade regulation, government contracting, banking, pension, payroll, employment and labor, and healthcare reimbursement and compliance professionals.

Aspen Publishers is a leading information provider for attorneys, business professionals and law students. Written by preeminent authorities, Aspen products offer analytical and practical information in a range of specialty practice areas from securities law and intellectual property to mergers and acquisitions and pension/benefits. Aspen's trusted legal education resources provide professors and students with high-quality, up-to-date and effective resources for successful instruction and study in all areas of the law.

Kluwer Law International supplies the global business community with comprehensive English-language international legal information. Legal practitioners, corporate counsel and business executives around the world rely on the Kluwer Law International journals, loose-leafs, books and electronic products for authoritative information in many areas of international legal practice.

Loislaw is a premier provider of digitized legal content to small law firm practitioners of various specializations. Loislaw provides attorneys with the ability to quickly and efficiently find the necessary legal information they need, when and where they need it, by facilitating access to primary law as well as state-specific law, records, forms and treatises.

Wolters Kluwer Law & Business, a unit of Wolters Kluwer, is headquartered in New York and Riverwoods, Illinois. Wolters Kluwer is a leading multinational publisher and information services company.

Check Out These Other Great Titles:

BLOND'S LAW GUIDES

Comprehensive, Yet Concise . . . JUST RIGHT!

Each Blond's Law Guide book contains: Black Letter Law Outline · EasyFlow™ Charts · Case Clips · Mnemonics

Available titles in this series include:

Blond's Civil Procedure

Blond's Constitutional Law

Blond's Contracts

Blond's Criminal Law

Blond's Criminal Procedure

Blond's Evidence

Blond's Property

Blond's Torts

Law school is very different from your previous educational experiences. In the past, course material was presented in a straightforward manner both in lectures and texts. You did well by memorizing and regurgitating. In law school, your fat casebooks are stuffed with material, most of which will be useless when finals arrive. Your professors ask a lot of questions but don't seem to be teaching you either the law or how to think. Sifting through voluminous material seeking out the important concepts is a hard, time-consuming chore. We've done that job for you. This book will help you study effectively. We hope to teach you the law and how to think.

Preparing for Class

Most students start their first year by reading and briefing all their cases. They spend too much time copying unimportant details. After finals they realize they wasted time on facts that were useless on the exam.

Case Clips

Case Clips help you focus on what your professor wants you to get out of your cases. Facts, Issues, and Rules are carefully and succinctly stated. Left out are details irrelevant to what you need to learn from the case. In general, we skip procedural matters in lower courts. We don't care which party is the appellant or petitioner because the trivia is not relevant to the law. Case Clips should be read before you read the actual case. You will have a good idea what to look for in the case, and appreciate the significance of what you are reading. Inevitably you will not have time to read all your cases before class. Case Clips allow you to prepare for class in about five minutes. You will be able to follow the discussion and listen without fear of being called upon.

"Should I read all the cases even if they aren't from my casebook?"

Yes, if you feel you have the time. Most major cases from other texts will be covered at least as a note case in your book. The principles of these cases are universal and the fact patterns should help your understanding. The Case Clips are written in a way that should provide a tremendous amount of understanding in a relatively short period of time.

EasyFlow™ Charts

A very common complaint among law students is that they "can't put it all together." When you are reading 400 pages a week it is difficult to remember how the last case relates to the first and how November's readings relate to September's. It's hard to understand the relationship between different torts topics when you have read cases for three or four other classes in between. Our EasyFlow™ Charts will help you put the whole course together. They are designed to help you memorize fundamentals. They reinforce your learning by showing you the material from another perspective.

Outlines

More than 100 lawyers and law students were interviewed as part of the development of this series. Most complained that their casebooks did not teach them the law and were far too voluminous to be useful before an exam. They also told us that the commercial outlines they purchased were excellent when used as hornbooks to explain the law, but were too wordy and redundant to be effective during the weeks before finals. Few students can read four 500-page outlines during the last month of classes. It is virtually impossible to memorize that much material and even harder to decide what is important. Almost every student interviewed said he or she studied from homemade outlines. We've written the outline you should use to study.

"But writing my own outline will be a learning experience."

True, but unfortunately many students spend so much time outlining they don't leave time to learn and memorize. Many students told us they spent six weeks outlining, and only one day studying before each final!

Mnemonics

Most law students spend too much time reading, and not enough time memorizing. Mnemonics are included to help you organize your essays and spot issues. They highlight what is important and which areas deserve your time.

EASYFLOW™ CHARTS

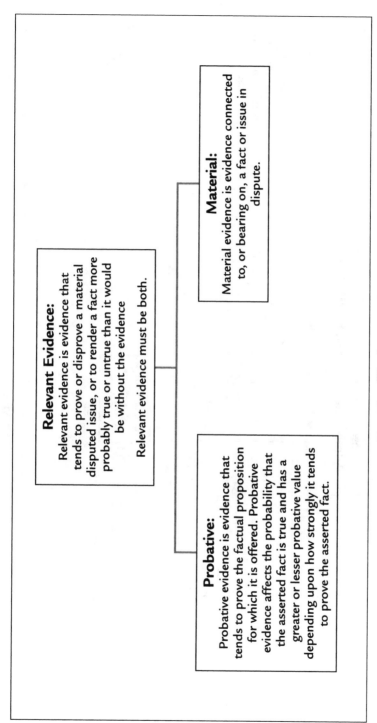

Relevant Evidence:

Relevant evidence is evidence that tends to prove or disprove a material disputed issue, or to render a fact more probably true or untrue than it would be without the evidence

Relevant evidence must be both.

Material:

Material evidence is evidence connected to, or bearing on, a fact or issue in dispute.

Probative:

Probative evidence is evidence that tends to prove the factual proposition for which it is offered. Probative evidence affects the probability that the asserted fact is true and has a greater or lesser probative value depending upon how strongly it tends to prove the asserted fact.

EasyFlow™ Chart 3.1

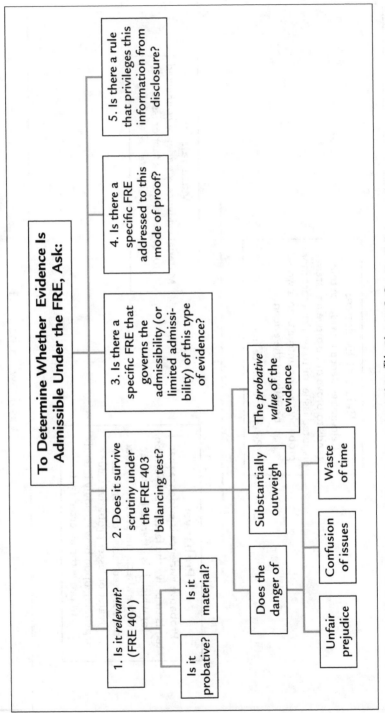

EasyFlow™ Chart 3.2

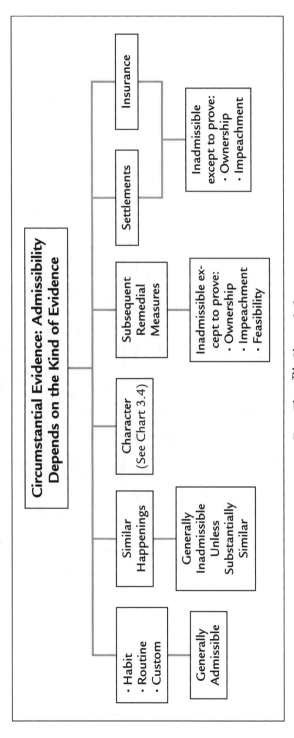

Circumstantial Evidence: Admissibility Depends on the Kind of Evidence

- Habit
- Routine
- Custom

Generally Admissible

Similar Happenings

Generally Inadmissible Unless Substantially Similar

Character (See Chart 3.4)

Subsequent Remedial Measures

Inadmissible except to prove:
- Ownership
- Impeachment
- Feasibility

Settlements

Insurance

Inadmissible except to prove:
- Ownership
- Impeachment

EasyFlow™ Chart 3.3

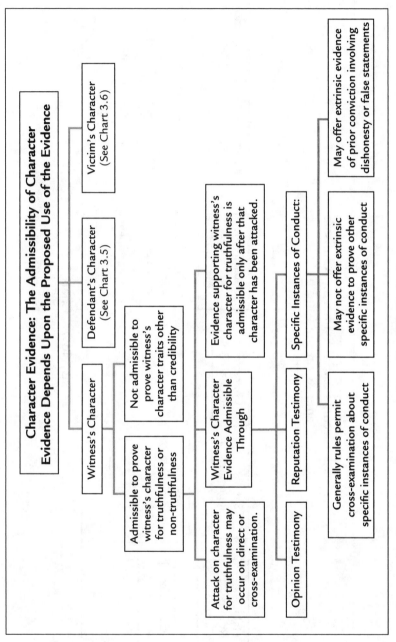

Character Evidence: The Admissibility of Character Evidence Depends Upon the Proposed Use of the Evidence

Witness's Character

Defendant's Character (See Chart 3.5)

Victim's Character (See Chart 3.6)

Admissible to prove witness's character for truthfulness or non-truthfulness

Not admissible to prove witness's character traits other than credibility

Attack on character for truthfulness may occur on direct or cross-examination.

Witness's Character Evidence Admissible Through

Evidence supporting witness's character for truthfulness is admissible only after that character has been attacked.

Opinion Testimony

Reputation Testimony

Specific Instances of Conduct:

Generally rules permit cross-examination about specific instances of conduct

May not offer extrinsic evidence to prove other specific instances of conduct

May offer extrinsic evidence of prior conviction involving dishonesty or false statements

EasyFlow™ Chart 3.4

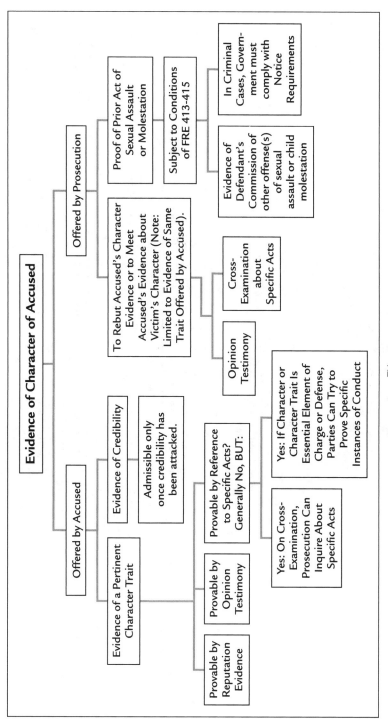

Evidence of Character of Accused

Offered by Accused
- Evidence of a Pertinent Character Trait
  - Provable by Reputation Evidence
  - Provable by Opinion Testimony
  - Provable by Reference to Specific Acts? Generally No, BUT:
    - Yes: On Cross-Examination, Prosecution Can Inquire About Specific Acts
    - Yes: If Character or Character Trait Is Essential Element of Charge or Defense, Parties Can Try to Prove Specific Instances of Conduct
- Evidence of Credibility
  - Admissible only once credibility has been attacked.

Offered by Prosecution
- To Rebut Accused's Character Evidence or to Meet Accused's Evidence about Victim's Character (Note: Limited to Evidence of Same Trait Offered by Accused).
  - Opinion Testimony
  - Cross-Examination about Specific Acts
- Proof of Prior Act of Sexual Assault or Molestation
  - Subject to Conditions of FRE 413-415
    - Evidence of Defendant's Commission of other offense(s) of sexual assault or child molestation
    - In Criminal Cases, Government must comply with Notice Requirements

EasyFlow™ Chart 3.5

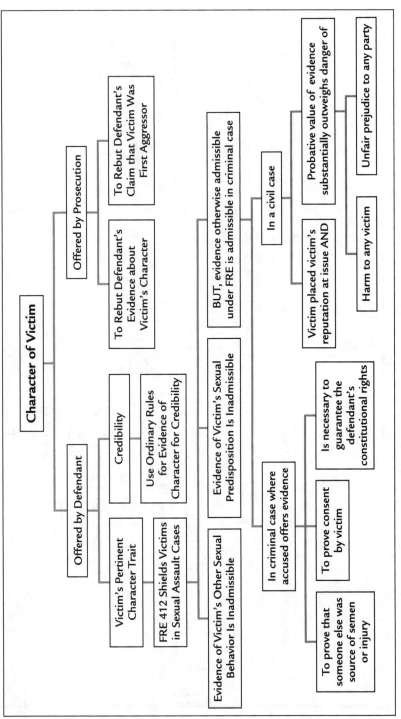

EasyFlow™ Chart 3.6

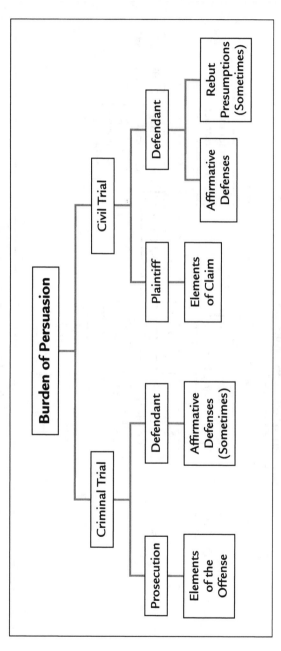

EasyFlow™ Chart 4.1

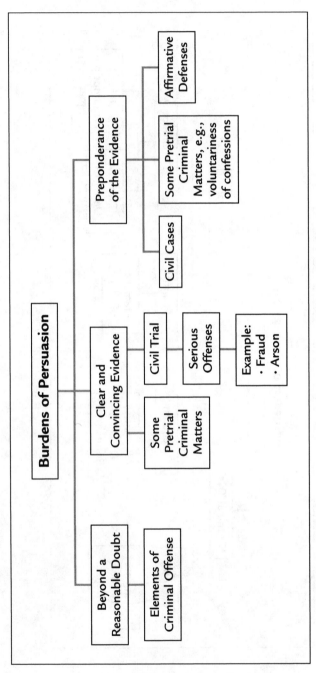

EasyFlow™ Chart 4.2

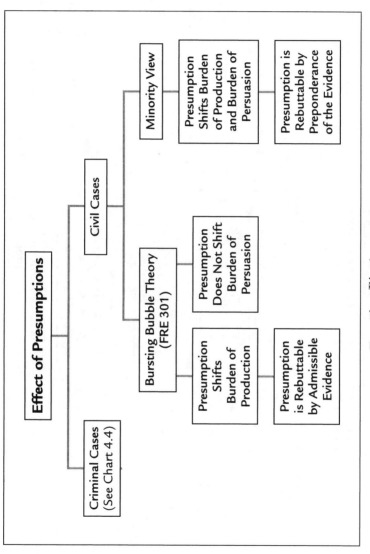

EasyFlow™ Chart 4.3

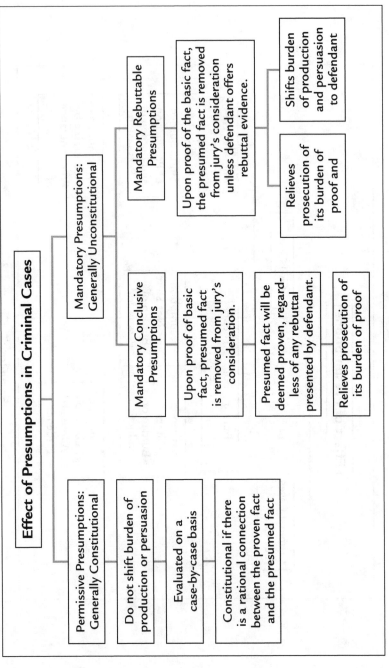

Effect of Presumptions in Criminal Cases

Permissive Presumptions: Generally Constitutional

- Do not shift burden of production or persuasion
- Evaluated on a case-by-case basis
- Constitutional if there is a rational connection between the proven fact and the presumed fact

Mandatory Presumptions: Generally Unconstitutional

Mandatory Conclusive Presumptions

- Upon proof of basic fact, presumed fact is removed from jury's consideration.
- Presumed fact will be deemed proven, regardless of any rebuttal presented by defendant.
- Relieves prosecution of its burden of proof

Mandatory Rebuttable Presumptions

- Upon proof of the basic fact, the presumed fact is removed from jury's consideration unless defendant offers rebuttal evidence.
- Relieves prosecution of its burden of proof and
- Shifts burden of production and persuasion to defendant

EasyFlow™ Chart 4.4

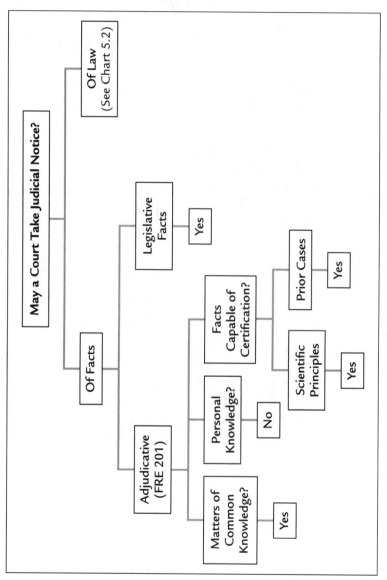

EasyFlow™ Chart 5.1

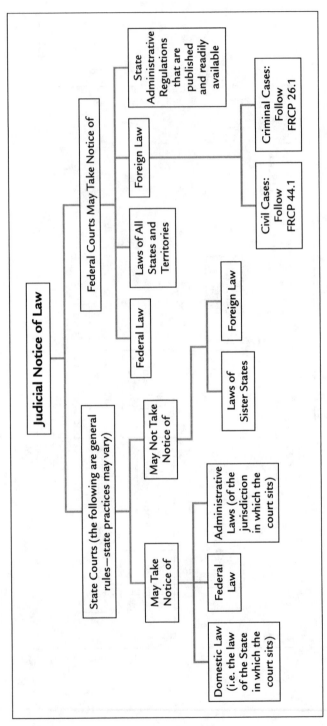

EasyFlow™ Chart 5.2

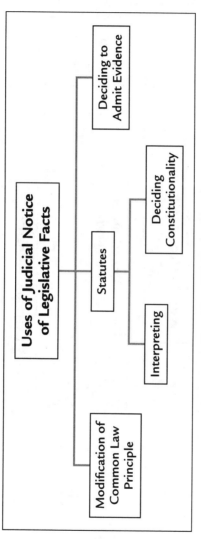

EasyFlow™ Chart 5.3

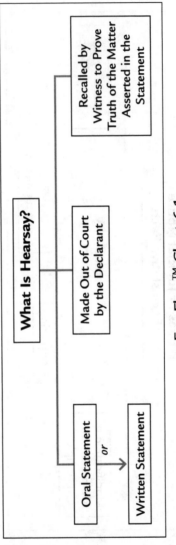

EasyFlow™ Chart 6.1

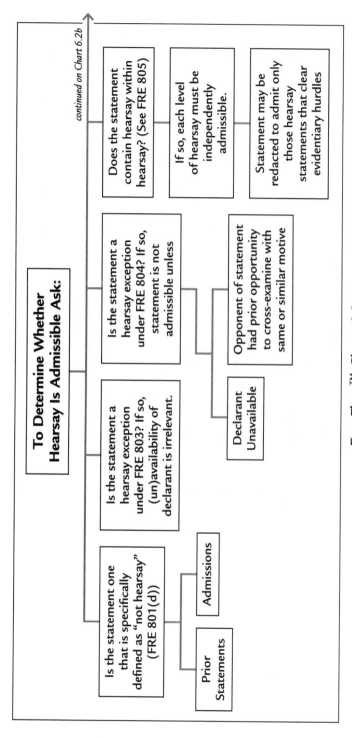

continued on Chart 6.2b

To Determine Whether Hearsay Is Admissible Ask:

Is the statement one that is specifically defined as "not hearsay" (FRE 801(d))

Prior Statements

Admissions

Is the statement a hearsay exception under FRE 803? If so, (un)availability of declarant is irrelevant.

Is the statement a hearsay exception under FRE 804? If so, statement is not admissible unless

Declarant Unavailable

Opponent of statement had prior opportunity to cross-examine with same or similar motive

Does the statement contain hearsay within hearsay? (See FRE 805)

If so, each level of hearsay must be independently admissible.

Statement may be redacted to admit only those hearsay statements that clear evidentiary hurdles

EasyFlow™ Chart 6.2a

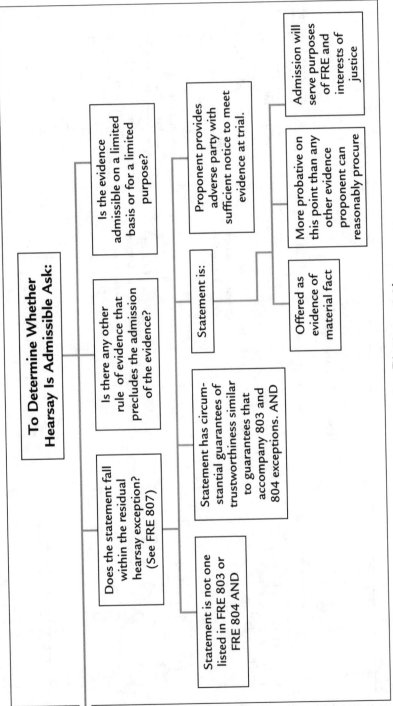

To Determine Whether Hearsay Is Admissible Ask:

Is the evidence admissible on a limited basis or for a limited purpose?

Is there any other rule of evidence that precludes the admission of the evidence?

Does the statement fall within the residual hearsay exception? (See FRE 807)

Proponent provides adverse party with sufficient notice to meet evidence at trial.

Admission will serve purposes of FRE and interests of justice

More probative on this point than any other evidence proponent can reasonably procure

Offered as evidence of material fact

Statement is:

Statement has circumstantial guarantees of trustworthiness similar to guarantees that accompany 803 and 804 exceptions. AND

Statement is not one listed in FRE 803 or FRE 804 AND

EasyFlow™ Chart 6.2b

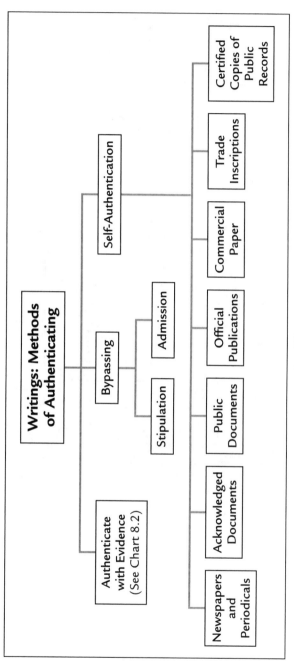

EasyFlow™ Chart 8.1

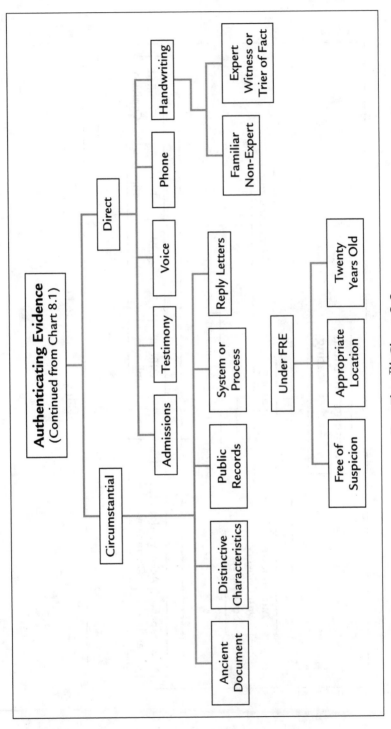

EasyFlow™ Chart 8.2

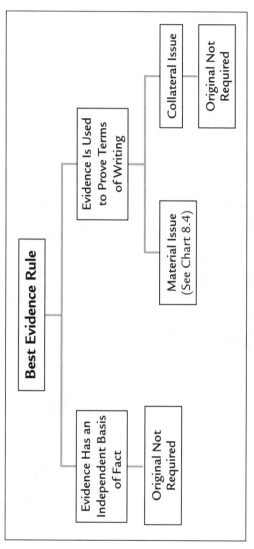

EasyFlow™ Chart 8.3

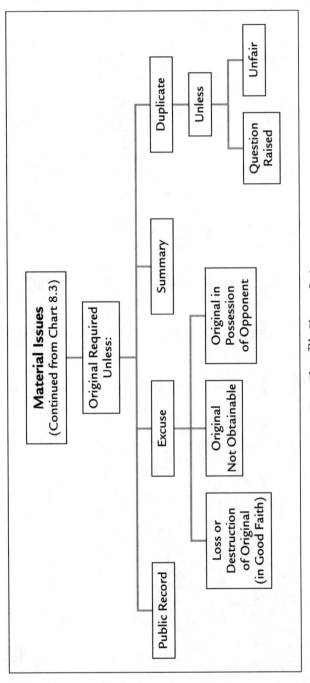

EasyFlow™ Chart 8.4

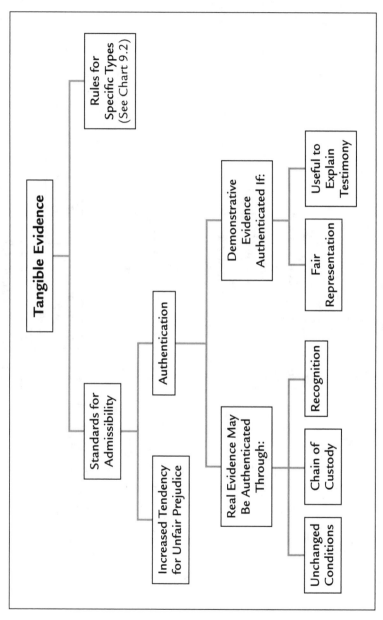

EasyFlow™ Chart 9.1

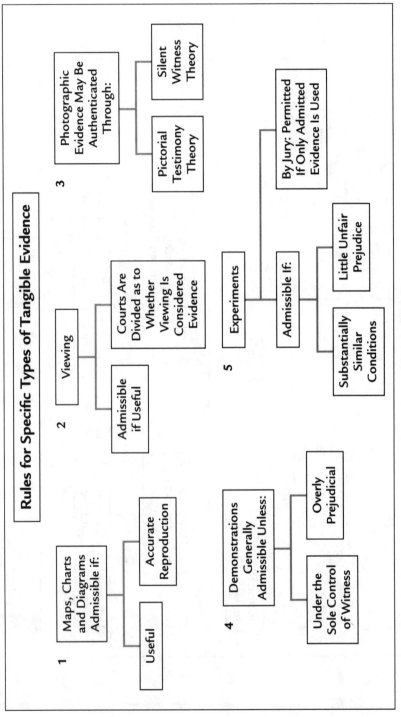

EasyFlow™ Chart 9.2

General Principles

I. RULES OF EVIDENCE

A. Rules of evidence are standards that regulate how parties prove facts to a fact finder. Our legal system requires, with rare exceptions, that the fact finder base its decisions solely on the evidence presented in court. The rules of evidence were developed to restrict courtroom evidence to reliable evidence that is relevant to the disputed issue(s).

B. Federal Rules of Evidence ("FRE")

1. The Federal Rules of Evidence are the most important and influential source of evidence law. The Federal Rules became effective in 1975 and have since been revised many times, most recently in 2006. A majority of states have adopted the FRE.

2. The FRE are applicable in all federal courts, in both civil and criminal cases. They also govern in bankruptcy courts and in proceedings held before United States Magistrate-Judges. See FRE 101.

3. The FRE are designed to be liberally construed to promote flexibility, fairness, judicial economy, and just outcomes. See FRE 102. On occasion, application of the FRE might require determination of a state law issue. See also FRE 302 and 501.

C. State Evidence Rules

1. As already noted, most states have adopted the FRE. Some states continue to derive their rules of evidence from state statutes and common law sources.

II. TYPES OF EVIDENCE

A. Real and Demonstrative Evidence

1. Generally

Real and demonstrative evidence are two different types of tangible evidence.

a. Real Evidence

Tangible evidence that is the actual substance, document, item, or other material from the core matter of the litigation is real evidence.

b. Demonstrative Evidence
Tangible evidence that illustrates, explains, or summarizes the position of the party that offers it into evidence is demonstrative evidence.

2. Examples
Consider a homicide trial at which the prosecution introduces the alleged murder weapon and a schematic drawing of the path the defendant allegedly followed to access the victim's home.

a. The murder weapon is *real* evidence.

b. The schematic drawing is *demonstrative* evidence.

B. Direct and Circumstantial Evidence

1. Direct Evidence
Direct evidence is evidence that, if credited by the fact finder, will resolve a factual issue without requiring the fact finder to draw any inferences.

2. Circumstantial Evidence
Circumstantial evidence is evidence that, even if credited by the fact finder, will not resolve a factual issue. Circumstantial evidence requires the fact finder to draw inferences to reach a conclusion about a disputed matter. Like other kinds of evidence, circumstantial evidence must be both material and probative of the proposition it is offered to prove.

3. Examples
Consider a robbery case. A witness testifies that he saw the defendant put a gun in a store cashier's face, and heard the defendant say "This is a stick-up." The cashier testifies that someone that she cannot identify pointed a gun at her face and said "This is a stick-up" and took $325. A police officer testifies that he arrested the defendant later the same day that the cashier stated that the robbery occurred, and the defendant had $325 in his pocket.

a. The witness's testimony, "I saw defendant stick a gun in the cashier's face and heard him say 'this is a stick-up'," is direct evidence that the defendant committed a robbery.

b. The police officer's testimony is circumstantial evidence that the defendant committed a robbery.

c. The cashier's testimony is
   i. direct evidence that a robbery occurred; and,
   ii. combined with the police testimony is circumstantial evidence that defendant was the robber.

C. Oral Evidence
  1. Generally
    Oral evidence consists of statements made by a witness, under oath, in the presence of the fact finder, at a proceeding designed to address the disputed matter.
  2. Changing Terminology
    Older cases might use the terms "testimonial evidence" or "testimonial proof" to refer to oral evidence. However, recent Supreme Court Confrontation Clause jurisprudence uses the term "testimonial evidence" to refer to out-of-court statements subject to confrontation. Students should be alert to this important change in terminology.

III. LIMITED ADMISSIBILITY

A. Generally
  When evidence is admitted for one purpose, but not for another purpose, that evidence has limited admissibility.
B. Federal Rules
  FRE 105 addresses the admission of evidence for limited purposes. In particular, FRE 105 provides that, upon request of a party, the trial court shall:
  1. Restrict evidence to "its proper scpe" and
  2. Instruct the jury as to the limited admissibility of the evidence.
C. Examples
  1. Joint Trials
    In a trial that includes more than one defendant or plaintiff, evidence is of limited admissibility if it is admissible against one party but not against another. For example, in most civil cases an admission by one party might not be used to prove that another party is liable.

IV. ROLE OF JUDGE AND JURY

A. The Judge
  1. Generally
    Typically, a judge resolves all questions of law and a limited number of factual matters:
    a. Preliminary Questions of Fact
      Judges resolve a wide range of preliminary questions of fact, such as whether particular matters are privileged, whether a witness is competent to testify, whether a witness can offer expert testimony, and whether a confession was made voluntarily. See FRE 104(a) and (b).

b. Judge Trials

At a judge trial ("bench trial") the judge is the sole finder of fact.

c. Directed Verdict

In limited circumstances, at a jury trial, the trial judge can remove one or more questions from the jury and resolve them herself.

2. Verdicts

As noted previously, in a bench trial, a judge renders the verdict by considering the law and the evidence and reaching a conclusion about whether the moving party has met its burden of proof

B. The Jury

1. Generally

The jury determines issues of fact. For example:

a. The jury decides whether to credit any or all of a witness's testimony.

b. The jury decides whether the evidence has established that agency relationship exists between two parties. Whereas the judge:

i. Makes a preliminary determination of whether there is sufficient evidence of an evidentiary relationship to merit an instruction on the law of agency.

ii. Judge instructs the jury on the law of agency, prior to the jury rendering a verdict.

2. Verdicts

When a jury renders a verdict, the judge instructs the jury about the law. The jury then considers the evidence, decides what evidence to accept or reject, and then applies the law to the evidence to reach a verdict as to whether the moving party has met its burden of proof.

CHAPTER 2

Competency of a Witness to Testify

I. INTRODUCTION

A. Generally

Whether a witness is competent to testify is a threshold question that determines whether a witness will be allowed to provide oral evidence.

B. Standard of Review

The competency of a witness to give testimony at trial is a matter within the discretion of the trial court and a trial court will be reversed in this area only if the appellate court finds that the trial court abused its discretion.

II. COMMON LAW

A. Generally

At common law, there were many bases for finding witnesses incompetent to testify. Modern common and statutory law have eliminated or restricted most of those grounds for per se incompetence.

B. Older Common Law

Historically, a witness was incompetent to testify if

1. the witness did not believe in God;
2. the witness was a convicted felon;
3. the witness was a young child;
4. the witness was insane; or
5. the witness or the witness' spouse had an interest in the case.

C. Modern Common Law

1. Generally

Modern common law eschews automatic disqualifications based on a witness's age, mental illness, religious beliefs, or interest in the case. Instead, modern common law typically permits a judge to make an individual determination.

2. Three-Factor Competence Test

Modern common law typically relies on a three-factor competence test. A witness is competent if a judge determines that

a. the witness can offer testimony that is meaningful to the fact finder; and

b. the witness can understand and honor his or her oath; and

c. the witness is capable of understanding, remembering, and describing facts relevant to the disputed issue.

3. Terminology

a. Offering Testimony Meaningful to the Fact Finder

The witness must be able to offer testimony that is meaningful to the fact finder. In general, this means that

i. the witness had the ability to accurately observe and perceive the event(s) about which the witness will testify.

ii. the witness has the ability to coherently convey his testimony to the trier of fact.

b. Oath or Affirmation

i. The practice in most courts is that the witness makes an oath or affirmation confirming the witness's commitment to telling the truth.

ii. The witness must understand the obligation of giving truthful testimony.

iii. The witness must be able to distinguish between truth and untruth. In this regard, youth, mental impairment, or senility may disqualify a witness.

c. Ability to Recount Facts

i. The witness must be able, at the time of trial, to recall the events about which the witness will testify.

D. Specific Issues of Witness Competence in Modern Common Law

1. Infants (Minors)

Modern common law no longer uses a specific age "cut-off" to determine when a child becomes competent to testify. The competency of a child is determined by the trial court using the three factors already described.

2. The Mentally Ill and the Developmentally Delayed

Witnesses who suffer from mental deficiencies or mental illnesses are not thereby rendered incompetent to testify. Rather, the trial court must consider the nature of the witness's mental illness or impairment to determine whether the witness is competent to testify. Typically, mental illness or defect only affects the weight of the witness's testimony and not his or her competence to testify. However, if the mental illness or defect is one that will frustrate effective cross-examination, the witness will be deemed incompetent.

E. State Laws on Competence
1. Dead Man's Statutes
Many jurisdictions have a Dead Man's statute that makes the surviving party to a transaction incompetent to testify against the estate of a deceased party to the transaction regarding any matter about which the deceased party might have offered contradictory evidence.
a. Rationale
The policy consideration that justifies the Dead Man's statutes is an equitable one: The deceased party is not able to speak at a trial; therefore, the interested surviving party should not be able to speak at a trial.
b. Exceptions
i. The surviving party may testify as to facts that can be corroborated by independent evidence.
ii. The surviving party may testify as to independent physical facts such as the party's own actions.
2. Hypnotically Refreshed Recollection
a. Jurisdictions take varying stances on the competence of posthypnotic witnesses.
i. Some jurisdictions have declared that a posthypnotic witness is competent to testify only to those facts that the witness can show that he remembered prior to hypnosis.
ii. A middle-ground view of the competency of posthypnotic testimony is the "safeguard" approach. The "safeguard" approach establishes specific guidelines regarding the pre- and posthypnotic interviews. If the hypnotic interviews comport with the established guidelines, the witness is fully competent to testify.
iii. Other jurisdictions deem all posthypnotic witnesses incompetent to testify. This restriction on the competence of posthypnotic testimony does not apply to a criminal defendant. The Constitution guarantees a criminal defendant the right to testify on his or her own behalf.

III. COMPETENCE UNDER THE FEDERAL RULES OF EVIDENCE

A. Generally
The Federal Rules of Evidence set out the standards for witness competence in FRE 601 and 602. The principles behind the FRE approach to witness competence are

1. deference to applicable state law; and
2. belief that cross-examination will enable the fact finder to adequately assess the witness's credibility and accuracy.

B. Competence Under the FRE
   1. Presumption of Competence
      FRE 601 states that every witness is competent to testify unless
      a. "otherwise" provided by the FRE; or
      b. prohibited by State law in a civil case in which State law provides the rule of decision as to a claim or defense.
   2. Personal Knowledge Requirement
      FRE 602 adds the additional restriction that, regardless of a witness's general competence to testify, a lay witness must have personal knowledge of the matter about which the witness will testify. As discussed in Chapter 3 there are separate rules that govern expert testimony.
   3. Oath or Affirmation Requirement
      FRE 603 requires evey witness to take an oath or affirmation to the effect that the witness will testify truthfully.
   4. Presiding Judge Incompetent to Testify
      FRE 605 prohibits the presiding judge at a trial from testifying as a witness at that trial.
   5. Competence of Jurors
      a. At Trial
         FRE 606(a) prohibits a juror from testifying as a witness at the trial of a case on which the juror is sitting.
      b. Impeaching the Jury Verdict
         i. Generally
            FRE 606(b) provides that a juror is incompetent to testify about that juror's mental processes in rendering a verdict.
         ii. Outside Influences or Extraneous Prejudicial Information
            FRE 606(b) states that a juror is competent to testify as to
            (1) whether the jury was subject to extraneous prejudicial information;
            (2) whether the jury was subject to improper outside influence;
            (3) whether there was a mistake in entering the verdict on the verdict form.

C. Competence of Person with Diminished Capacity
   A witness's diminished capacity or mental impairment typically goes to the weight of the witness's testimony and not its admissibility.

CASE CLIPS

Rock v. Arkansas, 483 U.S. 44 (1987)

Facts: Rock was charged with manslaughter in the shooting death of her husband. Because she could not remember the details of the shooting, she underwent hypnosis to try to refresh her memory. As a result of the hypnosis sessions, Rock was able to remember that, at the time of the incident, she had her thumb on the hammer of the gun, but did not have her finger on the trigger. As a result of those details, Rock's attorney arranged for a firearms expert to examine the handgun. The expert's inspection revealed that the gun was defective and, when hit or dropped, prone to fire without the trigger being pulled. The prosecution filed a motion in limine to exclude testimony obtained through the hypnosis session, and the trial judge granted that motion.

Issue: Whether an evidentiary rule prohibiting the admission of a defendant's hypnotically refreshed testimony violates the defendant's constitutional right to testify in her own defense.

Rule (Blackmun): A State cannot, on a per se basis, exclude all hypnotically refreshed testimony. The rule proceeds on the assumption that hypnotically refreshed testimony is always unreliable. The complete inadmissibility of a defendant's testimony is an arbitrary restriction on the right to testify in the absence of obvious evidence by the State repudiating the validity of the testimony. Possible inaccuracies in hypnotically refreshed testimony can be reduced by the use of procedural safeguards, and information obtained from hypnosis may be verified by corroborating evidence. If the State can prove in a particular case that the testimony is unreliable, then the exclusion may be justified.

Dissent (Rehnquist): An individual's right to present evidence is always subject to reasonable restrictions. Hypnotic testimony is inherently unreliable. No set of procedures can ensure against this.

Tanner v. United States, 483 U.S. 107 (1987)

Facts: A jury found Tanner guilty of mail fraud. After the trial, the defense became aware that many of the jurors had used drugs or alcohol during the trial. Tanner requested an evidentiary hearing into the conduct of the jury, that he had been deprived of his Sixth Amendment right to a trial by a competent jury. The government argued that, pursuant to FRE 606(b), the trial jurors were incompetent to testify about jurors' conduct. The District Court agreed that, under FRE 606(b), juror testimony about intoxication was inadmissible to impeach the jury's verdict.

Issue: Under Rule 606(b), may a juror may testify as to drug and alcohol use by members of the jury?

Rule: FRE 606(b) prohibits testimony by a juror regarding juror conduct during jury deliberations, except that a juror may testify about whether extraneous prejudicial information was improperly brought to the jury's attention or whether any outside influence was improperly brought to bear on any juror. Legislative history confirms that drug and alcohol use is not an "outside influence" about which a juror is competent to testify.

Dissent: If the policy considerations that underlie FRE 606(b) conflict with the Sixth Amendment right to trial by a fair, mentally competent, and impartial jury, the Rule must yield. As a common sense matter, drugs and alcohol are outside influences on jury members.

Zeigler v. Moore, 335 P.2d 425 (Nev. 1959)

Facts: Plaintiff sued Defendant's estate for damages, alleging that her car was struck by a car negligently operated by Defendant. At the trial, under the "Dead Man's rule," the court excluded Plaintiff's testimony and the testimony of Plaintiff's witness, a sheriff.

Issues:

1. Does a Dead Man's statute preclude the admission of the Sheriff's testimony?
2. Does a Dead Man's statute preclude the admission of Plaintiff's testimony concerning matters within his own knowledge that could not have been contradicted by the deceased?

Rule:

1. Under Nevada law, the Dead Man's statute does not apply to the testimony of disinterested third parties. Thus, the statute does not apply to the Sheriff's testimony.
2. The purpose of the Dead Man's statute is to prevent the living from obtaining unfair advantage because of the opposing party's death. However, when admission of testimony would not further those purposes, the living party's testimony should be admitted. Here, Plaintiff should have been permitted to testify about her own actions and about the road conditions prior to the accident. However, Plaintiff should not have been permitted to testify about matters as to which the decedent, of his own knowledge, could have contradicted her testimony.

State v. Singh, 586 S.W.2d 410 (Mo. 1979)

Facts: Singh was charged with the murder of his wife. At the trial, the State presented the decedent's daughter as a witness. The daughter was five at the time of the incident, and six when she testified. On appeal, Singh claimed: (1) that the trial court erred in determining that the daughter was a competent witness, and (2) that the trial court erred by conducting "extensive cross-examination" of the daughter and thereby aided the State in establishing her competence.

Issues:

1. When is a child a competent witness?
2. Can the the trial court ask questions of the witness during a competency examination?

Rules:

1. There is no fixed age at which a child may be a competent witness. Competency is measured based on the facts and circumstances of each case. Generally, a child is competent to testify if, in the discretion of the court, the child (1) is able to understand the obligation to tell the truth, (2) had the mental capacity at the time to observe and register the occurrence, (3) has the memory to retain a recollection of the event, and (4) has the capacity to translate the memory into words.
2. The procedure for determining competency is a voir dire examination outside the presence of the jury. The conduct of this examination is within the control of the court. The court can either conduct the examination itself, or it can allow counsel to conduct it and ask questions as it sees fit.

Schneiderman v. Interstate Transit Lines, 69 N.E.2d 293 (Ill. 1946)

Facts: Schneiderman brought a suit against Defendant to recover damages for personal injuries he sustained when the car he was driving collided with one of Defendant's buses. Schneiderman's injuries affected his power to speak coherently and intelligently; he could only respond to simple questions. The court held that Schneiderman's mental condition rendered him incompetent to testify and thus none of his testimony should have been admitted. Schneiderman appealed.

Issue: Can a witness who suffers from a mental deficiency be competent to testify?

Rule: A witness who suffers from mental deficiency is competent to testify if that witness has the capacity to observe, recollect, and communicate. Any mental deficiency of the witness affects the weight and not the admissibility of the testimony.

Cramer v. Tyars, 588 P.2d 793 (Cal. 1979)

Facts: The District Attorney filed a petition for the commitment of Tyars as a mentally retarded person who was a danger to himself or others. At the hearing, Tyars was called as a witness. Because of his speech handicap, it was difficult to understand what he was saying, so the court engaged an "interpreter," a ward attendant who was familiar with Tyars's speech. The jury found that he was a mentally retarded person who was a danger to himself and others and he was ordered to be committed to a state hospital. **Issue:** Whether a mentally retarded person who is the subject of a petition for civil commitment can be called as a witness at the commitment hearing. **Rule:** Reason and common sense suggest that it is appropriate for a jury to be allowed to observe the person sought to be committed, and to hear him speak and respond to questions to make an informed judgment as to his level of mental and intellectual functioning. Tyars's speech handicap did not make him an incompetent witness because the court permitted a ward attendant who was very familiar with Tyars's speech to serve as an interpreter.

United States v. Ward, 989 F.2d 1015 (9th Cir. 1993)

Facts: Ward was indicted on tax evasion and failure to file income tax returns. He filed a "motion to challenge the oath," which proposed an alternative oath that replaced the word "truth" with the phrase "fully integrated honesty." Ward believed that honesty is superior to truth. The judge denied this motion. At his trial, Ward offered to take both the standard oath and his oath, but the judge refused to allow it. Ward did not testify, and was convicted. On appeal, Ward argued that the district court's refusal to allow him to swear to the alternate oath prevented him from testifying in his own defense. **Issue:** Can a court prevent a witness from testifying solely on the basis of the witness's religiously based objections to the form of the oath? **Rule:** Ward professes beliefs that are protected by the First Amendment, and the court's interest in administering its precise form of oath must yield to Ward's First Amendment rights. There is no constitutionally or statutorily required form of oath. FRE 603 requires only that a witness declare that he will testify truthfully, by oath or affirmation administered in a form calculated to awaken his conscience and impress his mind with the duty to do so. **Dissent:** Ward's proposed alternative oath does not contain an acknowledgment of the duty to speak truthfully and does not ensure that the defendant is aware of the cost of dishonesty. The majority's accommodation of his concerns will result in numerous wasteful and time-consuming attacks on the standard oath.

State v. Ranieri, 586 A.2d 1094 (R.I. 1991)

Facts: Rape victim was assaulted but never saw her assailant and was unable to identify him for 18 months after the attack. During that time,

Defendant was arrested and charged with the assault and burglary. A local newspaper published his picture several times. On date of trial, victim had suddenly identified Defendant as her attacker. Defendant was convicted. On appeal, Defendant challenged the admission of the victim's identifications, alleging that because she had no personal knowledge of her assailant's identity and had an insufficient opportunity to view the assailant, she was not a competent witness.

Issue: Is a witness who lacks personal knowledge of a matter incompetent to testify with respect to that matter?

Rule: A witness cannot testify to a matter unless evidence is introduced sufficient to support a finding that the witness has personal knowledge of the matter. If the witness lacks personal knowledge, then the witness is incompetent to testify with respect to that matter. In deciding whether a witness is competent, the judge must determine whether a witness had a sufficient opportunity to perceive the subject matter about which he or she is testifying.

Rosen v. United States, 245 U.S. 467 (1918)

Facts: Defendants were accused of conspiring to steal mail. Cooperating co-conspirator pled guilty and testified for the government against other conspirators. Defendants objected that the witness was not competent to testify because he had previously been convicted of forgery. The objection was overruled.

Issue: Is a convicted felon competent to serve as a witness?

Rule (Clarke): A felon is competent to serve as a witness. The general evidentiary trend is to remove disabilities from witnesses. This is driven by the belief that the truth is more likely to be arrived at by hearing the testimony of all persons of competent understanding who have knowledge of the facts in a case, and that the jury should decide the credibility and weight of the testimony.

United States v. Hickey, 917 F.2d 901 (6th Cir. 1990)

Facts: Defendant was indicted for conspiring to distribute cocaine and using a communication facility to facilitate a crime. A government witness testified against Defendant as part of his own plea bargain. On cross-examination, Defendant exposed witness's addiction, his claimed lack of memory, his uncertainty as to details, and inconsistencies in his testimony. On appeal, Defendant argued that the court committed reversible error in allowing the jury to hear and consider witness's testimony.

Issue: Is a witness whose perception is sometimes impaired competent to testify?

Rule: FRE 602 provides that a witness may not testify to a matter unless evidence is introduced sufficient to support a finding that the witness has personal knowledge of the matter. Testimony should not be excluded for lack of personal knowledge unless no reasonable juror could believe that the witness had the ability and opportunity to perceive the events about which he will testify.

United States v. Allen J., 127 F.3d 1292 (10th Cir. 1997)

Facts: District court found that Defendant committed aggravated sexual abuse of a developmentally disabled child and adjudged him a juvenile delinquent. On appeal, Defendant argues that the trial court erred in finding the victim competent to testify.
Issue: Is a developmentally delayed child competent to testify?
Rule: The competency of a child witness depends on the capacity and intelligence of the child, the child's appreciation of the difference between truth and falsehood, and the child's appreciation of his or her duty to tell the truth.

People v. Fleiss, No. BO93373 (Cal. Ct. App. 1996)

Facts: Fleiss was convicted of three counts of pandering and acquitted of one count of drug dealing. She subsequently brought a motion for a new trial, in support of which five jurors filed declarations alleging juror misconduct. Specifically, the declarations stated that jurors had traded "not guilty" votes on the drug charge in exchange for "guilty" votes on the pandering charge.
Issue: Does the bartering of votes constitute prejudicial jury misconduct?
Rule: Trading votes constitutes prejudicial misconduct. The jurors in this case took a solemn duty to impartially dispense justice and turned it into advocacy for a cause. The verdict in this case resulted not from the evidence, but from extraneous and improper considerations.

United States v. Ewing, 979 F.2d 1234 (7th Cir. 1992)

Facts: Police executing a search warrant at Defendant's home found cocaine packaged in plastic bags, along with other evidence of drug trafficking. Defendant was convicted of drug trafficking. On appeal, Defendant argued that the district court erred in not allowing defense counsel to testify about allegations that the government tampered with the evidence used against him.
Issue: Can an attorney testify at trial about allegations that the government tampered with evidence used against her client?

Rule: Under the Illinois Rule of Professional Conduct, a lawyer cannot be both witness and counsel in the same case, except in exceptional circumstances. This rule gives the trial court the discretion to determine whether counsel may appear as a witness without withdrawing from the case. Here, the attorney's paralegal testified that she and the attorney had examined the physical evidence. Additionally, a handwriting analyst testified that Defendant did not write the words on the front of the notebooks. Thus, the attorney's testimony merely would have been cumulative.

State v. Moore, 902 A.2d 1212 (N.J. 2006)

Facts: Victim was sexually assaulted in her home in the middle of the night. Victim was unable to provide sufficient information to develop a composite sketch, so she underwent hypnosis, following which she identified Defendant from a photo array. At trial, the court permitted Victim's testimony as refreshed recollection and permitted the State to play a portion of the recording of the hypnotic session. Defendant was convicted, but the case was reversed on other grounds. On remand, the trial court determined that Victim's testimony should be barred because the doctor who conducted the hypnotic session did not comply with the *Hurd* guidelines for the admissibility of hypnotically refreshed testimony.
Issue: Is the hypnotically refreshed testimony of a witness admissible in a criminal trial?
Rule: The hypnotically refreshed testimony of a witness generally is inadmissible in a New Jersey criminal trial. Scientific evidence justifies abandoning the template established in *Hurd* for the admissibility of hypnotically refreshed testimony as it cannot meet the general acceptance standard of admissibility. There is a lack of empirical evidence that hypnosis actually improves recall, and the probative value of hypnotically refreshed testimony is outweighed by the inherent risks of distorted recollection and false confidence.

Washington v. Texas, 388 U.S. 14 (1967)

Facts: Defendant was charged with a shooting. At his trial, he sought to have a co-defendant corroborate his defense by testifying about the events leading up to the shooting. Co-defendant's testimony was excluded, however, because of two Texas statutes that provided that persons charged or convicted as co-participants in the same crime could not testify for one another, although they could testify for the State. Defendant was convicted.
Issue: Whether a state procedural statute providing that persons charged as principals, accomplices, or accessories in the same crime cannot be introduced as witnesses for each other violates the right of a defendant

to have compulsory process for obtaining witnesses in his favor under the Sixth Amendment.

Rule: The rule disqualifying an alleged accomplice from testifying on behalf of the defendant is absurd. The accomplice can be called by the prosecution to testify against the defendant. Common sense suggests that the accomplice would have a greater interest in lying in favor of the prosecution than against it, especially if he is still awaiting trial or sentencing. The rule is also at odds with the principle that the truth is more likely to be arrived at by hearing the testimony of all competent persons who may have knowledge of the fact involved in a case, leaving the weight of such testimony to the jury.

Gordon v. Idaho, 778 F.2d 1397 (9th Cir. 1985)

Facts: Gordon appeared at a deposition, but, because of his religious beliefs, refused to swear under oath or make an affirmative affirmation. He was cited for civil contempt and imprisoned for 12 days. He then filed a civil suit, alleging a violation of his First Amendment rights. The district court dismissed his action for Gordon's failure to comply with the discovery order, directing him to take an oath or make an affirmation.

Issue: Is a promise to tell the truth sufficient to ensure truthful testimony at trial?

Rule: Any statement indicating that the deponent is impressed with the duty to tell the truth and understands that he can be prosecuted for perjury for failure to do so satisfies the requirement for an oath or affirmation under Fed. R. Civ. P. 30(c) and 43(d).

Dissent: Gordon's demand trivializes the purposes of the Free Exercise Clause. Yielding to his demand will invite demands for special formulations in future cases and cause needless delay.

United States v. Heinlein, 490 F.2d 725 (D.C. Cir. 1973)

Facts: Defendants were convicted of felony murder and assault with intent to rape while armed. The only alleged eyewitness to the events was Harding, a chronic alcoholic. During trial, the defense attempted to demolish Harding's credibility by introducing evidence of Harding's prior convictions for drunkenness, assault with intent to commit rape, forgery, and larceny. Defendants also moved, midtrial for a psychiatric evaluation of Harding's competence to testify. On appeal, the Defendants argued that the court erred in denying their motion for a competency examination.

Issue: Whether the decision to order a psychiatric examination of a witness is within the discretion of the trial court.

Rule: The competency of the witness to testify before the jury is a question within the discretion of the trial court. Although Harding's testimony did contain some inconsistencies and gaps, the trial court concluded that these differences were not enough to seriously undermine Harding's account of what happened. Therefore, the trial court acted within its discretion in denying the motion for a competency hearing.

Borawick v. Shay, 68 F.3d 597 (2d Cir. 1995)

Facts: Plaintiff began to experience panic attacks and, after seeking psychological treatment, was referred to a hypnotist. Before these hypnosis sessions, Plaintiff had no recollection of abuse. During her sessions, Plaintiff allegedly revealed to hypnotist that she had been sexually abused by her aunt and uncle. Hypnotist did not tell Plaintiff what she had described during the sessions. Several months after her final hypnotic session, Plaintiff experienced nonhypnotic memories of sexual abuse and brought a diversity action against her aunt and uncle.

Issue: Whether testimony about memories of childhood sexual abuse that are recalled for the first time in adulthood following the use of hypnosis is admissible.

Rule: A lower court should conduct a case-by-case analysis considering the following factors: (1) whether the purpose of the hypnosis was to refresh a witness's memory of an accident or crime or whether it was conducted as part of a therapy, (2) whether the witness received any suggestions from the hypnotist or others prior to or during hypnosis, (3) whether a permanent record was made of the hypnosis session, (4) whether the hypnotist was appropriately qualified by training in psychology or psychiatry, (5) whether corroborating evidence exists to support the reliability of the hypnotically refreshed memories, (6) the subject's hypnotizability, and (7) whether the procedures used were reliable. The court should weigh the factors in favor of and against the reliability of the hypnosis procedure. The party attempting to admit the testimony bears the burden of persuading the court that the balance tips in favor of admissibility.

CHAPTER 3

Relevance, Admissibility, and Common Types of Evidence

I. RELEVANCE

A. Defined

Evidence is relevant when it has the tendency to prove or disprove a material issue, or to render a fact more probably true or untrue than it would be without the evidence. In addressing whether evidence is relevant, courts consider its materiality and its probative value.

1. Materiality

If evidence proves a fact that is connected to the issue in dispute, that evidence is material. To be admissible, evidence must be linked to a material issue in the case.

2. Probative Value

The probative value of evidence is the degree to which evidence proves the factual proposition for which it is offered. Evidence has a greater or lesser probative value depending on how strongly it tends to prove the existence of the asserted fact. In some instances, otherwise relevant evidence is excluded because its probative value is not high enough to outweigh its prejudicial impact on other matters in dispute.

II. RELEVANCE UNDER THE FRE

A. Generally

1. FRE 401 states that "[r]elevant evidence means evidence having any tendency to make the existence of any fact that is of

consequence to the determination of the action more probable or less probable than it would be without the evidence."

2. FRE 402 states that all relevant evidence is admissible "except as otherwise provided" by the FRE, federal statute, or constitutional law.

3. FRE 403 states that relevant evidence may be excluded if its probative value is "substantially outweighed by the danger of unfair prejudice, confusion of the issues, or misleading the jury, or by considerations of undue delay, waste of time, or needless presentation of cumulative evidence."

   a. Unfair Prejudice
      Evidence is unfairly prejudicial if it encourages a decision based on illegal inferences, bias, or emotion.

   b. Confusion of Issues
      Relevant evidence may be excluded if it confuses or distracts the jury from the main issues.

   c. Waste of Time
      Evidence may be excluded if it is so cumulative that it wastes the jury's time.

III. CHARACTER EVIDENCE

A. Generally
   1. Defined
      Character evidence is evidence that proves that a party or witness possesses a certain character or personality trait. Character evidence is offered to prove that, on a particular occasion relevant to the dispute, a party or witness acted in conformity with a particular character trait.

   2. Admissibility
      a. Because character evidence can be very prejudicial, its admissibility is highly regulated.

      b. The rules governing the admissibility of character evidence vary according to whether the evidence is being offered against party or a witness. In addition, there are special rules that apply in criminal cases.

B. Admission Against a Witness
   Generally, character evidence is not admissible against a witness except character evidence for truthfulness or untruthfulness.

   1. Specific instances of a witness's prior conduct are admissible when the conduct is
      a. relevant and
      b. probative to the witness's character for truthfulness or untruthfulness; and

c. the truthful character of the witness has been challenged by the opposing party.

2. The Extrinsic Evidence Rule

Generally, evidence of specific instances of witness conduct may not be proven by extrinsic evidence; however, on cross-examination, counsel may inquire about

a. Specific instances of conduct that reflect on the testifying witness's character for truthfulness; or

b. Specific instances of conduct that reflect upon the truthful character of another witness, about whom the testifying witness has already given evidence.

C. Admission Against a Party

Character evidence is generally not admissible against a party unless the party's character is a material issue in the case. (A defamation action is an example of a case in which a person's character is at issue). (See FRE 405(b).)

D. Special Rules in Criminal Cases

1. Character of Accused

a. Generally

FRE 404(a)(1) authorizes introduction of evidence of "a pertinent character trait" if it is

i. Offered by the Accused

An accused may offer evidence of his own relevant character or character trait(s). FRE 404(a)(1); or

ii. Offered by the Prosecution

(1) To Rebut Accused's Character Evidence

If the accused offers evidence of his or her own character or character trait(s), the prosecution may offer relevant evidence to rebut the character evidence offered by the accused. FRE 404(a)(1); or

(2) Meet Accused's Evidence About Victim's Character

If the accused offers evidence about the character trait of a victim (see FRE 404(a)(2)), the prosecution may offer evidence of the same character trait in the accused. This is sometimes referred to as "opening the door" to otherwise inadmissible evidence about the accused's character.

iii. For a discussion of prior bad acts and their admissibility against the accused, see below.

2. Character of Victim

a. Pertinent character traits of an alleged victim may be admissible such as the victim's character for truthfulness, untruthfulness, or peacefulness, see FRE 404(a)(2).

b. In a sex offense case, there are limits to the relevance of a victim's alleged sexual predisposition or character.

E. Methods of Proving Character Evidence

1. Generally

a. Reputation

Character evidence is proved by reputation when a party introduces oral testimony that describes a person's reputational within a particular community. A witness who provides testimony about a person's reputation need not have personal knowledge about that person's character; instead the witness must have personal knowledge of the reputational evidence about which he or she is testifying.

b. Opinion

Character evidence is proved by opinion when a party introduces oral testimony from a witness who describes his or her personal opinion about the person's character.

c. Specific Acts

Character is proved by specific acts when a party offers evidence of a person's specific acts on particular occasions to support allegations about that person's character. Proof of character by reference to specific acts is generally authorized only when the character evidence is central to the issues in dispute in the case (e.g., in a defamation action).

2. Methods of Proving Character Evidence Under the FRE

In all cases in which the FRE permit the use of character evidence, it may be proven by:

a. Reputation

Under FRE 405(a), a party may introduce, on direct examination, proof of character by testimony about a person's reputation.

b. Opinion

Under FRE 405(a) a party may introduce, on direct examination, proof of character by a testifying witness's opinion of a person's character.

c. Specific Instances of Conduct

i. On Direct Examination

FRE 405(b) authorizes proof of character by testimony about specific instances of conduct when the character or character trait of a person is "an essential element of a charge, claim or defense."

ii. On Cross-Examination

Following a party's introduction of character evidence by reputation or opinion, the opposing party may, on cross-examination, inquire about relevant specific instances of conduct.

IV. EVIDENCE OF PRIOR ACTS ADMISSIBLE FOR REASONS OTHER THAN CHARACTER

A. Evidence of defendant's other acts may be admissible when those acts are relevant to an issue other than the defendant's character.

B. FRE 404(b) provides an illustrative list of reasons why other act evidence may be relevant and admissible:

1. Motive

   Evidence of other acts might reveal a motive that is probative of a person's conduct or intent.

2. Opportunity

   Evidence of other acts may be used to show that the person had access to the scene of a crime or was present at a specific event.

3. Intent

   The specific intent required for a crime may be shown by evidence of specific acts of misconduct, such as other crimes.

4. Preparation

   Evidence of other acts may be used to show preparation for the act in dispute.

5. Plan

   Evidence of other acts may be used to demonstrate that the prior act and the act at issue were both parts of a common scheme.

6. Knowledge and Absence of Mistake

   Evidence of other acts may be used to prove that the crime was not committed accidentally.

7. Identity

   If the identity of the person who committed an act is in dispute, evidence of other acts may be used to establish an actor's identity (this is sometimes referred to as use to establish as modus operandi).

8. Context

   If the other act is closely linked with the act in dispute, the other act may be admitted to put the disputed act in context.

C. Prerequisites for Admission of Evidence of Other Acts

1. The proponent of the other act evidence must establish that a jury could conclude, by a preponderance of the evidence, that the other act evidence was committed by the person about whom it is offered. FRE 404(b).

2. The evidence must be admissible under FRE 403.

   a. If the probative value of the other act evidence is substantially outweighed by the danger of unfair prejudice, jury confusion, or waste of time, the other act evidence is not admissible.

      b. Some common considerations implicated by the 403 balancing test include:
        i. the degree of similarity between the acts;
        ii. the time interval between the acts;
        iii. the proponent's need for the evidence; and
        iv. the availability of other evidence on the same issue.
D. Scope of Rule FRE 404(b)
  1. Applicability
    It is a common misconception that FRE 404(b) applies only to criminal acts in criminal cases. FRE 404(b) applies to all prior acts, in any type of case, unless another rule or statute supplants the 404(b) analysis.
  2. There is some dispute in the case law about the proper application of FRE 404(b) to prior act evidence in sexual assault and child molestation cases.
E. Procedure
  Rule 404(b) requires that, upon the request of the accused, the prosecution must provide reasonable pretrial notice of any "prior bad act" evidence that it intends to introduce at trial.

V. IMPEACHMENT

A. Defined
  To impeach a witness is to attack the accuracy of the witness's testimony by challenging the witness's knowledge, accuracy of perception, or credibility. Impeachment is usually accomplished through cross-examination and the presentation of extrinsic evidence. There are several forms of impeachment evidence.
B. Impeachment by Prior Inconsistent Statements
  1. Generally
    To impeach a witness with prior inconsistent statements means to show, either through cross-examination or extrinsic evidence, that the witness previously made a statement inconsistent with, or contrary to, the testimony given at trial.
  2. Foundation
    To impeach a witness with extrinsic evidence of a prior inconsistent statement, the examiner must first offer an opportunity to the witness to explain the alleged inconsistency. The witness should be questioned regarding the existence of the statement, and informed of the time, place, and content.
  3. Exception to Hearsay Rule
    Prior inconsistent statements used to impeach a witness may be admitted as an exception to the hearsay rule.

C. Evidentiary Effects
  1. Majority View
     Prior inconsistent statements are only admissible for impeachment purposes; they have no independent evidentiary value.
  2. Minority View
     A minority of jurisdictions allow jurors to attribute independent evidentiary value to prior inconsistent statements that were admitted for impeachment purposes.
D. Impeachment by Character
  1. General Rule
     FRE 404(a) prohibits a party from using character evidence to prove that, on a particular occasion, a person acted in conformity with his or her alleged character trait(s) on a particular occasion. Major exceptions are discussed below.
     a. Character of the Accused
        i. General Rule: As a general matter, it is impermissible to use character evidence against an accused for the purpose of showing that the accused acted, in conformity with that character.
        ii. Exceptions (FRE 404(b)): Because of the high risk of prejudice associated with the use of character evidence against an accused, Rules 404(b) and 609(a)(1) impose express limitations on the use of character evidence to impeach an accused.
     b. Character of the Victim (FRE(a)(2))
        i. Offered by the Accused: The accused may offer evidence about a victim's pertinent character trait(s), subject to FRE 412 limitations on evidence about a victim's (a) past sexual behavior and (b) alleged sexual predisposition.
        ii. Offered by the Prosecution to
           (1) Rebut accused's evidence about victim's character: If the accused offers evidence about the victim's character trait(s), the prosecution may offer evidence to rebut that evidence.
           (2) Invoke the First Aggressor Rule: If a defendant is accused of homicide and argues that the victim was the first aggressor, the prosecution may introduce rebuttal evidence of the victim's "peaceful" character.
     c. Character of Witnesses
        i. Credibility of Witness: Evidence of prior bad acts:
           (1) may be used to impeach the credibility of a witness, but
           (2) may not be proved by extrinsic evidence.

This means that a party may cross-examine a witness about prior bad acts, but must "live with" the witness's answer and may not introduce other, extrinsic evidence of those acts, even if the witness falsely denies them. See FRE 608(a).

    ii. Credibility of Person About Whom Witness Has Testified: A party may cross-examine a witness about specific acts that illustrate the credibility of a person about whose character the witness has already testified. See FRE 608(b).

E. Impeachment by Evidence of Character for Untruthfulness

    1. A witness may be impeached by evidence that tends to show that the witness has an untruthful character. This impeachment may arise from evidence of reputation or opinion.

    2. A criminal defendant who testifies on his own behalf is not exempt from impeachment by opinion or reputation testimony.

F. Impeachment by Evidence of Defect of Capacity

    1. Perception

    A witness may be impeached by evidence of some sensory defect that rendered the witness incapable of perceiving the events the witness describes.

    2. Memory

    A witness may be impeached by evidence that the witness has an impaired memory and therefore cannot reliably relate past events.

    3. Mental Illness or Disability

    A witness may be impeached by evidence of mental illness, disability, or diminished capacity that distorts either the witness's perception or recollection of reality.

G. Specific Contradiction by Another Witness

    1. A witness may be impeached by another witness's testimony that contradicts the testimony of the first witness.

    2. However, a party may not introduce extrinsic evidence of contradictions between witnesses if the contradictions relate to collateral matters.

H. Bias or Motive to Lie

    1. A witness may be impeached by evidence showing that the witness is biased or prejudiced for or against one of the parties to the case. In addition, a witness may be impeached by evidence that the witness has a motive to falsify testimony.

    2. Extrinsic Evidence Admissible

    Witness bias is not collateral to the litigation; therefore a party may impeach a witness by introducing extrinsic evidence of bias or motive to lie.

I. Impeachment by Means of Prior Convictions

1. FRE 609 governs the admission of prior convictions in the federal courts, and has been adopted by many states.
2. FRE 609(b) provides for the admission of evidence that any witness has been convicted of a crime that involved dishonesty or false statements.
3. FRE 609(a) distinguishes between impeachment of witness and impeachment of defendants.
   a. Witnesses
      Evidence of a witness's prior conviction shall be admitted if
      i. The prior conviction carried a possible punishment of at least one year of incarceration.
      ii. The evidence satisfies the 403 balancing test.
   b. The Accused
      Evidence of the accused's prior conviction shall be admitted if
      i. The prior conviction carried a possible punishment of at least one year of incarceration; and
      ii. The court determines that the probative value of the evidence of prior conviction outweighs its prejudicial effect on the defendant.
4. FRE 609 Limits on Admissibility of Ten-Year-Old Convictions
   a. If more than ten years have passed since the commission of the prior crime, evidence of the commission of that crime is not admissible unless:
      i. The court determines that, in the interests of justice, the probative value of the evidence, supported by specific facts and circumstances, substantially outweighs its prejudicial effect.
      ii. In addition, the proponent of such evidence must give the adverse party advance written notice, sufficient to allow a fair opportunity to contest the use of such evidence.

J. Balancing Test Under FRE 609
When balancing probative value against prejudice, the court must consider:
1. The Impeachment Value of Prior Crime
   This factor requires the court to assess the probative value of the prior conviction in showing a lack of veracity in the witness.
2. Age of the Conviction/Subsequent History
   This factor requires the judge to consider the age of the crime. Crimes that approach the ten-year mark have very little probative value for the veracity of the witness. The judge should also consider whether the witness has any subsequent criminal history.

3. Similarity to Crime Charged

This factor requires the court to assess the similarity of the prior crime and the crime charged. Prior convictions for the same or similar crimes are generally very prejudicial, as the jury might tend to decide that if the defendant "did it before, he did it this time." (Many state jurisdictions forbid impeachment by the same or similar crime if there is any other prior conviction available for use as impeachment material.)

4. Importance of the Defendant's Testimony

If a defendant informs the court that he or she will not testify for fear of being impeached by a prior conviction, the court should consider how important the defendant's testimony would be in establishing the defense. Note: A defendant who declines to testify because the court has authorized his impeachment by prior crime evidence waives his appeal on this issue.

5. Centrality of the Credibility Issue

The court should consider how central the issue of credibility is to the case.

K. Other FRE 609 Limitations on Convictions Available for Use as Impeachment Evidence

1. A conviction that has been the subject of a pardon, certification of rehabilitation, or other similar process is not admissible if the person has not been convicted of any new crime.

2. A conviction has been the subject of pardon or clemency based on a finding of innocence.

3. BUT, when an appeal is pending, the conviction is not inadmissible. However, evidence of the pending appeal is also admissible.

4. A juvenile adjudication is typically not available for use as impeachment evidence. However, in a criminal case, the court may allow the impeachment of a witness, other than the accused, by evidence of a juvenile adjudication if:

   a. The crime at issue in the adjudication is one that would be admissible to attack the credibility of an adult; and

   b. The evidence is necessary to a fair determination of guilt or innocence.

L. Impeachment in Cases of Sexual Assault or Child Molestation

1. Generally

Many jurisdictions have enacted rape shield laws that protect the victim of a rape from impeachment by evidence of prior sexual misconduct.

2. Federal Rules: FRE 412–415 contain special rules authorizing the use of character evidence in civil and criminal cases in which the defendant is accused of sexual assault or child molestation.

Those rules

a. forbid the use of opinion or reputation testimony regarding the past sexual behavior of the alleged victim, and

b. permit other evidence regarding the alleged victim's past sexual behavior in three specific situations, and under strict procedural guidelines.

   i. Past Sexual Behavior with persons Other Than the Defendant

    Admissible to show that the defendant was *not* the source of the semen or injury.

   ii. Past Sexual Behavior with the Defendant

    Admissible only to show consent.

   iii. Other Past Sexual Behavior

    Admissible only as constitutionally required.

c. Victim's Nonsexual Misconduct

   Evidence of the victim's nonsexual misconduct is subject to the general rules that govern admissibility of other acts evidence.

3. Prior False Accusations

a. A defendant is almost always entitled to show that an alleged victim has a reputation for making false accusations of rape, especially when this showing is supported by independent evidence.

b. In an effort to develop that theory, the court usually permits the defendant to question the witness and to offer evidence that establishes a bias or motive for fabricating the accusation.

Note: By their own terms, FRE 412 and 415 apply in civil cases involving claims of sexual assault or child molestation. Some courts have held that FRE 413 and 414 also apply in civil cases that present issues similar to those raised in a criminal case.

M. Impeachment of One's Own Witnesses

Traditionally, a party was bound by the testimony of its witnesses and a party could not impeach its own witness.

1. Surprise or Hostility

Many jurisdictions permit a party to impeach its own witness if the witness offers unexpected testimony or becomes hostile and uncooperative on the witness stand.

2. Adverse Party

If a party calls an adverse party as a witness, or a hostile witness, the proponent of the witness may seek to impeach that witness.

3. Minority View

Several states have now adopted the view that a party may always impeach its own witnesses.

N. Rehabilitation
  1. Generally
     If a witness's credibility has been attacked on cross-examination, the proponent of the witness may rehabilitate the witness on redirect. Rehabilitation may be by
     a. Prior Consistent Statements
        Prior consistent statements may only be used to rebut a charge of recent fabrication or improper influence or motive. FRE 801(d)(1).
     b. Explanation of Prior Inconsistent Statement
        On redirect examination, a witness is permitted to explain a prior inconsistent statement.
     c. Explanation of Prior Conviction or Misconduct
        Witnesses are permitted to testify as to the circumstances of a prior conviction or act of misconduct if the explanatory testimony will help shore up their credibility.
     d. Character Support
        After an opposing party has attacked a witness's character, the proponent of the witness may elicit evidence to support the character of its witness.

VI. EVIDENCE OF HABIT, ROUTINE, CUSTOM

A. Under the FRE
  1. Habit
     a. Defined
        Habit evidence is evidence of a person's regular response to a specific set of circumstances or a person's regular conduct in a specific set of circumstances.
     b. Distinguished from Character Evidence
        Habit evidence is more specific than character evidence inasmuch as character evidence goes to a person's general disposition.
     c. Admissibility
        FRE 406 authorizes the admission of evidence of habit to prove that the conduct of a person on a particular occasion was in conformity with the habit.
  2. Routine
     a. Defined
        Evidence of routine is evidence that relates to an organization's established routine or practice.

      b. Admissibility
      FRE 406 permits the admission of evidence for the purpose
      of showing that the organization acted in conformity with
      the established practice or routine.

B. Common Law
  1. Trade Custom
    a. Defined
    Evidence of trade custom is evidence that shows the actions
    of others in the same industry.
    b. Admissibility
    Trade custom evidence is relevant — and therefore admissible —
    only if the proponent of the evidence can demonstrate that
    the custom was prevalent
      i. in the relevant locality
      ii. at the time of the disputed event.
  2. Similar Happenings
    a. Defined
    Evidence of similar happenings is evidence of a similar hap-
    pening such as a similar claim, event, or nonevent.
    b. Inadmissibility
    Evidence of similar happenings is generally inadmissible;
    however, there are limited circumstances in which a court
    may admit such evidence.
      i. Exception for Substantial Showing
      If the proponent of the evidence relating to the prior
      similar claim can make a substantial showing that the
      similar prior claims were false claims, the evidence is usu-
      ally relevant and admissible.
      ii. Exception for Prior Similar Accidents
      Evidence of prior similar accidents is admissible when the
      prior accidents were caused by the same condition or
      conditions as the incident in dispute, and this evidence
      is offered to prove
      (1) That the alleged condition(s) existed; or
      (2) That the defendant had knowledge of the condi-
          tion(s) that caused the current injury.
    c. Absence of Prior Similar Events
      i. General Rule
      Evidence about the absence of prior, similar accidents or
      claims is generally inadmissible.
      ii. Exception; Prior Contracts
      Evidence of prior contract is usually admissible so long as
      the contract was between the parties to the litigation, and
      not third persons.

VII. OTHER FRE PROVISIONS

A. Settlement Offers
1. General Rule
Settlement offers are generally inadmissible.
2. Examples
a. FRE 408
Under FRE 408, evidence of compromises or offers to compromise are inadmissible to prove liability for, or invalidity of, a claim.
b. FRE 409
Under FRE 409, evidence of an offer to pay for medical or hospital expenses is not admissible to prove liability.
3. Rationale
a. Unreliability
Statements made during settlement negotiations are not considered to be reliable because they might have been made in an effort to avoid litigation.
b. Public Policy
Moreover, public policy favors settlements and a contrary rule would discourage such settlement discussions.
B. Guilty Pleas
1. FRE 410
Under FRE 410, neither withdrawn guilty pleas nor offers to plead guilty are admissible. Moreover, statements made during plea negotiations are similarly inadmissible.
2. Exceptions
a. FRE 410 authorizes the introduction of statements made in connection with plea discussions if another statement made in connection with the plea or offer to plea has been introduced and fairness requires that the fact finder consider the complete statement(s).
b. FRE 410 makes evidence of a withdrawn guilty plea admissible in a prosecution for perjury or false statement.

VIII. SUBSEQUENT REMEDIAL MEASURES

A. FRE 407
FRE 407 makes subsequent remedial measures inadmissible to prove negligence or culpable conduct. In 1997 FRE 407 was amended to apply in product liability cases.
B. Rationale
Repairs and remedial measures should be encouraged.

C. Exceptions
Subsequent remedial measures may be admissible to
1. Show
    a. ownership, or
    b. feasibility of repair, or
2. impeach a witness.
D. Liability Insurance
The admissibility of liability insurance turns upon the purpose for
which the evidence is introduced.
1. Inadmissible Under FRE 411
    Evidence of a party's liability insurance is not admissible to
    demonstrate
    a. whether the party acted wrongfully, or
    b. whether the party has the ability to pay damages.
2. Admissible Under FRE 411
    Evidence of a party's insurance may be admissible for other
    purposes, such as to
    a. prove ownership or control,
    b. impeach a witness, or
    c. flesh out an admission of liability.

IX. OPINION TESTIMONY

A. Common Law
1. Generally
    Common law typically prohibits lay witnesses from giving opin-
    ion testimony. At common law, this rule against lay opinions is
    strictly construed, subject to certain exceptions.
2. Exceptions
    a. Witness's Perception
        A witness may testify about his or her perceptions, so long as
        the proposed testimony is, indeed, rationally related to the
        witness's perception.
    b. "Collective Facts" or "Short-Hand" Facts Theory
        This theory authorizes the admission of opinion testimony
        by lay witnesses when it is difficult or impossible to separate
        the witness's opinion from the testimony about facts the
        witness observed or perceived. For example, when a witness
        describes someone as ill, the witness is both reporting his
        or her observation and drawing an inference from that
        observation.
    c. Other Examples
        Other examples of admissible opinion testimony from lay
        witnesses may include evidence of a witness's perception of

sensory matters, including speed (e.g., of a vehicle), volume, force, and so on, intoxication, or identification.

B. Under the Federal Rules

   1. General Rule

      As a general matter, a lay witness testifying in federal court may not testify about the witness's opinions or inferences.

   2. Exception

      A lay witness may provide the jury with those opinions and inferences that are rationally based on the witness's perceptions; helpful to the jury in understanding the witness's testimony or determining a fact in dispute; and not based on the type of scientific, technical, or other expert knowledge addressed in FRE 702.

   3. Examples

      Examples of lay opinions admissible under FRE 702:

      a. Estimate of witness's lost profits

      b. Identification of person on surveillance video

      c. Opinion that person was sane or insane

C. Ultimate Issue

   Unlike an expert witness, a lay witness may offer an opinion on the ultimate issue.

D. Expert Testimony

   In many cases, the nature of some of the facts is such that the jury might need the assistance of an expert to properly evaluate the facts and draw conclusions from them. In these cases one or both parties will call an expert witness to give expert testimony.

CASE CLIPS

Doe v. United States, 666 F.2d 43 (4th Cir. 1981)

Facts: Black was charged with rape. He submitted a pretrial motion to admit evidence about, and permit cross-examination concerning, the victim's past sexual behavior.

Issue: Is evidence of the past sexual behavior and habits of the victim admissible in a rape trial?

Rule: Rule 412 excludes reputation or opinion evidence of the past sexual behavior of the rape victim.

Huddleston v. United States, 485 U.S. 681 (1988)

Facts: Huddleston was charged with selling stolen goods in interstate commerce and possessing stolen property in interstate commerce. At trial, the prosecution sought to introduce evidence of prior similar transactions by Huddleston. The court allowed the evidence.

Issue: Whether, before admitting prior acts to show motive or knowledge under FRE 404(b), a court must make a preliminary finding that the Government has proved the "other act" by a preponderance of the evidence.

Rule (Rehnquist): Evidence of similar acts should be admitted under Rule 404(b) if there is sufficient evidence to support a finding by the jury, by a preponderance of the evidence, that the defendant committed the similar act. The court should first determine whether the evidence is probative of a material issue other than character.

Michelson v. United States, 335 U.S. 469 (1948)

Facts: Michelson was charged of bribing a federal revenue agent. He claimed entrapment, and called five witnesses to testify as to his good character and reputation. All the witnesses were asked by the prosecution if they had heard that Michelson had been arrested for receiving stolen goods 20 years earlier.

Issue: May the prosecution question character witnesses concerning past events or crimes that would tend to damage the defendant's reputation?

Rule (Jackson): A defendant may call various witnesses to testify as to his general character. However, once the defendant opens the door by introducing testimony of his reputation, his witnesses may be cross-examined as to acts that, if they were aware of them, might tend to damage defendant's character in the community. These questions may also shed light on factors the witnesses may have used to form their opinion and on how well they really know the defendant.

People v. Adamson, 165 P.2d 3 (Cal. 1946)

Facts: Adamson was accused of murdering a woman. Underneath the victim's body was the lower part of a silk stocking with the top part torn off. The tops of three women's stockings were found in Adamson's room; however, none of the stocking tops from the room matched with the bottom part of the stocking found under the body. The stocking tops were admitted in evidence at trial. Adamson objected, contending that the evidence was unfairly prejudicial.

Issue: Whether real evidence that tends to prove a material issue is inadmissible because it is also highly prejudicial to the defendant.

Rule: Except in rare cases of abuse, demonstrative evidence that tends to prove a material issue or clarify the circumstances of the crime is admissible despite its prejudicial tendency. In this case, proof that the defendant had a use for women's stockings was a "logical link in the chain of evidence" that made the proof probative and material. The risk of prejudice did not outweigh the probative value of the proof.

People v. Collins, 438 P.2d 33 (Cal. 1968)

Facts: Collins and his wife were on trial for robbery. The prosecution experienced some difficulty in establishing that they were the perpetrators of the crime. In an attempt to bolster the identifications, the prosecutor called a mathematics instructor at a state college who testified about the mathematical probability that persons other than the Collinses possessed their unusual personal characteristics. The witness inferred that there was a one in 12 million chance that Collins and his wife were innocent and that another couple with equally distinctive characteristics actually committed the robbery.

Issue: May evidence of mathematical probability be introduced in a criminal case?

Rule: The application of mathematical techniques in a criminal case must be critically examined in view of the substantial unfairness to the defendant that could result. The testimony here lacked an adequate foundation both in evidence and in statistical theory. The jurors were most likely impressed by the mystique of the mathematical demonstration but were unable to assess its relevancy or value.

People v. Zackowitz, 172 N.E. 466 (N.Y. 1930)

Facts: Zackowitz was charged with murder. At trial, the main issue was his state of mind at the moment of the murder. The prosecution was allowed to introduce evidence that Zackowitz owned three other pistols and a tear gas gun, the possession of which, it was argued, characterized him as "a desperate type of criminal," and a "person criminally inclined."

Issue: May evidence of other crimes be admitted if there is no connection to the charges?

Rule: Evidence of another crime that has no connection to the current charges is not relevant to any issue in dispute. The evidence is relevant only to the defendant's criminal disposition and is inadmissible because it creates an impermissible inference.

Dissent: The defendant was presented to the jury not as a man of dangerous disposition in general, but as one who, having an opportunity to select a weapon to carry out his threats, proceeded to do so.

United States v. Abel, 469 U.S. 45 (1984)

Facts: Defendant was convicted of bank robbery. The prosecution attempted to prove the bias of a major defense witness by showing that the witness was a member of the Aryan Brotherhood, a secret and violent prison gang.

Issue: May extrinsic evidence be presented to impeach a witness for bias?

Rule (Rehnquist): Extrinsic evidence may be presented to impeach a witness for bias if the evidence is sufficiently probative of a witness's possible bias for or against a party. Under the Federal Rules of Evidence, it is permissible to impeach a witness by showing his bias because this affects his or her credibility as a witness.

Denver City Tramway Co. v. Lomovt, 126 P. 276 (Colo. 1912)

Facts: Witness gave oral testimony at trial. On cross-examination, Witness denied having made prior statements that contradicted his trial testimony.

Issue: If a witness denies making prior inconsistent statements, may a party introduce extrinsic evidence of the alleged prior inconsistent statements?

Rule: If a witness denies having made prior inconsistent statements, the cross-examining party may impeach the witness by introducing extrinsic evidence of those statements.

United States v. Owens, 21 M.J. 117 (U.S. Ct. of Military App. 1985)

Facts: Defendant was accused of shooting and killing his wife after a domestic quarrel. On cross-examination, the prosecutor attempted to impeach Owens by eliciting his admission to a prior act of intentional falsehood.

Issue: May counsel impeach a witness during cross-examination by eliciting Defendant's admission to a prior bad act of intentional falsehood?

Rule: Under FRE 608(b), counsel is authorized to impeach a witness by extracting, on cross-examination, his or her admission to a prior act of intentional falsehood. The evidence must be relevant and its probative value must outweigh the risk of undue prejudice to the witness. Counsel is not permitted to introduce extrinsic evidence of the specific conduct.

Commonwealth v. Holden, 134 A.2d 868 (Pa. 1957)

Facts: Defendant was convicted of murder. At trial, a witness testified that while he was being questioned by the police, Defendant winked at him in an attempt to tell him to create an alibi.

Issue: Whether a witness can testify as to the meaning manifested by the defendant in a nonverbal signal communicated to the witness.

Rule: A witness can state facts, but cannot interpret them.

State v. Brewer, 505 A.2d 774 (Me. 1985)

Facts: Defendant was convicted of driving while intoxicated despite his contention that Pratt was the driver. Defendant's guilt was inferred from Defendant's failure to call Pratt as a witness.

Issue: May the failure of a party to call a witness permit the inference that the witness's testimony would be unfavorable?

Rule: Under the rules of evidence, neither party vouches for any witness's credibility. Therefore, a party's decision not to call a witness cannot be treated as an evidentiary fact that permits any inference as to whether the witness's testimony would be unfavorable.

State v. Rolls, 389 A.2d 824 (Me. 1978)

Facts: Defendant objected to testimony that indicated that only 5 percent of the population had the victim's blood type, which was also found on Defendant's pants. Defendant asserted that the report was hearsay.

Issue: Is the testimony of an expert witness concerning the percentage of the population that has a blood characteristic inadmissible because it is based on the reports of others?

Rule: Testimony from expert witnesses concerning blood characteristics of the population is not considered hearsay and is admissible.

People v. Santarelli, 401 N.E.2d 199 (N.Y. 1980)

Facts: Defendant shot and killed his brother-in-law with no apparent motive. At trial, he contended his conduct should be excused because he was legally insane at the time of the crime. The prosecution, in an effort to rebut this claim, sought to establish that the shooting was a product of Defendant's "explosive personality," and offered proof through the testimony of witnesses that Defendant had committed a number of unprovoked violent acts in the past.

Issue: If a defendant claims he was legally insane at the time of the offense, can the government introduce evidence of uncharged criminal or immoral conduct that has a tendency to disprove the defendant's claim?

Rule: Evidence of uncharged criminal or immoral conduct may be admitted as part of the prosecution's case on rebuttal if it has a tendency to disprove the defendant's claim that he was legally insane at the time of the crime. However, a defendant who asserts an insanity defense opens the door to the prosecution's character evidence only to the extent that such evidence has a natural tendency to disprove his specific claim.

Dissent: The majority's new rule is too restrictive. It has long been recognized that the scope of evidence that is admissible on the issue of insanity is very broad.

United States v. Figueroa, 618 F.2d 934 (2d Cir. 1980)

Facts: Defendant, who was charged with selling heroin, objected to evidence of his prior conviction for the same offense. The prior conviction was introduced to show intent, although no issue concerning Defendant's intent had been raised.

Issue: When is evidence of a defendant's similar crimes or acts admissible at trial?

Rule: To be admissible, evidence of a defendant's similar crimes or acts must be relevant to some disputed issue in the trial, and its probative value must not be substantially outweighed by the risk of unfair prejudice. Here, it was an error to admit Defendant's prior conviction because his attorney had made it clear that Defendant had not brought his intent into dispute.

State v. Bock, 39 N.W.2d 887 (Minn. 1949)

Facts: At Defendant's forgery trial, the prosecution introduced testimony that Defendant had been identified as a person who attempted to pass forged checks on nonexistent accounts on three subsequent occasions.

Issue: Is it an error to admit evidence of collateral crimes with which the defendant is neither charged nor convicted?

Rule: Evidence of separate and independent crimes is generally inadmissible to prove the guilt of a person charged with having committed a crime. However, evidence of collateral crimes is admissible if it is necessary to prove the identity of a person. Similarly, evidence of other similar crimes of the accused closely connected in time, place, and manner is admissible. The evidence is also admissible to show a common system, scheme, or plan.

Specht v. Jensen, 853 F.2d 805 (10th Cir. 1988)

Facts: Plaintiffs brought a suit for damages arising out of allegedly invalid searches of their home and office. Plaintiffs called an attorney as an expert witness. Expert answered a series of hypothetical questions and offered legal conclusion that Defendants conducted an illegal search.

Issue: Does FRE 702 permit an attorney, called as an expert witness, to state his or her view of the law that governs the verdict and give his or her opinion as to whether Defendants' conduct violated that law?

Rule: Expert witnesses may not give their opinions on ultimate questions of law.

Halloran v. Virginia Chemicals, Inc., 361 N.E.2d 991 (N.Y. 1977)

Facts: Plaintiff sued for injuries he sustained while using Defendant's product. The trial court refused to permit Defendant to admit evidence that Plaintiff had, on previous occasions, ignored the label warnings on Defendant's product.

Issue: Is evidence of habit admissible to prove that a person followed that habit on a particular occasion?

Rule: Evidence of habit or regular usage involves a repetitive pattern of conduct and is therefore predictive of conduct on a particular occasion. Where the issue involves proof of a deliberate and repetitive practice, a party may introduce evidence of such habit to allow the inference of its persistence.

Old Chief v. United States, 117 S. Ct. 644 (1987)

Facts: Defendant was accused of being a felon in possession of a firearm. One element of that crime is proof, beyond a reasonable doubt, that the defendant has a prior felony conviction. Defendant sought to minimize prejudicial impact of the jury learning about his felony record by offering to stipulate that he had previously been convicted of a crime. The prosecution refused to stipulate and argued that it had the right to prove its case in the manner it chose — in this case through the introduction of evidence about Defendant's prior conviction.

Issue: Did the district court abuse its discretion when it permitted the prosecutor to introduce relevant evidence of a prior conviction, where the offered proof was highly prejudicial and Defendant had offered to stipulate to it?

Rule (Souter): Evidence of the name or nature of a prior offense generally carries a risk of unfair prejudice to the defendant. The government was presented with alternative, relevant, admissible evidence of the prior conviction by Old Chief's offer to stipulate. There was no cognizable difference between the evidentiary significance of an admission and the legitimately probative component of the official record the prosecution preferred to place in evidence. The risk of unfair prejudice here substantially outweighed the discounted probative value of the record of conviction, and thus it was an abuse of discretion to admit the record when an admission was available.

Dissent (O'Connor): The government was entitled to offer evidence to directly prove a necessary element of its case. Any incremental harm resulting from proving the name or the basic nature of the prior felony can be properly mitigated with limiting jury instructions.

White v. State, 598 A.2d 187 (Md. 1991)

Facts: Defendants were charged with rape. At trial, defendants claimed that the victim fabricated rape charge after they refused to obtain cocaine for her. In support of this claim, defendants sought to introduce testimony of witness who claimed that victim had previously offered or exchanged sex for drugs. The trial court excluded the evidence on the ground that such testimony would violate Maryland's rape shield statute.

Issue: In rape cases, is evidence that the victim had, in the past, exchanged sex for drugs, relevant to establish victim's bias or motive to make false accusation, even in violation of state's rape shield statute?

Rule: The rape shield law provides that evidence relating to a victim's reputation for chastity is not admissible in any prosecution of a rape or sexual offense. Evidence of specific instances of the victim's prior sexual conduct are only admissible if the judge finds that the evidence is relevant and material to a fact in issue in the case, and that its inflammatory or prejudicial nature does not outweigh its probative value. Here, the probative value of testimony about rape victim's prior exchange of sex for drugs was far outweighed by its prejudicial impact. Accordingly, testimony was inadmissible.

Johnson v. Elk Lake School District, 283 F.3d 138 (3d Cir. 2002)

Facts: A former student sued a high school guidance counselor, school district, school board, and school superintendent, claiming that the counselor had sexually harassed and abused her. Pursuant to FRE 415, plaintiff's lawyer sought to demonstrate defendant's propensity toward sexual abuse by introducing evidence that the counselor had touched a co-worker in the crotch area.

Issue: What are the standards for the admission of prior sexual misconduct evidence under FRE 415?

Rule: A court may admit the evidence as long as it is satisfied that the evidence is relevant, with relevancy determined by whether a jury could reasonably conclude by a preponderance of the evidence that the past act was a sexual assault and that it was committed by the defendant. Even when the evidence of a past sexual offense is relevant, the trial court retains discretion to exclude it under Rule 403 if the evidence's probative value is substantially outweighed by the danger of undue prejudice, confusion, or delay. In cases where the past act is demonstrated with specificity and is substantially similar to the charged acts, it is Congress's intent that the probative value of the similar act be presumed to outweigh Rule 403's concerns.

United States v. Mezzanatto, 513 U.S. 196 (1995)

Facts: Defendant was accused of violating federal narcotics laws. Prior to trial, Defendant engaged in plea negotiations with the government. During those negotiations, Defendant signed a waiver, consenting to the prosecution's subsequent use of his statements at any trial that might occur. The plea negotiations were unsuccessful and Defendant went to trial and testified in his own defense. On cross-examination, the government sought to inquire about statements Defendant had made during the plea negotiations. Defendant objected, arguing that FRE 410 operates as an absolute bar to the use of those statements.

Issue: Can a defendant's waiver authorize the admission of statements that are otherwise made inadmissible by FRE 410?

Rule: Nothing in FRE 410 or in the parallel provisions of the Federal Rules of Criminal Procedure prohibits a party from entering into a stipulation as to the admissibility of certain evidence. Where, as here, Defendant acted voluntarily and with the assistance of counsel, the rules of evidence do not preclude a waiver of the protections extended by FRE 410.

Dissent: FRE 410 does not create a personal right that can be waived by a criminal defendant. Congress's enactment of FRE 410 reflects a general policy decision about the best means of promoting plea bargaining. Had Congress intended to create a waivable right, Congress would have written the possibility of waiver into the rule itself.

General Electric Company v. Joiner, 522 U.S. 136 (1997)

Facts: Electrician sued manufacturers, arguing that manufacturers' products contained PCBs and derivative chemicals that had caused his lung cancer. Plaintiff sought to introduce expert testimony in support of his theory that PCBs and derivative chemicals had caused his illness. The trial court concluded that the studies on which Plaintiff's expert relied did not support Plaintiff's expert's opinion. Accordingly, the trial court did not admit Plaintiff's expert testimony. The appellate court reversed, holding that the district court should only have considered whether the studies themselves were reliable and not whether they supported the expert's conclusions.

Issue: What standard should an appellate court apply in reviewing a trial court's decision to admit or exclude expert testimony under *Daubert*?

Rule: *Daubert* did not change the district court's fundamental role as "gatekeeper" and the "abuse of discretion" standard remains the proper standard for appellate review of a district court's evidentiary ruling. Neither *Daubert* nor the FRE require a district court to admit expert evidence that is connected to the existing data only by the *ipse dixit* of the expert. Here, the district court concluded that there was too great an analytical gap between the data and the opinion proffered to warrant the admissibility of the opinion under FRE 702 and the *Daubert* inquiry. This was an appropriate exercise of the court's discretion.

Kumho Tire Company, Ltd. v. Carmichael, 526 U.S. 137 (1999)

Facts: Carmichael's car crashed after a tire on his car blew out. Carmichael and others sued defendants who had manufactured and distributed the tire. Plaintiffs' cases rested, in significant part, on the opinion of an engineering expert who had concluded that the blowout was caused by a design defect in the tire. Defendants moved to exclude Plaintiffs' expert testimony, arguing that the expert's methodology failed to satisfy FRE 702. Relying on its gatekeeper role, the district court granted Defendants' motion. Plaintiffs appealed. The appellate court reversed, holding that *Daubert* applied only to scientific evidence and not to engineering expertise based on skill or experience.

Issue: Whether the "gatekeeping obligation" of *Daubert* and Rule 702 applies only to scientific testimony or to all expert testimony.

Rule: Consideration of the *Daubert* factors is not limited to cases involving scientific evidence. Rather, a district court's use of relevant *Daubert* factors is appropriate when the court considers the admissibility of any specialized evidence, such as technical or mechanical evidence.

Daubert v. Merrill Dow Pharmaceuticals, Inc. 509 U.S. 579 (1993)

Facts: Petitioners were children born with serious birth defects. Petitioners and their parents sued Defendants in federal court, alleging that

Bendectin, a prescription drug marketed by Defendants, had caused the birth defects. Both sides sought to introduce expert scientific testimony on the issue of whether Bendectin can cause birth defects. The federal district court used the *Frye* general acceptance theory to exclude Defendants' proposed expert testimony. Defendants appealed, arguing that FRE 702 supplanted the common law rule of *Frye*.

Issue: Under the FRE, when is scientific evidence admissible?

Rule: Scientific evidence is not admissible under FRE 702 unless the trial court finds that it is both relevant and reliable. To make that determination, a federal district court must engage in a flexible inquiry about both the reliability of the underlying scientific reasoning or methodology and the reliability of its application to the particular facts at issue in the case before it. The district court should consider factors such as whether the theory or technique in question can be (and has been) tested, whether it has been subjected to peer review and publication, the extent of its known or potential error rate, the existence and maintenance of standards controlling its operation, and whether it has attracted widespread acceptance within a relevant scientific community. Even if expert testimony satisfies the requirements of FRE 702, it is still subject to the other rules of evidence. For example, if the expert opinion is based on otherwise inadmissible hearsay, it should only be admitted if the facts or data are "of a type reasonably relied upon by experts in the particular field in forming opinions or inferences upon the subject" (FRE 703). Moreover, under FRE 403, the district court may exclude relevant and reliable expert evidence "if its probative value is substantially outweighed by the danger of unfair prejudice, confusion of the issues, or misleading the jury."

State v. Chapple, 660 P.2d 1208 (Ariz. 1983)

Facts: Chapple was convicted of murder. On appeal, he contended that the trial court erred by admitting pictures of victim's charred body and skull.

Issue: When is inflammatory evidence admissible?

Rule: Where the evidence is of a nature that might incite passion or inflame the jury, the court must go beyond the question of relevancy and consider whether the probative value of the evidence outweighs the danger of prejudice created by admission of the evidence.

Tuer v. McDonald, 701 A.2d 1101 (Md. 1997)

Facts: Plaintiff's husband died while awaiting cardiac surgery. Plaintiff brought a medical malpractice suit against hospital and cardiac surgeons. Plaintiff's husband had been taking Heparin but was taken off the drug on the morning his surgery was supposed to occur. After his death, the hospital changed its protocol with respect to discontinuing Heparin and continued its administration until cardiac patients went into the operating room. Defendants filed a motion to exclude any reference to the change in protocol as an inadmissible subsequent remedial measure.

Issue: When is evidence of a subsequent remedial measure admissible?

Rule: Subsequent remedial measure evidence is not ordinarily admissible for impeachment if it is offered for simple contradiction of a defense witness's testimony. However, if the feasibility of a subsequent remedial measure is controverted, then evidence of subsequent remedial measures is admissible to prove feasibility.

United States v. Lipscomb, 702 F.2d 1049 (D.C. Cir. 1983)

Facts: Lipscomb was accused of possession of heroin with intent to distribute. Lipscomb made a motion in limine to prevent the prosecution from cross-examining him about his eight-year-old robbery conviction. After the district court denied Lipscomb's motion, Lipscomb declined to testify. Lipscomb then appealed, arguing that the district court failed to properly inquire into the underlying facts of the conviction and therefore abused its discretion in admitting the evidence.

Issue: How much information about a prior felony conviction must the trial court have before it decides whether to admit that prior conviction into evidence?

Rule: To meet its burden of justifying the admission of the conviction, the government at a minimum must give the court the name of the crime and the date of the conviction. The court has discretion to inquire into the facts and circumstances underlying a prior conviction. However, the court also has discretion to determine how extensive this inquiry should be. Here, the government provided the court with basic information about the crime; therefore, the court did not abuse its discretion in declining to engage in further inquiry.

Luce v. United States, 469 U.S. 38 (1984)

Facts: Luce was indicted on charges of conspiracy and possession of cocaine with intent to distribute. During his trial, he moved to preclude the government from using a prior state conviction to impeach him. The court ruled that the prior conviction fell within the category of permissible impeachment evidence under FRE 609. After hearing the court's ruling, Luce decided not to testify.

Issue: Whether a defendant who did not testify at trial is entitled to review of the district court's ruling denying his in limine motion to preclude impeachment by his prior conviction.

Rule (Burger): To raise and preserve for review the claim of improper impeachment with a prior conviction, a defendant must testify at trial. Any possible harm flowing from a district court's ruling permitting impeachment by a prior conviction is wholly speculative if the defendant does not testify.

Harris v. New York, 401 U.S. 222 (1971)

Facts: Harris was charged with selling heroin. He took the stand in his own defense. On cross-examination, the prosecutor asked him about certain statements he had allegedly made after his arrest but before receiving his *Miranda* warnings.

Issue: Are statements obtained in violation of *Miranda* admissible for impeachment purposes?

Rule (Burger): Statements obtained in violation of *Miranda* are admissible for impeachment purposes. The shield provided by *Miranda* is not a license to commit perjury.

Dissent (Brennan): The values underlying the Fifth Amendment are jeopardized if an exception against admission of tainted statements is made for impeachment purposes.

Jenkins v. Anderson, 447 U.S. 231 (1980)

Facts: Jenkins stabbed and killed a man. Two weeks later, he turned himself in to the authorities. At his trial, Jenkins contended that the killing was in self-defense. On cross-examination, the prosecutor elicited testimony that Jenkins failed to go to the police immediately after the stabbing. In closing arguments, the prosecution also referred to Jenkins's failure to inform the authorities as a form of impeachment of his credibility.

Issue: Does the use of prearrest silence to impeach a defendant's credibility violate the Fifth or Fourteenth Amendments?

Rule (Powell): Neither the Fifth nor Fourteenth Amendment is violated by the use of prearrest silence to impeach a defendant's credibility. Having voluntarily taken the stand, the defendant is under an obligation to speak truthfully, and the prosecution may use the traditional truth-testing devices of the adversary process to ensure this occurs. Attempted impeachment on cross-examination may enhance the reliability of the criminal process.

Dissent (Marshall): There are three problems with this holding. First, prearrest silence is so unlikely to be probative of the defendant's untruthfulness that its use for impeachment purposes is contrary to due process. Second, drawing an adverse inference from the failure to volunteer incriminating statements infringes the privilege against self-incrimination. Third, the availability of the inference for impeachment purposes impermissibly burdens the decision to exercise the constitutional right to testify in one's own defense.

United States v. Havens, 446 U.S. 620 (1980)

Facts: Defendant was convicted of importing, conspiring to import, and intentionally possessing a controlled substance. He was arrested when customs officials found cocaine sewn into an accomplice's t-shirt. The t-shirt was suppressed prior to trial. At trial, Havens testified in his own defense and denied knowledge of the t-shirt during cross-examination. On rebuttal, the government introduced the shirt to impeach his credibility.

Issue: Whether evidence suppressed as the fruit of an illegal seizure may still be used to impeach a defendant's trial testimony.

Rule (White): A defendant's statements made in response to cross-examination are subject to impeachment by the government. If a defendant chooses to testify and lies, the government should be able to rebut the testimony, even with evidence that has been illegally obtained.

Dissent (Brennan): The government should not be able to use cross-examination as a vehicle to admit otherwise inadmissible evidence.

United States v. Medical Therapy Sciences, 583 F.2d 36 (2d Cir. 1978)

Facts: Defendant and his company, Medical Therapy Services, were convicted of filing false claims for Medicare payments. An unindicted co-conspirator testified for the government. On appeal, Berman argued that the trial judge erred in permitting the prosecutor to call character witnesses to bolster the unindicted co-conspirator's credibility.

Issue: When may character evidence be introduced to bolster the credibility of a witness?

Rule: Under FRE 608, character evidence is admissible only after the character of the witness for truthfulness has been attacked.

United States v. Ince, 21 F.3d 576 (4th Cir. 1994)

Facts: Defendant was indicted for assault with a dangerous weapon, with intent to do bodily harm. At trial, the government called an eyewitness who said she could no longer remember details of what she heard and saw. The government then called the officer who had taken the witness's statement to impeach her.

Issue: May a prior inconsistent statement be introduced to impeach one's own witness?

Rule: Under FRE 607, the credibility of a witness may be attacked by any party, including the party calling the witness. However, at a criminal trial, there are limits on the government's power to impeach its own witness by presenting prior inconsistent statements. In determining whether a government witness's testimony offered as impeachment is admissible, or on the contrary is actually a subterfuge to get substantive evidence that is otherwise inadmissible hearsay before a jury, a trial court must apply Rule 403 and weigh the testimony's impeachment value against its tendency to prejudice the defendant unfairly or to confuse the jury.

United States v. Dotson, 799 F.2d 189 (5th Cir. 1986)

Facts: Defendant, a convicted felon, was charged with three counts of receiving firearms. Defendant testified at trial that following his release from prison, he was faced with serious and repeated threats to his physical safety and had purchased the weapons for his protection. As part of its rebuttal to Defendant's defense of necessity, the government called four government agents to testify that, in their opinion, Defendant and his witnesses were of untruthful character.
Issue: May a witness offer character evidence by way of an opinion that lacks any foundation?
Rule: In the absence of some underlying basis to demonstrate that the opinions were more than bare assertions that the defendant and his witnesses were incredible, the opinion evidence should not have been admitted. The court should have required that the witnesses identify the basis or source of their opinions.

Phar-Mor, Inc. v. Goff, 594 So. 2d 1213 (Ala. 1992)

Facts: Plaintiff fell in a Phar-Mor store and alleged that Phar-Mor's negligence was the proximate cause of her injuries. She claimed her foot was caught under a display basket that was negligently maintained in the store aisles. At trial, Phar-Mor's store manager testified that the basket had been erected in accordance with the manufacturer's instructions. The trial court allowed Goff to introduce photos that showed subsequent remedial measures — specifically that Phar-Mor baskets were stored differently at the time of the trial.
Issue: When may evidence of subsequent remedial measures be introduced to impeach a defendant's testimony?
Rule: To impeach the credibility of a witness through the introduction of a subsequent remedial measure, the testimony providing grounds for impeachment must have been initiated by the witness.

United States v. Alexander, 816 F.2d 164 (5th Cir. 1987)

Facts: Defendant was convicted of robbery. On appeal, he argued that the district court erred in excluding the testimony of two witnesses who were crucial to his defense of mistaken identity. These witnesses would have testified as to the difficulties and inaccuracies involved in comparing photographs of Defendant with pictures of the robber taken by bank surveillance cameras.

Issue: If visual identification is crucial to a defense, is expert identification testimony admissible?

Rule: FRE 702 provides that if scientific, technical, or other specialized knowledge will assist the trier of fact to understand the evidence or to determine a fact in issue, a witness qualified as an expert can testify as to that knowledge. The entire case against Defendant turned on the photographic identification, and it was an error for the court to exclude without good reason relevant expert testimony bearing directly on that issue.

United States v. Chischilly, 30 F.3d 1144 (9th Cir. 1994)

Facts: Defendant was charged with aggravated sexual assault and murder. Prior to trial, he filed a motion in limine requesting a hearing to examine the admissibility of DNA profiling analysis. The trial court denied his motion.

Issue: Is DNA testing admissible under FRE 702 and *Daubert*?

Rule: DNA evidence is admissible under Rule 702 and *Daubert*. Objections to the reliability of DNA testing go to the weight of the evidence rather than to its admissibility.

United States v. Scop, 846 F.2d 135 (2d Cir. 1988)

Facts: Defendants were indicted for mail fraud, securities fraud, and conspiracy. At their trial, the government called a Securities and Exchange Commission investigator as an expert witness. Over defense objections, the investigator was allowed to give his opinion as to whether there was a scheme to defraud investors.

Issue: May experts offer opinions embodying legal conclusions?

Rule: FRE 704 is not intended to allow experts to offer opinions embodying legal conclusions. Doing so invades the province of the court to determine the applicable law and to instruct the jury as to that law.

United States v. West, 962 F.2d 1243 (7th Cir. 1992)

Facts: West was indicted for robbery. At trial, he offered an insanity defense. An examining expert determined that West understood the wrongfulness of his actions at the time of the crime; thus he was not legally insane. As a result, the trial court excluded all of the psychiatrist's testimony. Based on the expert's conclusion on the insanity issue, the trial court refused to charge the jury on the insanity defense.

Issue: Whether a psychiatrist's testimony may be excluded on the basis of his or her inadmissible opinion on the ultimate issue.

Rule: The psychiatrist's opinion on the ultimate issue should play no role in determining whether the psychiatrist can still testify as to the defendant's mental state. FRE 704(b) makes it possible for juries to find a defendant not guilty by reason of insanity even if no expert would draw that same conclusion. Conversely, the rule permits juries to find a defendant sane and guilty notwithstanding an expert's contrary opinion.

Pelster v. Ray, 987 F.2d 514 (8th Cir. 1993)

Facts: Plaintiffs sued Defendants for fraud, alleging Defendants knowingly sold a car with a fraudulent odometer reading. At trial, Plaintiffs' expert testified about automobile theft and odometer fraud. He described the various investigative techniques he used in his work, and how people alter or roll back a car's odometer.

Issue: When is expert testimony admissible?

Rule: FRE 702 provides for the admission of expert testimony where it will "assist the trier of fact to understand the evidence or to determine a fact in issue." If the subject matter is within the knowledge or experience of lay people, expert testimony is superfluous.

Christophersen v. Allied-Signal Corp., 939 F.2d 1106 (5th Cir. 1992)

Facts: Christophersen died from a rare form of cancer and his survivors sued his employer, arguing that his illness was caused by exposure to toxic fumes at his workplace. Plaintiffs attempted to establish medical causation of a toxic tort through the testimony of an expert witness. The district court held that the basis of the expert's opinion was insufficiently unreliable because it was premised on factual data that came from the affidavit of another employee.

Issue: When is an expert opinion based on unreliable facts and therefore inadmissible?

Rule: Pursuant to FRE 703, expert testimony must be based on acts and data of a type reasonably relied on by experts in the particular field in forming opinions or inferences on the subject. Judges may reject opinions founded on critical facts that are untrustworthy, mainly because such opinions cannot be helpful to the jury.

People v. Anderson, 495 N.E.2d 485 (III. 1986)

Facts: Anderson shot and killed the manager of the apartment building where he lived and worked. At trial, he raised the defense of insanity and called a psychiatrist as an expert witness. The trial judge refused to allow any disclosure of the contents of the reports on which the psychiatrist relied in forming his opinion.

Issue: Whether an expert witness may explain the basis of his or her opinion by referring to matters contained in reports that are otherwise inadmissible.

Rule: An expert may utilize reports made by others in forming his or her opinion as long as experts in the field reasonably rely on such materials. An expert should be allowed to reveal the contents of materials on which he or she reasonably relies to explain the basis of his or her opinion. Absent a full explanation of the expert's reasons, including underlying facts and opinions, the jury has no way of meaningfully evaluating the expert testimony.

Burchett v. Commonwealth, 98 S.W.3d 492 (Ky. 2003)

Facts: Burchett ran a stop sign and collided with the victim's truck. He was indicted for manslaughter. At trial, the court allowed the State to introduce evidence of Burchett's daily use of marijuana to support the State's contention that he was under the influence of marijuana at the time of the collision.

Issue: Is evidence that a defendant smoked marijuana on a daily basis admissible to prove that he smoked marijuana on the day of the incident?

Rule: The habit evidence rule encourages a dangerous non sequitur: Because a defendant regularly performs a particular act, he also did so on this particular occasion. Evidence of habit can be unduly prejudicial to the defendant. Confusion of the issues and delay are additional unwarranted, but unavoidable, consequences of the introduction of habit evidence. Accordingly, the evidence should not have been admitted.

Dissent: The evidence excluded here would satisfy the definition of relevant evidence.

United States v. Saunders, 943 F.2d 388 (4th Cir. 1991)

Facts: Defendant was charged with aggravated sexual abuse. Defendant sought to offer evidence that the victim was a prostitute who traded sex for drugs. The court permitted Defendant to testify as to his own prior sexual relations with the victim, but excluded testimony by defense witnesses about their sexual relations with victim.

Issue: Whether evidence of the victim's prior sexual acts with a third party is admissible to prove the defendant's state of mind about the victim's consent.

Rule: FRE 412 provides that reputation and opinion evidence about a victim's past sexual behavior is never admissible, and evidence of specific prior acts is limited to directly probative evidence. When consent is an issue, Rule 412 permits only evidence of the defendant's past experience with the victim.

The Rule manifests the policy that it is unreasonable for a defendant to base his belief of consent on the victim's past sexual experiences with third persons; it is unacceptable to suggest that, because the victim is a prostitute, she is assumed to have consented with anyone at any time.

Olden v. Kentucky, 488 U.S. 227 (1988)

Facts: Defendants were indicted for kidnapping, rape, and forcible sodomy. The trial court refused to allow the defense to impeach the victim's testimony by introducing evidence supporting the victim's motive to lie.
Issue: Whether the Confrontation Clause entitles a defendant to cross-examine a rape witness about her motive to testify falsely.
Rule (Per curiam): The Confrontation Clause includes the right to conduct reasonable cross-examination. The exposure of a witness's motivation is a proper and important function of the right of cross-examination. The trial court erred.

United States v. Cunningham, 103 F.3d 553 (7th Cir. 1996)

Facts: Defendant was charged with tampering with Demerol at the hospital at which she worked. Defendant had a prior conviction for stealing Demerol from another hospital and her nurse's license had been suspended, but had been reinstated. The trial court admitted evidence of the license suspension as well as evidence of Defendant's addiction to Demerol and her falsification of drug test results.
Issue: Is evidence of prior bad acts admissible to show a defendant's motive?
Rule: FRE 404(b) forbids the introduction of evidence of a person's prior conduct for the purpose of showing a propensity to act in accordance with that character. However, evidence of prior conduct can be introduced for other purposes, such as to show the defendant's motive for committing the crime with which he or she is charged.

United States v. Sanders, 964 F.2d 295 (4th Cir. 1992)

Facts: Defendant, a prison inmate, was charged with assault with a dangerous weapon with intent to do bodily harm and possession of contraband. Before trial, he filed a motion in limine to exclude evidence of his prior convictions. Citing FRE 609(a) and 404(b), the court permitted the government to cross-examine Sanders about his prior assault and contraband convictions.
Issue: May a prior felony conviction be used to attack the credibility of a witness?

Rule: Under Rule 609(a)(1), the district court was required to balance the probative value of the evidence of the prior convictions against its prejudicial effect in determining admissibility. However, admission of evidence of a similar offense undoubtedly prejudices the defendant. Thus, the evidence here was inadmissible because of the high likelihood of prejudice.

United States v. Peoples, 250 F.3d 630 (8th Cir. 2001)

Facts: Defendants were indicted for aiding and abetting the murder of a federal government witness. At trial, an FBI agent testified in connection about recorded conversations between Defendants. The agent did not participate in the conversations nor was she present to observe either of the defendants as they spoke. Agent gave her opinion regarding the meaning of words and phrases used by the defendants and her opinion about what the defendants were thinking during the conversations.

Issue: Are lay opinions offered by a law enforcement officer admissible if the officer does not have personal knowledge of the matters about which he or she is testifying?

Rule: When a law enforcement officer is not qualified as an expert by the court, her testimony is admissible as a lay opinion only when the officer is a participant in the conversation, has personal knowledge of the facts being relayed in the conversation, or observed the conversations as they occurred.

State v. Porter, 698 A.2d 739 (Conn. 1997)

Facts: Defendant retained a polygrapher to evaluate Defendant's claim of innocence. Polygrapher concluded that Defendant was telling the truth and Defendant moved to admit polygraph results. Trial court denied the motion in view of Connecticut's traditional per se ban on the admissibility of polygraph evidence.

Issue: Is polygraph evidence per se inadmissible in Connecticut courts?

Rule: Polygraph evidence invades the fact-finding province of the jury, which has traditionally been the sole arbiter of witness credibility. The prejudicial impact of polygraph evidence greatly exceeds its probative value. Thus, polygraph evidence should remain per se inadmissible in all trial court proceedings in Connecticut courts.

United States v. Scheffer, 523 U.S. 303 (1998)

Facts: Defendant was an Air Force airman who volunteered to work as an drug informant. After providing a urine sample but before knowing the results, Scheffer was asked to take a polygraph test. In the opinion of the examiner, the test "indicated no deception" when Scheffer denied using drugs since joining the Air Force. However, the results of the urinalysis

revealed the presence of drugs. Scheffer was tried by general court-martial on various charges, including using methamphetamine. At trial, he claimed "innocent ingestion" of the drugs and sought to introduce the polygraph evidence to support his testimony. The military judge denied the motion, relying on Military Rule of Evidence 707, which provided that the results of a polygraph examination cannot be admitted into evidence. **Issue:** Whether Military Rule of Evidence 707, which makes polygraph evidence inadmissible in court-martial proceedings, unconstitutionally abridges an accused's right to present a defense.
Rule (Thomas): Rule 707 is constitutional. The government has a legitimate interest in ensuring that reliable evidence is presented to the trier of fact in a criminal trial. There is no consensus that polygraph evidence is reliable. Thus, Rule 707 is a rational and proportional means of advancing a legitimate governmental interest. Rule 707 also preserves the court members' core function of making credibility determinations in criminal trials.
Dissent (Stevens): The court ignores the strength of the defendant's interest in having polygraph evidence admitted in certain cases. There is no legal requirement that expert testimony satisfy a particular degree of reliability to be admissible.

United States v. Smithers, 212 F.3d 306 (6th Cir. 2000)

Facts: Defendant was convicted of bank robbery. At his trial, three eyewitnesses identified Smithers as the robber, even though two had earlier failed to select his picture in a photo spread. The trial court refused to allow the defense to call an expert witness to testify about the factors that could affect eyewitness accuracy.
Issue: Does a court abuse its discretion by excluding expert evidence about eyewitness testimony without first conducting a *Daubert* hearing?
Rule: The district court abused its discretion in excluding the expert's testimony without first conducting a hearing pursuant to *Daubert*. Under *Daubert*, a trial court should consider (1) whether the reasoning or methodology underlying the expert's testimony is scientifically valid, and (2) whether that reasoning or methodology properly could be applied to the facts at issue to aid the trier of fact. In neglecting to undertake a *Daubert* analysis, the court failed to take these factors into consideration.
Dissent: The certainty of the testimony of social scientists is limited by the nature of their field.

State v. Kinney, 762 A.2d 833 (Vt. 2000)

Facts: Kinney was charged with kidnapping, sexual assault, and lewd and lascivious behavior. The State called an expert to testify about rape trauma syndrome, the characteristics and conduct of rape victims, and statistics regarding the rate of false reporting of rape.

Issue: Whether expert evidence of rape trauma syndrome and the associated behavior of rape victims are admissible.

Rule: Expert evidence of rape trauma syndrome and the associated typical behavior of adult rape victims are admissible to assist the jury in evaluating the evidence and to respond to defense claims that the victim's behavior after the alleged rape was inconsistent with the claim that a rape occurred. However, the expert's testimony about the incidence of false reporting by rape victims should not have been admitted. This testimony was tantamount to an expert opinion that the victim was telling the truth and thus invaded the province of the jury.

Ballou v. Henri Studios, Inc., 656 F.2d 1147 (5th Cir. 1981)

Facts: The plaintiffs filed a suit against Henri Studios, alleging that Ballou's death was proximately caused by the negligence of one of Henri Studios' employees. Plaintiffs filed a motion to prevent the introduction at trial of the results of a blood alcohol test that showed that Ballou was intoxicated at the time of his accident. Relying on FRE 403, the district court precluded admission of the blood test because its prejudicial impact outweighed its probative value.

Issue: In weighing the probative value of evidence under FRE 403, may a court consider the credibility of the evidence?

Rule: FRE 403 does not permit a court to consider the credibility of evidence when weighing its probative value. Weighing the probative value under Rule 403 means the probative value with respect to a material fact if the evidence is believed.

United States v. Carrillo, 981 F.2d 772 (5th Cir. 1993)

Facts: Defendant was charged with distribution of heroin and cocaine. At his trial, he offered a defense of mistaken identity. The district court allowed the government to present evidence that Defendant had participated in two other sales of controlled substances to help establish his identity as the drug seller in the present case.

Issue: When is evidence of extrinsic acts admissible under FRE 404(b)?

Rule: Under Rule 404(b), evidence of other crimes or acts is not admissible to prove the character of a person to show conformity therewith. However, it may be admissible for other purposes, such as proof of motive, opportunity, intent, preparation, plan, knowledge, identity, or absence of mistake or accident. The admissibility of extrinsic act evidence under Rule 404(b) is determined by a two-part test. First, it must be determined that the extrinsic offense evidence is relevant to an issue other than the defendant's character. Second, the evidence must possess probative value that is not substantially outweighed by its undue prejudice and must meet the other requirements of Rule 403.

United States v. Beasley, 809 F.2d 1273 (7th Cir. 1987)

Facts: Beasley, a chemist, was charged with seven counts of obtaining Dilaudid, a controlled substance, with intent to distribute. At his trial, the prosecution offered evidence that Beasley continued to deal in other drugs after the period covered by the indictment. The decision to admit this evidence was based on a belief that the bad acts showed a "pattern" of crimes "especially close in time"; however, during the trial the judge told the jury the evidence was admitted to show Beasley's intent.

Issue: Whether evidence of other crimes or acts is admissible to prove a pattern of behavior or the intent of the accused.

Rule: Patterns of acts may show identity, intent, plan, absence or mistake, or one of the other listed grounds in FRE 404(b), but a pattern is not itself a reason to admit certain evidence. The evidence of intent creates a risk of the forbidden inference that a person who violates the law at one time has a bad character and thus violated the law at a different time. So although the prior acts were relevant to show intent, their probative value was far outweighed by their potential for unfair prejudice.

Perrin v. Anderson, 784 F.2d 1040 (10th Cir. 1986)

Facts: Plaintiff alleged that Defendants — members of the Oklahoma Highway Patrol — deprived his deceased son of his civil rights when they shot and killed him. During the trial, the court allowed four police officers to testify that, during previous encounters with the decedent, he had been uncontrollable and violent. Defendants offered this evidence to prove that decedent was the first aggressor in the fight with Defendants.

Issue: Can the FRE 404(a) criminal case exceptions be invoked in a civil case?

Rule: FRE 404(a)'s general ban on character evidence permits a criminal defendant to offer evidence of the victim's character to show that the victim was the first aggressor. Although the rule only literally applies to criminal cases, when the central issue involved in a civil case is criminal in nature, the defendant may invoke the exception.

Simon v. Kennebunkport, 417 A.2d 982 (Me. 1980)

Facts: Simon, an elderly woman, sued the Town of Kennebunkport after she fell on a sidewalk. She alleged that her injury was proximately caused by a defect in the design or construction of the sidewalk. The trial court excluded evidence that during the two years prior to the accident many other persons stumbled or fell at the same location.

Issue: Is evidence of similar happenings admissible to show a defective or dangerous condition?

Rule: In a negligence action, evidence of other similar accidents or occurrences may be relevant circumstantially to show a defective or dangerous condition, notice thereof, or causation on the occasion in question. The absence of other accidents or occurrences may also be probative on these issues. When a party seeks to introduce evidence of other accidents, the presiding judge must determine its relevance by considering whether there is a substantial similarity between the offered evidence and the case at bar, and whether the evidence is probative on a material issue in the case.

United States v. Hogan, 763 F.2d 697 (5th Cir. 1985)

Facts: Defendants were indicted for drug offenses. The majority of the government's proposed proof came from a statements made by a cooperating witness who had made key statements while he was incarcerated in Mexico. Following Witness's release, Witness denied any involvement in drug offenses, denied Defendants participated in drug activities, and insisted that his prior statements were the result of torture. Knowing that Witness had changed his statements, the government nevertheless called Witness to testify at Defendants' trial. Government then impeached Witness with his prior inconsistent statements and called Drug Enforcement Agency and embassy officials to impeach Witness's story of torture and fabrication.

Issue: Whether the government may call a hostile witness for the primary purpose of impeaching him with otherwise inadmissible hearsay testimony.

Rule: The government may call a witness it knows might be hostile, and it might impeach the witness's credibility. However, the prosecution may not call a witness it knows to be hostile for the primary purpose of eliciting otherwise inadmissible impeachment testimony, for this scheme serves as a subterfuge to avoid the hearsay rule.

State v. Oswalt, 381 P.2d 617 (Wash. 1963)

Facts: Defendant was charged with robbery and burglary. At trial, he presented an alibi witness who testified that Defendant was in Oregon on the day of the crime. On cross-examination, alibi witness testified that Defendant had been in Oregon every day for the past few months. The State attempted to impeach alibi witness by presenting the testimony of a police officer who said that he had seen Defendant in Washington one month before the crime.

Issue: Can a witness be impeached on matters that are collateral to the principal issue being tried?

Rule: A witness cannot be impeached on matters that are collateral to the principal issues being tried. To determine whether a matter is collateral, the court should consider whether the facts as to which error is predicated, have been shown in evidence for any purpose independent of the impeachment.

United States v. Saada, 212 F.3d 210 (3d Cir. 2000)

Facts: Defendants were convicted of various fraud charges arising out of a scheme to cheat an insurance company. The government produced evidence that they staged a flood in their business. The defendants then submitted inflated claims for compensation for the damaged merchandise. An eyewitness to the crime made a statement supporting Defendants' version of events. However, the eyewitness died before trial. At trial, the eyewitness's statement was admitted under the excited utterance exception in FRE 803(2). The court allowed the government to impeach credibility of the deceased hearsay witness by introducing extrinsic evidence of specific instances of the eyewitness's misconduct.

Issue: Whether extrinsic evidence of a hearsay declarant's prior bad acts is admissible to impeach the credibility of an unavailable declarant.

Rule: FRE 608 bans the use of extrinsic evidence of prior misconduct; this rule applies to hearsay declarants.

United States v. Lindstrom, 698 F.2d 1154 (11th Cir. 1983)

Facts: Defendants were indicted for mail fraud and conspiracy. At trial, they sought to impeach the government's key witness by introducing proof of her psychiatric history, which included manipulative and destructive conduct. The trial court limited defense questioning concerning the witness's prior psychiatric treatment and confinement.

Issue: May psychiatric evidence be used to impeach a witness?

Rule: A goal of effective cross-examination is to impeach the credibility of opposing witnesses. Certain forms of mental disorder have high probative value on the issue of credibility. Accordingly, a witness may be impeached by evidence of mental disorder or psychiatric condition.

State v. Odom, 560 A.2d 1198 (N.J. 1989)

Facts: Defendant was convicted of possession with intent to distribute controlled substances. At trial, the court qualified a police officer as an expert and permitted him to testify that in his opinion, the facts and circumstances surrounding the crime indicated that Defendant possessed the drugs for distribution and not for personal use.

Issue: Whether a duly qualified expert's conclusion that a defendant possessed drugs with the intent to distribute was improper because it answered an ultimate issue reserved to the jury.

Rule: An expert's testimony that expresses a direct opinion that a defendant is guilty of the crime is improper. However, as long as an expert does not express his opinion of the defendant's guilt, but simply characterizes the defendant's conduct based on the facts in evidence in light of his specialized knowledge, the opinion is not objectionable even though it embraces ultimate issues that the jury must decide.

Ingram v. McCuiston, 134 S.E.2d 705 (N.C. 1964)

Facts: Plaintiff sued for personal injuries sustained when the Defendant's car collided with her car. At trial, in an effort to establish the cause of Plaintiff's injuries, Plaintiff's counsel asked the treating orthopedic specialist a hypothetical question that covered six pages in the record. The Defendant's objections to this question were overruled.

Issue: What are the requirements for the proper use of a hypothetical question?

Rule: A hypothetical question may include only facts that are already in evidence or those that the jury might logically infer from the question. Although an expert may base his or her opinion on facts testified to by another expert, the witness may not have submitted to him or her, as a part of the facts to be considered in the formation of his or her inference and conclusion, the opinion of the other such expert.

United States v. Tran Trong Cuong, 18 F.3d 1132 (4th Cir. 1994)

Facts: Defendant was accused of unlawfully prescribing controlled substances to patients who were known drug abusers. At trial, the government called a medical expert who had prepared a written report summarizing information about Defendant's patients. He also testified as to the qualifications of another expert who had also prepared a report on some of Defendant's patients. It was the first expert's opinion that his findings and the second expert's findings were "essentially the same." The defense objected to this testimony.

Issue: Whether an expert opinion is inadmissible if the expert has relied on underlying data that is not of the type reasonably relied on by experts in the field.

Rule: Under FRE 703, an expert's opinion must be based on underlying data that is of the type reasonably relied on by experts in the field.

No foundation was laid for determining that second expert's report was "of a type reasonably relied upon by experts in a particular field in forming opinions or inferences upon the subject." Furthermore, it is doubtful that the report would have met this requirement because it was prepared at the request of the prosecution. Reports specifically prepared for purposes of litigation are not of a type reasonably relied on by experts in the particular field.

United States v. Saelee, 162 F. Supp. 2d 1097 (D. Alaska 2001)

Facts: Defendant was charged with importing drugs through the mail. The government hired a forensic document analyst to compare the handwriting exemplars provided by Defendant with the handwriting on the address labels on the packages in question. Expert concluded that Defendant wrote one of the labels and was probably the writer of another. The court granted Defendant's motion in limine to exclude the handwriting comparison evidence at trial.

Issue: Was the testimony of the forensic document analyst admissible under the Federal Rules of Evidence?

Rule: The government failed to meet its burden of establishing that the expert testimony in this case is admissible under Rule 702. *Daubert* sets forth a nonexclusive list of factors for courts to consider in determining whether expert evidence is reliable, none of which indicate that the particular testimony here is reliable. There is a lack of empirical evidence on the proficiency of document examiners and little empirical testing done on the basic theories on which the field is based. There is little known about the error rates of forensic document examiners. The field also suffers from a lack of controlling standards. The evidence does indicate that there is general acceptance of the theories and techniques involved in the field of handwriting analysis among the closed universe of forensic document examiners, which indicates nothing. Lastly, there is also no proof that expert's proposed testimony as to similarity between known and questioned documents would be the product of reliable principles and methods.

United States v. Piccinonna, 885 F.2d 1529 (11th Cir. 1989)

Facts: Piccinonna was convicted of two counts of knowingly making false material statements to a grand jury. On appeal, he argued that the trial court erred in refusing to admit his polygraph expert's testimony and test results.

Issue: When is polygraph expert testimony and examination evidence admissible at trial?

Rule: Polygraph expert testimony will be admissible in this circuit when both parties stipulate in advance as to the circumstances of the test and as to the scope of its admissibility. It will also be admissible when used to impeach or corroborate the testimony of a witness at trial.

City of Cleveland v. Peter Kiewit Sons' Co., 624 F.2d 749 (6th Cir. 1980)

Facts: Plaintiff and Defendant entered into a contract permitting Defendant to use a portion of the City's dock. Shortly after Defendant surrendered possession to the City, portions of the dock collapsed. The City filed suit against Defendant. At trial, counsel for the City repeatedly made reference to the fact that Defendant was one of the nation's largest construction companies, and that Kiewit had an extensive general public liability insurance policy, and had been awarded a $9 million contract. The jury returned a verdict for the City and the Defendant appealed, arguing that the court improperly permitted the Plaintiff to introduce evidence of Defendant's wealth and ability to pay.

Issue: Whether evidence of the poverty or wealth of a party is admissible in a negligence action.

Rule: Evidence as to the poverty or wealth of a party to an action is inadmissible in a negligence action. Appealing to the sympathy of jurors through references to financial disparity is improper.

Reed v. General Motors Corp., 773 F.2d 660 (5th Cir. 1985)

Facts: Plaintiff's car was struck from behind by Boudreaux's car. All of Plaintiff's passengers were seriously injured. At the time of the accident, Boudreaux was engaged in an illegal race with his friend Meche. The Plaintiff sued Boudreaux, Meche, and their insurers. At the time the case was tried, Louisiana courts permitted a defendant to try to mitigate the damages by introducing evidence of his or her poverty and inability to pay a large verdict. For this purpose, Boudreaux sought to introduce evidence of the limits of his insurance coverage, which were clearly inadequate to compensate the Plaintiff. The trial court then permitted Plaintiff to introduce evidence of Meche's coverage, which was significantly higher.

Issue: Whether the amount of a defendant's insurance coverage is relevant evidence.

Rule: FRE 411 prohibits the admission of evidence that a person was or was not insured against liability on the issue of whether he or she acted negligently or wrongfully. The state statute allowing for the joinder of insurance companies made the existence of insurance coverage relevant. However, the fact that the existence of insurance was admissible did not mean that the court was bound, or even permitted, to admit the amount of coverage.

Jones v. Pak-Mor Manufacturing Co., 700 P.2d 819 (Ariz. 1985)

Facts: Plaintiff sued Defendant for injuries suffered while working on equipment manufactured by Defendant. Before trial, Plaintiff moved to exclude all evidence of the absence of prior, similar accidents. The trial court granted the motion.

Issue: Is the absence of prior accidents admissible evidence in a products liability case involving a claim of defective design?

Rule: In product liability cases involving a claim of defective design, the trial court has discretion under FRE 403 to admit evidence of safety history concerning both the existence and nonexistence of prior accidents, provided that the proponent establishes the necessary predicate for the evidence. The evidence of safety history is admissible on issues pertaining to whether the design caused the product to be defective, whether the defect was unreasonably dangerous, whether it was a cause of the accident, or whether the defendant should have foreseen that the design of the product was not reasonably safe for its contemplated uses.

United States v. Azure, 845 F.2d 1503 (8th Cir. 1988)

Facts: Defendant was charged with sexual abuse of a ten-year-old girl. Prior to trial, he sought to introduce evidence of past sexual relations between the victim and her friend.

Issue: Is evidence of a victim's past sexual behavior admissible under FRE 412 if offered to show the source of the injury to the victim?

Rule: Evidence of specific instances of a victim's past sexual behavior is admissible under Rule 412(b)(2)(A) if offered "upon the issue of whether the accused was or was not, with respect to the alleged victim, the source of semen or injury."

Redmond v. Kingston, 240 F.3d 590 (7th Cir. 2001)

Facts: Redmond, a counselor at an institution for drug- and alcohol-abusing minors, was accused of statutory rape of a 15-year-old resident of the institution. Eleven months earlier, the victim had told her mother she had been raped but later admitted making up the story to get her mother's attention. At trial, Redmond sought to cross-examine the victim about this lie in on the theory that the alleged victim would lie about a sexual assault to get attention, and thus had a motive to accuse him falsely. The trial judge refused to permit this cross-examination.

Issue: Did the exclusion of the evidence of the alleged victim's prior allegation and recantation of rape violate the defendant's constitutional right of confrontation?

Rule: Redmond's right of confrontation was infringed by the exclusion of the alleged victim's prior allegation and subsequent recantation. This was highly probative, nonconfusing, nonprejudicial evidence that was vital to the central issue in the case. The evidence was not cumulative or peripheral; indeed, that victim's credibility was of critical importance because her testimony was virtually the only evidence offered by the prosecution.

United States v. LeMay, 260 F.3d 1018 (9th Cir. 2001)

Facts: Defendant was charged with two counts of child molestation. Before trial, the prosecution gave notice of its intent to introduce, under FRE 414, evidence of Defendant's prior acts of sexual misconduct.

Issue: Whether allowing prior acts of child molestation as propensity evidence under Rule 414 violates fundamental fairness.

Rule: Courts have routinely allowed propensity evidence in sex offense cases even while disallowing it in other criminal prosecutions. Evidence of a defendant's prior acts of sexual misconduct is commonly admitted in prosecutions for offenses like rape, incest, adultery, and child molestation. The introduction of acts of prior sexual misconduct can amount to a constitutional violation only if their prejudicial effect far outweighs their probative value. As long as the protections of Rule 403 remain in place so that judges retain the authority to exclude potentially devastating evidence, Rule 414 is constitutional.

United States v. Robinson, 161 F.3d 463 (7th Cir. 1998)

Facts: Robinson was indicted on charges stemming from two bank robberies. He allegedly robbed the Americana Bank, then robbed the Harrington Bank ten days later. He pleaded guilty to robbing Harrington Bank, but went to trial for the first robbery. The prosecution offered evidence of the Harrington Bank robbery at the trial for the Americana Bank robbery.

Issue: Is evidence from a prior similar crime admissible in the trial for another crime?

Rule: Evidence may be admissible under FRE 404(b) to demonstrate modus operandi, or evidence that shows a defendant's distinctive method of operation. The evidence must bear a singular strong resemblance to the pattern of the offense charged and the similarities must permit an inference of pattern. This evidence was admissible to prove identity.

In re Air Crash Disaster, 86 F.3d 498 (6th Cir. 1996)

Facts: Following a crash of a Northwest Airlines plane, Plaintiffs sued Northwest Airlines and McDonnell Douglas, the plane's manufacturer. Northwest sought to introduce evidence relating to its postaccident rewiring of the plane's Central Warning System as proof that the initial system had been unsafe. McDonnell Douglas filed a motion in limine to exclude that evidence and the district court granted the motion on the grounds that it was inadmissible as a subsequent remedial measure under FRE 407.

Issues:

1. Whether Rule 407's rule of exclusion applies to subsequent remedial measures taken by a third party.
2. Whether Rule 407's rule of exclusion applies to subsequent remedial measures taken after the design of a product, but before the incident at issue at trial.
3. Whether a memorandum, which was written after the accident, that recommends a change in policy, is considered a subsequent remedial measure under Rule 407.

Rules:

1. Yes. There is nothing in the text of Rule 407 that limits its application to measures by a "responsible" party — measures by a party against whom the evidence is offered. By its terms, the Rule seems to exclude evidence of remedial measures regardless of who undertook them.
2. No. Rule 407 bars the admission of evidence of remedial measures taken after an event that would have made the event less likely to occur. Measures taken after the design of a product but before the accident fall outside the reach of Rule 407.
3. Yes. Under Rule 407, a change in policy after an accident is a subsequent remedial measure within the meaning of the Rule.

McInnis v. A.M.F., Inc. 765 F.2d 240 (1st Cir. 1985)

Facts: Plaintiff was injured when her motorcycle was involved in an accident with a car driven by Poirier. She settled with Poirier prior to instituting suit against A.M.F. At trial, A.M.F. was allowed to introduce evidence of the settlement.

Issue: Is evidence of a settlement between a plaintiff and a third party admissible under FRE 408?

Rule: Rule 408 bars evidence of settlements between plaintiffs and third-party joint tortfeasors or former co-defendants. The Rule is commonly invoked to bar the admission of agreements between a defendant and a third party to compromise a claim arising out of the same transaction being litigated. The policies underlying Rule 408 also prohibit the admission of evidence of a settlement between the plaintiff and a third party against whom he has a claim.

Affiliated Manufacturers, Inc. v. Aluminum Co. of America, 56 F.3d 521 (3d Cir. 1995)

Facts: Plaintiff brought suit alleging that Defendant owed additional money on a contract between the two parties. Pursuant to FRE 408, Defendant brought a motion in limine to exclude certain documents and deposition testimony as evidence of settlement negotiations. The documents included Defendant's employees' evaluation of one of the two disputed invoices.

Issue: Whether evidence that demonstrates an apparent difference of opinion between the parties as to the amount of a claim is excluded under Rule 408.

Rule: The application of Rule 408 is limited to evidence concerning settlement or compromise of a claim, where the evidence is offered to establish liability or the validity or amount of the claim. Additionally, Rule 408 has been interpreted as applicable to a dispute or apparent difference of view between the parties concerning the validity or amount of a claim.

Krueger v. State Farm Mutual Auto Insurance Co., 707 F.2d 312 (8th Cir. 1983)

Facts: Decedent was killed when he was struck by Batchman's car. A witness to the collision testified as to his estimate of the distances and speeds involved. However, he was not permitted to testify as to his opinion about whether Batchman could have stopped and prevented the accident. On appeal, Plaintiff argued that Witness was qualified, pursuant to FRE 701, to render such an opinion.

Issue: When is lay opinion testimony admissible?

Rule: Under Rule 701, lay opinions are admissible if they are (a) rationally based on the perception of the witness, and (b) helpful to a clear understanding of his or her testimony or the determination of a fact in issue. Witness's opinion would not have been helpful. The jury had already heard evidence about the distances, speeds, and conditions that set the stage for the collision. Witness's further conclusions would have been superfluous.

People v. Kelly, 549 P.2d 1240 (Cal. 1976)

Facts: Defendant allegedly made a series of anonymous, threatening phone calls. The police obtained a tape recording of the calls and submitted it for spectrographic analysis. A police lieutenant testified that among those who were familiar with and used voice identification analysis, the technique was considered reliable and concluded that the voices on the two tapes were that of the same person.

Issue: Whether a foundation for the admission of expert testimony can be laid even if the witness does not show the requisite academic qualifications enabling him or her to express an expert opinion.

Rule: The witness did not possess the necessary academic qualifications that would have enabled him to express a competent opinion on the issue of the general acceptance of the voiceprint technique in the scientific community. Witness had impressive qualifications as a technician and law enforcement officer, but not as a scientist.

Elock v. Kmart Corp., 233 F.3d 734 (3d Cir. 2000)

Facts: Plaintiff brought a suit for personal injuries she sustained as the result of a slip and fall at a Kmart store. Before and during trial, Kmart sought to exclude the testimony of Plaintiff's expert in vocational rehabilitation on the grounds that he was not qualified as an expert in the field. The district court conducted a voir dire on the expert's qualifications and found that he was qualified to testify about vocational rehabilitation.

Issue: Whether a witness who lacks formal training and credentials in a particular field may testify as an expert in that field.

Rule: Before an expert witness may offer an opinion pursuant to FRE 702, he or she must have "specialized knowledge" regarding the area of testimony. The basis of this specialized knowledge can be practical experience, as well as academic training and credentials. The specialized knowledge requirement is interpreted liberally. At a minimum, a proffered expert witness must possess skill or knowledge greater that of than the average layman.

State v. Green, 428 P.2d 540 (Wash. 1967)

Facts: Defendant was charged with burglary, but contended that two companions had actually committed the crime. One of those companions, Gaither, was called by the prosecution as a witness. The prosecution had not interviewed him before trial. Gaither testified that Green was innocent, after which the prosecutor claimed surprise and unexpected hostility from the witness, and laid a foundation for impeachment by establishing that Gaither had earlier made a written statement incriminating Green as an accomplice.

Issue: Could the prosecution legitimately claim surprise when it had neither interviewed the witness nor otherwise made inquiries as to whether the witness would adhere to his pretrial statement concerning the defendant?

Rule: A party is permitted to impeach its own witness in the event of genuine surprise and hostility. If there weren't an exception to the general rule that a party vouches for the credibility of his witness, a party would be left in a position of hopeless betrayal by a witness on whom he had good reason to rely. Here, the prosecutor had Gaither's detailed pretrial statement. Gaither had never repudiated the statement, nor had he intimated to the prosecutor that he intended to do so. The prosecution had a right to undo the damage done by attempting to impeach the witness, thus canceling the effect of the surprisingly hostile testimony.

State v. Morgan, 340 S.E.2d 84 (N.C. 1986)

Facts: Defendant was on trial for murder. Defendant argued that he had shot the victim in self-defense. On cross-examination the trial court permitted the prosecutor to question Defendant about a prior act of assaultive conduct.

Issue: Are past incidents of assaultive conduct probative of a person's veracity and thus admissible under FRE 608(b)?

Rule: Evidence of assaultive behavior is not probative of the witness's character for truthfulness or untruthfulness. Thus, the evidence was not admissible under Rule 608(b).

CHAPTER 4

Burden of Proof and Presumptions

I. BURDEN OF PROOF

A. Burden of proof is an ambiguous term used to encompass two separate ideas: the burden of producing evidence and the burden of persuading the factfinder.

1. Burden of Producing Evidence

The burden of producing evidence, sometimes referred to as the burden of going forward, is the responsibility of providing some evidence from which it can be concluded that the fact at issue exists. When a party fails to satisfy the burden of producing evidence, the fact does not go to the jury, and the party risks a directed verdict.

2. Burden of Persuading the Factfinder

The burden of persuasion is the responsibility of persuading the trier of fact that the fact at issue is true. The party that bears the burden of persuasion must satisfy that burden to prevent a decision in the other party's favor.

B. Allocation of the Burden of Proof

1. Burden of Producing Evidence

The burden of producing evidence is usually allocated to a party that asserts an affirmative fact or proposition that must be proved. For this reason, the burden of producing evidence might shift back and forth during the course of a trial.

a. Civil Cases

In civil cases, the burden of producing evidence is originally carried by the plaintiff. Once the plaintiff has satisfied the burden, and made out a prima facie case, the burden usually shifts to the defendant. The defendant must then produce evidence either to support a defense or to rebut the evidence produced by plaintiff. The burden of producing evidence may shift back and forth several times in this manner.

b. Criminal Cases
   i. At Trial
      In a criminal trial, the burden of producing evidence is originally carried by the prosecution. The defendant only carries the burden of producing trial evidence if he or she wishes to assert an affirmative defense. In some jurisdictions the prosecution bears the burden of producing evidence to establish the nonexistence of an affirmative defense.
   ii. In Pre- and Posttrial Matters
      In pretrial and posttrial proceedings, the question of who bears the burden of production varies according to the issue in dispute. For example, the prosecution bears the burden of producing evidence that a defendant should be detained prior to his trial. Once the defendant has been detained prior to trial, the defendant bears the burden of producing evidence justifying reconsideration of his detention.

2. Burden of Persuasion
   Unlike the burden of producing evidence, the burden of persuasion generally remains with one party throughout the proceedings. The burden of persuasion usually lies with that party that wishes to change the status quo.
   a. Civil Cases
      In civil cases, the burden of persuasion is almost always allocated to the plaintiff. Not only must the plaintiff persuade the trier of fact that the facts are as he claims, but the plaintiff must also persuade the trier of fact of the nonexistence of any defense raised by the defendant. Occasionally, the law assigns the burden of persuasion to the defendant when asserting certain defenses. Legal presumptions (discussed below) may also shift the burden of persuasion.
   b. Criminal Cases
      The Fifth Amendment Due Process Clause requires that the prosecution prove all the elements of an offense beyond a reasonable doubt. This burden of persuasion never shifts to the defendant. However, once the prosecution presents its evidence, a defendant who asserts an affirmative defense, such as insanity, may carry the burden of persuasion as to that defense.

C. Satisfying the Burden of Production
   1. Quantity of Evidence
      To satisfy the burden of production, a party must produce affirmative evidence that makes it possible for a finder of fact to conclude that the proffered fact(s) exist.

The burden of production may be satisfied through direct or circumstantial evidence.

2. Quality of Evidence

The quality of the evidence required to satisfy the burden of production varies both by jurisdiction and by matter at issue.

a. Civil Trials

  i. Plaintiff

     The plaintiff in a civil trial satisfies the burden of production if it produces evidence that, if uncontested, would satisfy the plaintiff's burden of persuasion.

  ii. Defendant

     In many jurisdictions, the civil defendant satisfies the defendant's burden of production if it produces any admissible evidence as to the existence of the proffered fact. However, some jurisdictions require the defendant to produce evidence that meets the "preponderance of evidence" standard.

b. Criminal Trials

  i. Prosecution

     In a criminal trial, the prosecution must produce evidence that, if uncontested, would support a conviction by proof beyond a reasonable doubt.

  ii. Defendant

     Most jurisdictions require that any rebuttal evidence offered by the defendant meet the "preponderance of the evidence" standard.

D. Satisfying the Burden of Persuasion

A party satisfies the burden of persuasion by meeting one of three specified standards of proof: preponderance of the evidence, clear and convincing evidence, and proof beyond a reasonable doubt.

1. Preponderance of the Evidence

Proof by preponderance of the evidence is generally understood to be proof that shows that the existence of the claimed fact(s) is more probable than its nonexistence. The preponderance of the evidence standard is the standard generally required to satisfy the plaintiff's burden of persuasion in a civil trial. The "preponderance" standard may also suffice to establish an affirmative defense offered by a criminal defendant.

2. Clear and Convincing Evidence

The clear and convincing evidence standard requires a party to prove that the existence of the fact asserted is "highly probable." The clear and convincing standard is used in civil cases that raise issues similar to those litigated in criminal courts, and in civil cases that raise claims of fraud or deception. The clear and convincing standard is also used to determine some pretrial issues in criminal cases.

3. Beyond a Reasonable Doubt

The beyond a reasonable doubt standard requires that the proof be of a nature and quality that the fact would not hesitate to act on a proposition of equal certainty in his or her own life. The reasonable doubt standard is the standard of proof required to satisfy the prosecution's burden of persuasion in all criminal cases.

II. PRESUMPTIONS

A. Defined

A presumption is a procedural rule or process by which the existence of fact B may be presumed by proof of the existence of fact A.

B. Permissive Presumptions

1. Some presumptions merely authorize, but do not require, the finder of fact to infer the existence of fact B by proof of the existence of fact A.

2. Permissive Rebuttable Presumption

In criminal cases, permissible inferences may also be called permissive rebuttable presumptions. When a permissive rebuttable presumption exists, the finder of fact may accept or reject the inference of the existence of the presumed fact. The presumption is rebuttable because the opposing party has the right to introduce evidence that rebuts the presumption. This rebuttal evidence may either challenge the existence of fact A, challenge the validity of the inference that leads to fact B, or challenge the existence of fact B.

C. Mandatory Presumptions

1. Mandatory Presumptions Generally

When the law establishes a mandatory presumption, upon the proof of fact A, the trier of fact must presume the existence of fact B. Mandatory presumptions, especially those in criminal trials, are subject to constitutional scrutiny.

2. Conclusive Presumptions

When a presumption is not subject to rebuttal, that presumption is described as conclusive. Conclusive presumptions are subject to due process and equal protection considerations.

D. Majority View of the Effect of Presumptions: "Bursting Bubble" Theory

1. The majority opinion on the effect of presumptions was articulated by Professor Thayer and is alternately called the Thayer approach or the "bursting bubble" theory. This is the theory adopted in FRE 301 (above). According to this theory:

   a. A presumption operates to shift the burden of producing evidence to the party against whom the presumption operates; it does shift the burden of persuasion; rather

   b. Once the party opposing the presumption introduces evidence to support the nonexistence of the presumption, the presumption disappears and the burden of production shifts back to the other side.

2. Exceptions

   Even within those jurisdictions that adopt the Thayer approach there are certain exceptions:

   a. Where the fact at issue is one that a particular party is in a unique and peculiar position to know, the burden or persuasion may shift to that party.

   b. Certain jurisdictions adopt the "bursting bubble" approach but require an increased amount of evidence to rebut the presumption.

E. Minority Viewpoint

   Under the minority viewpoint, a presumption shifts both the burden of production and the burden of persuasion as to the non-existence of the presumption. Under this view, presumptions have evidentiary weight as well as procedural weight.

F. Effect of Presumptions in Civil Cases

   The effect of a presumption in a civil case varies with the laws of the particular jurisdiction. The FRE codify the law of presumptions in civil cases:

   1. In Federal Civil Actions

      FRE 301 provides that, in a federal civil case, a presumption

      a. imposes the burden of production upon the party seeking to rebut or defeat the presumption.

      b. Leaves the burden of persuasion untouched; that is, the burden of persuasion remains with the party that bore it at the commencement of the trial.

   2. State Claims and Defenses Tried in Federal Court

      When a case is tried in federal court, but State law supplies the claim or defense at issue, FRE 302 requires the federal court to apply State law concerning the allocation of burdens and presumptions.

G. Effect of Presumption in Criminal Cases

There are two types of presumptions identified in criminal law: permissive presumptions and conclusive presumptions.

1. Permissive Presumptions
   a. Generally
      A permissive presumption is one that the jury may, but need not accept. A permissive presumption does not shift the burden of proof. Rather, the trial court informs the jury that it may, but need not, presume the existence of fact B from the proof of fact A.
   b. Constitutionality of Permissive Presumption
      The constitutionality of a permissive presumption is evaluated on a case-by-case basis. A permissive presumption is constitutional so long as, in the case at issue, there is a rational connection between the proven fact and the presumed fact.

2. Mandatory Presumption
   a. Generally
      A mandatory presumption requires the jury to treat the presumed, upon proof of fact A, to treat fact B as proven. Mandatory presumptions of elemental facts are always unconstitutional, as they relieve the prosecution of its burden of proving all of the elements of a crime, by proof beyond a reasonable doubt.
   b. Two Types of Mandatory Presumptions
      There are two types of mandatory presumptions: mandatory conclusive presumptions and mandatory rebuttable presumptions.
      i. Mandatory Conclusive Presumptions
         Mandatory conclusive presumptions require the jury to treat presumed fact as proven. The presumption removes that fact from the jury's consideration, regardless of any evidence the defendant might produce to undermine the presumed fact. Mandatory conclusive presumptions of elemental facts are always unconstitutional.
      ii. Mandatory Rebuttable Presumptions
         Mandatory rebuttable presumptions require the jury to treat the presumed fact as proven unless the defendant rebuts that presumption. This "opportunity" to rebut the presumption not only relieves the prosecution of its burden of proof, but also constitutionally shifts the burden of proof to the defendant. Mandatory rebuttable presumptions of elemental facts are always unconstitutional.

CASE CLIPS

County Ct. of Ulster County v. Allen (S. Ct. 1979)

Facts: P was a passenger in an automobile stopped for speeding. Upon a search of the vehicle, two loaded handguns were found visible in the open purse of a female minor passenger. A machine gun and over a pound of heroin were found in the trunk. A New York statute provided that, with certain exceptions, the presence of a firearm in an automobile created a permissive presumption that the gun was possessed by all of the passengers of the automobile.

Issue: Does this presumption unconstitutionally relieve the prosecution of its burden of proof?

Rule (Stevens, J.): If there is a "rational connection" between the fact proven and the fact presumed, and the presumed fact is "more likely than not to flow" from the proven fact, the presumption does not relieve the prosecution of its burden of proof, and does not violate due process. As applied to the facts of this case, the presumption of possession was rational.

Dissent (Powell): The presumption was unconstitutional because it did not fairly reflect what common sense and experience tell us about passengers in cars and the possession of handguns. The presence of a person in a car, without more, does not indicate that he exercises "dominion or control over" everything within it.

Francis v. Franklin, 471 U.S. 307 (1985)

Facts: While visiting a dentist, Franklin, a prisoner, escaped from custody. During the course of his escape, he shot a local resident. Franklin claimed that the shooting was an accident. The trial judge gave two instructions to the jury to the effect that: (1) the acts of a person of sound mind are presumed to be the product of the person's will, but the presumption may be rebutted, and (2) a person of sound mind is presumed to intend the natural and probable consequences of his acts, but the presumption may be rebutted.

Issue: If intent is an element of the offense, can the law mandate presumption of a defendant's intent from other proven evidence?

Rule (Brennan, J.): Due process requires the prosecution to prove the intent beyond a reasonable doubt. The Due Process Clause prohibits the State from using evidentiary presumptions in a jury charge that have the effect of relieving the State of its burden of persuasion beyond a reasonable doubt of every essential element of the crime. Because a reasonable juror could have understood the challenged portions of the jury instruction as creating a mandatory presumption that shifted the burden of persuasion on the element of intent to the defendant, the jury charge violates the Due Process Clause.

Dissent (Rehnquist): One or two possibly misleading sentences out of jury instructions should not be the sole basis of a reversal. The jury was instructed four times that the State bore the burden of proof beyond a reasonable doubt.

Texas Department of Community Affairs v. Burdine, 450 U.S. 248 (1981)

Facts: Burdine sued the Texas Department of Community Affairs, alleging that its failure to promote her and the subsequent decision to terminate her had been predicated on gender discrimination in violation of Title VII. The District Court held that neither decision was based on gender discrimination.

Issue: What burden must an employer meet to rebut a prima facie case of employment discrimination in a Title VII suit?

Rule (Powell): The employer's burden is to rebut the presumption of discrimination by producing evidence that the plaintiff was rejected, or someone else was preferred, for a legitimate, nondiscriminatory reason. The employer does not have to actually persuade the court that it was motivated by those reasons; it just needs to raise a genuine issue of fact as to whether it discriminated.

Patterson v. New York, 432 U.S. 197 (1977)

Facts: Defendant shot Victim after seeing Victim and Defendant's estranged wife in a state of undress. Defendant was charged with second-degree murder and raised the affirmative defense of extreme emotional disturbance. The trial court instructed the jury that (1) the defendant had the burden of proving the affirmative defense by a preponderance of the evidence; and, (2) if the defendant met his burden, the jury had to find him guilty of manslaughter instead of murder. The jury found Defendant guilty of murder. On appeal, Defendant argued that the shift in the burden of persuasion violated his due process rights by improperly shifting the burden of persuasion from the prosecutor to the defendant.

Issue: Is it a violation of the Due Process Clause to require a defendant to bear the burden of proving an affirmative defense?

Rule (White): Due process does not require that the prosecution prove the nonexistence of the elements of affirmative defenses. The burden of persuasion for affirmative defenses may be placed on the defendant. In this case, the State proved, beyond a reasonable doubt, all of the elements necessary to convict Defendant of murder. The affirmative defense did not negate any facts of the crime that the State is required to prove to convict of murder. Therefore, it constitutes a separate issue on which the defendant may lawfully be required to carry the burden of persuasion.

Dissent (Powell): The Due Process Clause requires that the prosecutor bear the burden of persuasion beyond a reasonable doubt where, as here, the factor at issue makes a substantial difference in the punishment and stigma associated with the offense.

Martin v. Ohio, 480 U.S. 228 (1987)

Facts: Martin was charged with and tried for aggravated murder. She pleaded self-defense. Ohio law provides that self-defense is an affirmative defense, and that the defendant has the burden of proving it.

Issue: May a state constitutionally require a criminal defendant to meet the burden of proving an affirmative defense to the charged crime?

Rule (White): The state did not shift to Martin the burden of proving or disproving any of the elements composing the charged crime of murder. The burden of proving each element of the offense beyond a reasonable doubt still rested with the prosecution. Because proof of self-defense does not shift the burden to an element of the crime, the burden is not unconstitutionally placed on the defendant.

Dissent (Powell): In many cases, a defendant who finds himself or herself in immediate danger and reacts with deadly force will not have formed a prior intent to kill. The elements of the defense and the elements of the offense conflict; this conclusion should suggest that Ohio is prevented from shifting the burden as to self-defense.

United States v. Taylor, 464 F.2d 240 (2d Cir. 1972)

Facts: Defendant was stopped at a Canadian border crossing for routine questioning. Because Defendant had no proof of vehicle registration, customs agents inspected the car and discovered counterfeit money in a magazine and various road maps. Defendant moved for a directed verdict of acquittal. The trial court denied the motion and the jury convicted Defendant of possessing and concealing counterfeit bills.

Issue: What is the required standard for a judge to send a criminal case to the jury?

Rule: When deciding whether to send a criminal case to the jury, the judge must determine whether, with the evidence produced by the prosecution, a reasonable person might fairly conclude that the defendant's guilt had been proven, beyond a reasonable doubt. If the judge concludes that there is no evidence on which a reasonable mind might fairly conclude guilt beyond a reasonable doubt, the judge cannot send the case to the jury and must grant the motion of acquittal. However, if the judge concludes that on the evidence a reasonable mind could conclude guilt beyond a reasonable doubt, then the case must be sent to the jury.

In re Winship, 397 U.S. 358 (1970)

Facts: Minor was charged with delinquency based on his alleged theft of $120. The applicable statute required proof of delinquency by a preponderance of the evidence.

Issue: Must a juvenile conviction or delinquency finding be proven by proof beyond a reasonable doubt?

Rule (Brennan, J.): Guilt of a criminal charge, even against a juvenile, must be established by proof beyond a reasonable doubt.

Lego v. Twomey, 404 U.S. 477 (1972)

Facts: Defendant was arrested and charged with armed robbery. After arrest, Defendant made a statement confessing his involvement in the crime. At a pretrial hearing, Defendant sought to suppress the confession as an involuntary statement. The court found, by a preponderance of the evidence, the statement to be voluntary. Therefore, the statement was introduced at trial. On appeal Lego argued that he was not proven guilty beyond a reasonable doubt as required by *In re Winship*, 397 U.S. 358, because the confession used against him had been proved voluntary only by a preponderance of the evidence.

Issue: By what standard of proof must the prosecution prove the voluntariness of a confession?

Rule: The prosecution must prove, by a preponderance of the evidence, that the confession was voluntary; however, states are free to adopt a higher standard. Because the purpose that a voluntariness hearing was designed to serve has nothing to do with improving the reliability of jury verdicts, judging the admissibility of a confession by a preponderance of the evidence does not undermine *In re Winship*.

United States v. Jessup, 757 F.2d 378 (1st Cir. 1985)

Facts: The Bail Reform Act requires judicial officers making bail decisions to apply a rebuttable presumption that a person charged with a serious drug offense will likely flee before trial. Relying on this presumption, a federal magistrate judge detained Jessup. Jessup argued that the use of the presumption violates the Due Process Clause.

Issue: May the government use a mandatory rebuttable presumption to keep a defendant in custody to secure his presence at trial?

Rule: The presumption represents a reasonable congressional response to a problem of legitimate legislative concern. The government's interest in securing the appearance of a defendant at trial has been held to be important enough to warrant pretrial detention when there is a significant risk of flight. Congress held hearings and heard evidence that drug offenders posed a special risk of flight. The presumption does not significantly increase the risk of an erroneous deprivation of liberty because the defendant can rebut the presumption and is given the opportunity for a hearing.

Sandstrom v. Montana, 422 U.S. 510 (1979)

Facts: Sandstrom was on trial for murder. At trial, his attorney argued to the jury that, although Sandstrom admitted killing the victim, he did not do so "purposely or knowingly" and was not guilty of deliberate homicide, but of a lesser crime. The trial judge instructed the jury that "the law presumes that a person intends the ordinary consequences of his voluntary acts." Sandstrom was found guilty.

Issue: Whether, in a case in which intent is an element of the crime charged, the jury instruction "the law presumes that a person intends the ordinary consequences of his voluntary acts" violates the Fourteenth Amendment's requirement that the State prove every element of a criminal offense beyond a reasonable doubt.

Rule (Brennan): The question of whether the crime was committed purposely or knowingly was a fact necessary to constitute the crime of deliberate homicide. The challenged jury instruction had the effect of relieving the State of its burden of proof on the critical question of Sandstrom's state of mind. Because the State was not forced to establish every element of the crime by proof beyond a reasonable doubt, Sandstrom was deprived of his constitutional right to due process of law.

Hinds v. John Hancock Mutual Life Insurance Co., 155 A.2d 721 (Me. 1959)

Facts: Plaintiff was the beneficiary of his late father's life insurance policy. The policy provided for an additional death benefit if the death was due to bodily injuries sustained solely through "violent, external & accidental means." Decedent was killed by a gunshot wound and was extremely intoxicated at the time of his death. The physical evidence pointed toward suicide. However, Plaintiff sued to recover the additional death benefit.

Issue: Whether a rebuttable presumption against suicide ceases to operate if the party against whom it is asserted produces any evidence to contradict the presumed fact.

Rule: The death of the insured person by violent and external means was conceded. The burden was on the plaintiff to prove by a preponderance of the evidence that those means were also accidental. When no countervailing evidence is offered, or that which is offered amounts to surmise or speculation, the presumed fact stands as though proven and the jury will be so instructed. However, when the contrary evidence comes from such sources and is of such a nature that rational minds could not dispute the nonexistence of the presumed fact, the presumption will disappear as a matter of law. The presumed fact is controlling until the factfinder is convinced that the existence of the presumed fact is as likely as not.

O'Dea v. Amodeo, 170 A. 486 (Conn. 1934)

Facts: A statute provided that proof that the operator of a motor vehicle was the husband, wife, father, mother, son, or daughter of the owner raised a presumption that the motor vehicle was being operated as a family car within the general scope of authority of the owner, and imposed the burden of rebutting that presumption on the defendant. Plaintiff sued Defendants — driver and driver's father — after he was injured in a car accident with driver.

Issue: Whether presumptions that rest on the fact that the circumstances involved in the issue are peculiarly within the knowledge of one party are only rebuttable by that party's proof of countervailing circumstances.

Rule: When the circumstances involved are peculiarly within the knowledge of one party, in certain instances that party should have the burden not only of offering some substantial countervailing evidence, but also of proving such circumstances. The presumption will cease to operate when the adverse party has produced enough evidence that gives a basis for finding the circumstances relevant to the issue of the defendant's liability.

Rose v. Clark, 478 U.S. 570 (1986)

Facts: Defendant was charged with murder. The trial court instructed the jury that to convict Defendant of second-degree murder, malice must be shown. The court further instructed that malice is presumed in all homicides, thereby requiring Defendant to rebut that presumption. Defendant was convicted, and on appeal argued that the instructions were erroneous because they impermissibly shifted the burden of proof as to malice.

Issue: Do jury instructions that erroneously shift the burden of proof on an element of the crime necessarily constitute reversible error?

Rule (Powell): An otherwise valid conviction should not be set aside if the reviewing court may confidently say, based on the whole record, that the constitutional error was harmless beyond a reasonable doubt. However, some errors necessarily render a trial fundamentally unfair and require a reversal without regard to the evidence in the particular case. The erroneous instruction that shifted the burden of proof on malice is not "so basic to a fair trial" that it can never be harmless.

Dissent (Blackmun): Defendant was deprived of his right to a jury trial by this instruction. The jury was not compelled to perform its constitutionally required role and this rendered the trial fundamentally fair. The harmless error standard should not be applied.

In re Yoder Co., 758 F.2d 1114 (6th Cir. 1985)

Facts: Bankruptcy Court set a date for creditors to file proofs of claim against Yoder — the "bar date." Plaintiff filed a proof of claim about eight months after the bar date. Plaintiff later claimed he had never received notice of the bar date. The Bankruptcy Court made a factual finding that notice of the bar date had been sent to Bratton's lawyer, Ornstein. It relied primarily on a presumption of receipt that it held arose from the evidence that the notice was properly mailed.

Issue: Does a presumption have any probative effect once it has been rebutted?

Rule: Under Rule 301, a presumption has no probative effect once it is rebutted. In this context, testimony of nonreceipt, by itself, is sufficient to support a finding of nonreceipt. This testimony is sufficient to rebut the presumption of receipt. The Bankruptcy Court erred in relying on the presumption and notice of the hearing to establish receipt.

Dyer v. MacDougall, 201 F.2d 265 (2d Cir. 1952)

Facts: Plaintiff sued Defendant for libel and slander, alleging that Defendant had written a libelous letter about him and had made slanderous statements. At depositions, all witnesses denied hearing or reading the slanders. The trial court granted Defendant's motion for summary judgment, finding that there was no genuine issue of material fact under FRCP 56(c).

Issue: Should summary judgment be directed against a plaintiff who is unable to present any witnesses at trial to testify to his allegations?

Rule: If this case went to trial, Plaintiff would have no witnesses who would acknowledge the slanders alleged in the complaint. However, Plaintiff could put the witnesses on the stand and attempt to persuade the jury that they were lying about their ignorance of the alleged slanders. However, there could not be an effective appeal because demeanor evidence cannot be reflected in the record.

Legille v. Dann, 544 F.2d 1 (D.C. Cir. 1976)

Facts: Plaintiff sought an order directing the Commission of Patents, Legille, to reassign an earlier filing date to his patent application. The applications had been mailed on March 1, and were date-stamped March 8 by the Patent Office, which was the date of receipt. If the action of the Patent Office were to stand, three of the patent applications fail.

Dann requested a filing date of not later than March 6, on the basis that the law presumes that something mailed will be delivered in due course and without unreasonable delay. The district court held that the rebuttable presumption of delivery in due course could not be overcome by invoking another conflicting presumption, but had to be rebutted by positive evidence that the presumption was inapplicable in a particular case. Summary judgment was granted for Plaintiff.

Issue: Whether a summary disposition of a case may be made by deciding the relative strength of two contrary presumptions involved and deciding which one should prevail.

Rule: The prevailing view is the "bursting bubble" presumption — the presumption does not remain viable in the face of contradictory evidence. There is no legal or practical justification for preferring either of the two involved presumptions over the other.

In re Nicholas H., 46 P.3d 932 (Cal. 2002)

Facts: Nonbiological father filed an action to obtain custody of minor child while biological mother was in jail. Under state law, a man who receives a child into his home and openly holds the child out as his natural child is presumed to be the natural father of the child; however this presumption is rebuttable. The district court found that the presumption that the man was the child's natural father had been rebutted by his admission that he was not Nicholas's biological father.

Issue: Whether a presumption that a man is the natural father of a child whom he cares for is necessarily rebutted when the presumed father seeks parental rights but admits he is not the biological father of the child.

Rule: The statute says that the presumption is rebuttable, and may be rebutted in an appropriate action. When it used the limiting phrase "an appropriate action," the Legislature was unlikely to have had in mind an action like this, where no other man claims parental rights to the child and where a rebuttal of the presumption will render the child fatherless. It most likely had in mind an action where another candidate is vying for parental rights and seeks to rebut the presumption to perfect his claim.

Virginia v. Black, 538 U.S. 343 (2003)

Facts: A Virginia cross-burning statute made it a crime to burn a cross with the intent to intimidate and made the burning of a cross prima facie evidence of intent to intimidate. At Black's trial, the trial judge instructed the jury that the burning of a cross by itself was sufficient evidence from which they could infer the required intent.

Issue: Whether a statutory provision treating the act of cross-burning as prima facie evidence of intent to intimidate is constitutional.

Rule (O'Connor): The prima facie provision, as interpreted by the jury instruction, renders the statute unconstitutional. The provision allows the Commonwealth to arrest, prosecute, and convict a person based solely on the fact of cross-burning alone. It permits a jury to convict in every cross-burning case where defendants exercise their constitutional right not to put on a defense, and makes it more likely that the jury will find intent to intimidate regardless of the particular facts of the case.

Concurrence/Dissent (Scalia): The presentation of evidence that a defendant burned a cross in public is automatically sufficient on its own to support an inference that the defendant intended to intimidate only until the defendant comes forward with some evidence in rebuttal.

Dissent (Thomas): The fact that the statute permits a jury to draw an inference of intent to intimidate from the cross burning itself presents no constitutional problems. Not making a connection between cross burning and intimidation would be irrational.

McNulty v. Cusack, 104 So. 2d 785 (Fla. Dist. Ct. App. 1958)

Facts: Plaintiff sued Defendant after Defendant's car ran into the rear of Plaintiff's car at an intersection.

Issue: Does an unexplained rear-end collision give rise to a presumption of negligence?

Rule: When a car runs into another car from the rear, a presumption of negligence arises. The burden of going forward with the rebuttal evidence is on the party who ran into the preceding car from the rear.

State of Maryland v. Baltimore Transit Co., 329 F.2d 738 (4th Cir. 1964)

Facts: The plaintiff's intestate was killed when struck by a bus owned by the defendant. Witnesses testified that the decedent had crossed the street away from the intersection and without the invitation or protection of an electric pedestrian signal. The trial judge instructed the jury that a decedent is presumed to have exercised ordinary care for his own safety, but where evidence has been offered to show that the decedent failed to exercise ordinary care in a number of respects, the jury may not rely on the presumption. A general verdict was entered for the defendant.

Issue: Does a presumption survive, even after conflicting evidence has been offered, in cases where an injured person is unavailable because of injuries or death?

Rule: The presumption of due care may still be invoked where the injured person is unavailable because of the injuries suffered or because of death.

Scott v. Hansen, 289 N.W. 710 (Iowa 1940)

Facts: Passenger-Plaintiff sued a driver for personal injuries sustained when the driver collided with a cow that was crossing the highway. Plaintiff alleged that Defendant's operation of the car was reckless. Plaintiff testified that Defendant was traveling at approximately 70 miles per hour and never braked. Another witness testified that the cow bounced up and down like a rubber ball on impact. On the other hand, the physical evidence showed that the skid marks on the road extended for a distance of 354 feet before the collision, indicating that Defendant had attempted to stop the car long before he hit the cow.

Issue: Is a jury permitted to believe testimony that is contradicted by physical facts?

Rule: The testimony of Plaintiff and his witnesses is completely inconsistent with the undisputed and established physical facts that the inevitable conclusion is that Plaintiff and his witnesses were mistaken. The testimony was so lacking in probative force or effect that a jury's finding that the car's speed as it approached the cattle was not reduced would be unwarranted.

United States v. Nelson, 419 F.2d 1237 (9th Cir. 1969)

Facts: Nelson and Brewton were indicted for robbery. Brewton was found incompetent to stand trial. At Nelson's trial, the government introduced testimony that Brewton had entered and robbed the bank while an unidentified person sat in a car in an adjacent parking lot. After the robbery, the car fled at a high speed and was pursued by a police officer. The driver exited from the car and fled on foot. Nelson was later captured with $125 in his possession.

Issue: Is it proper to infer a fact at issue from other facts that have been established by circumstantial evidence?

Rule: Circumstantial evidence is not inherently less probative than direct evidence. Under some circumstances, it might be more reliable.

Smith v. Bell Telephone Co. of Pennsylvania, 153 A.2d 477 (Pa. 1959)

Facts: Plaintiff sued Bell Telephone, alleging that telephone conduit that crushed sewer line was responsible for driving seepage into his basement. After Plaintiff presented evidence, he was met with a compulsory nonsuit on the grounds that he had not made out a prima facie case.

Issue: When a plaintiff's case is based on circumstantial evidence, must that evidence be so conclusive as to exclude any other reasonable inference inconsistent with that evidence?

Rule: The evidence must be such that a jury can reach the conclusion sought by the plaintiff. It is not necessary that every fact point to liability. It is enough that there are sufficient facts for the jury to reasonably say that the preponderance of the evidence favors liability.

Delaware Coach Co. v. Savage, 81 F. Supp. 293 (D. Del. 1948)

Facts: Plaintiff's trolley coach and Defendants' truck collided, killing the driver of the trolley coach. At trial, a number of eyewitnesses testified and Defendants produced a greater number of disinterested witnesses supporting their position. The trial court found that because Plaintiffs failed to prove Defendants' negligence by a preponderance of the evidence, Plaintiff had failed to sustain its burden of persuasion. Judgment was entered for Defendants.

Issue: Which party bears the burden of proof in an ordinary civil case?

Rule: The burden of proof rests on the party asserting the affirmative of an issue, in this case, the negligence of the defendants. The party asserting the fact must prove it by a preponderance of the evidence. The burden of proof of such fact continues throughout the case and never shifts.

Riley Hill General Contractor, Inc v. Tandy Corp., 737 P.2d 595 (Or. 1987)

Facts: Plaintiff sought compensatory and punitive damages on fraud, breach of warranty, and negligence claims, arising out of Plaintiff's purchase of a computer that was manufactured and sold by Defendant. The jury returned a verdict for Plaintiff.

Issue: Whether the burden of persuasion for common law deceit should be by clear and convincing evidence, by a preponderance of the evidence, or by a combination of both concepts.

Rule: The burden of persuasion for common law deceit requires the proponent to prove each of the elements of deceit by clear and convincing evidence, but general or punitive damages arising out of that deceit need only be proved by a preponderance of the evidence.

CHAPTER 5

Judicial Notice of Facts

I. GENERALLY

Judicial notice occurs when a trial court accepts a fact as true without requiring either party to introduce evidence supporting that fact. Judicial notice is intended to save the parties, the court, and the jury the time and effort associated with proving facts that are a matter of common knowledge.

II. TERMINOLOGY

A. "Adjudicative" Facts
  1. Definition
     Adjudicative facts are facts that relate to the particular case before the court; they are facts that normally go to a jury in a jury case.
  2. Examples
     a. Notice of what action a party took
     b. Notice of a party's intention or motive
B. Legislative Facts
  Legislative facts are facts capable of universal application within the relevant jurisdiction. They are not unique to the parties or litigation before the court. Examples of legislative facts are:
  1. a legal principle
  2. a judicial ruling
  3. a court order
  4. a legislative enactment

III. NOTICE OF ADJUDICATIVE FACTS

A. Under the Federal Rules: FRE 201
   1. Generally
      a. FRE 201 is the federal rule governing judicial notice of adjudicative facts.
      b. N.B. The FRE approach to judicial notice is very similar to the common law approach.
   2. Scope
   FRE 201 applies to notice of adjudicative facts, but not to notice of legislative facts or notice of legal matters.
   3. Procedure
      a. Time of Taking Notice
      Judicial notice may be taken at any stage of the proceeding prior to the closing of the evidence.
      b. Opportunity to Be Heard
      Under the FRE, a party is entitled, upon timely request, to an opportunity to be heard as to the propriety of taking judicial notice. In the absence of prior notification (for example, when the court takes notice sua sponte), a party may make the request to be heard after the court has taken notice.
      c. Jury Instructions Regarding Effect of Judicial Notice
         i. Civil Cases
         In a civil action or proceeding, the court shall instruct the jury to accept as conclusive any fact judicially noticed.
         ii. Criminal Cases
         In a criminal case, the court shall instruct the jury that it may accept or reject any judicially noticed adjudicative fact.
   4. Substantive Limitations
      a. To be judicially noticed, an adjudicative fact must survive FRE 201's two-part test. The fact must be:
         i. One not subject to reasonable dispute, and
         ii. either:
            (1) Generally known within the territorial jurisdiction of the trial court, or
            (2) Capable of accurate and ready determination by resort to sources whose accuracy cannot reasonably be questioned.
      b. Clarification of Terms
         i. "Not Subject to Reasonable Dispute"
         Some commentators refer to this part of the test as "indisputability." A fact is "not subject to reasonable dispute"

when a court concludes that reasonable people agree about that fact.

   ii. "Well-Known Within the Territorial Jurisdiction of the United States"

A fact known only to the judge or to jurists is not a "well-known" fact. Rather, the fact must be one that is commonly known and understood without reference to outside materials or proof. In some circumstances, this might include evidence of trade custom that is generally known with the relevant trade community.

   iii. "Capable of Accurate and Ready Determination by Reference to Sources Whose Accuracy Cannot Be Reasonably Questioned"

This is technically a two-part test:

(1) The fact must be "capable of accurate and ready determination" and

(2) the source used to determine the accuracy of the fact must be one "whose accuracy cannot reasonably be questioned."

B. Particular Examples

  1. Scientific Principles and Methods

When authoritative studies show that a scientific principle is sound, the scientific principle can be judicially noticed. However, the judicial notice only extends to the accuracy of the scientific principle, not to its application in the case before the court.

  2. Prior Cases

A court can notice facts asserted in a prior judicial opinion; however, the court must clearly state the facts of which the court is taking notice and the relevant source of the court's knowledge.

C. Common Law

IV. NOTICE OF LEGISLATIVE FACTS

A. Generally

Legislative facts are facts capable of universal application within the relevant jurisdictional sphere.

B. Federal Rules

  1. Generally

There is no general federal evidence rule that addresses the notice of legislative facts. However, courts can and do take judicial notice of legislative facts. Legislative facts need not be indisputable to be noticed; the judge's belief in the legislative fact will usually suffice.

2. Foreign Law

The federal rules applicable to judicial notice of foreign law are found in Rule 44.1 of the Federal Rules of Civil Procedure and Rule 26.1 of the Federal Rules of Criminal Procedure.

C. Common Law Rule

At common law, courts were generally not allowed to take judicial notice of laws. More recently, most states have adopted statutes allowing courts to take judicial notice of statutes.

D. Analyzing Judicial Notice of Legislative Facts According to Type of Law

1. Judicial Notice of Domestic Law

Typically, the following rules apply to both state and federal courts:

   a. Domestic laws, including both state and federal law, may be subject to judicial notice.

   b. Administrative regulations may be noticed if they are published in a manner that makes them readily available.

   c. Municipal ordinances are generally not eligible for judicial notice; however, if they are published and readily available, some jurisdictions authorize judicial notice of those municipal ordinances.

2. Judicial Notice of Foreign Law

   a. State Courts

   Most states do not permit their judges to take notice of the laws of foreign countries.

   b. Federal Courts

   Federal judges can take notice of the laws of foreign countries.

      i. The party who wishes to raise the issue of foreign law must make this intention known in advance of the need for a ruling.

      ii. The rules applicable to judicial notice of foreign law in civil and criminal cases are found in Rule 44.1 of the Federal Rules of Civil Procedure and Rule 26.1 of the Federal Rules of Criminal Procedure, respectively.

E. Examples of Judicial Notice of Legislative Facts

1. Judicial Notice of the Constitutionality or Interpretation of a Statute

2. Judicial Notice of Evidentiary Privileges

FRE 501 permits federal judges to announce evidentiary privileges that are not codified, but that should be recognized in view of contemporary societal values.

3. Effect of Judicial Notice of Legislative Facts
Although a criminal jury cannot be instructed to treat adjudicative facts as conclusive, no such prohibition applies to legislative facts. A trial court may properly direct civil and criminal juries to accept as conclusive a judicially noticed legislative fact.

CASE CLIPS

United States v. Jones, 580 F.2d 219 (6th Cir. 1978)

Facts: Jones was convicted of illegally intercepting telephone calls and using the contents of the intercepted communications. He moved for a new trial on the ground that the government had failed to prove that the wiretapped communication came within the definition of the relevant statute because it failed to allege the telephone company's status as a common carrier providing facilities for interstate communications.

Issue: In a criminal case, may the prosecution's failure to plead a fact be cured by judicial notice?

Rule: Failure to plead a fact in a criminal proceeding may not be cured by judicial notice. Rule 201(f) permits the request of judicial notice at any stage of a civil proceeding, even on appeal. However, this provision must yield to the congressional intent expressed in Rule 201(g), which requires different standards for jury instructions in civil and criminal proceedings. In a civil action, a jury must accept as conclusive any fact judicially noticed, whereas in a criminal case, a jury *may* but is *not required* to accept a judicially noticed fact as conclusive.

In re Marriage of Tresnak, 297 N.W.2d 109 (Iowa 1980)

Facts: In a custody dispute, the trial court took judicial notice that the mother's plans to go to law school would result in her spending a great deal of time away from her children. The court then concluded that the mother's plans to attend law school were not in the best interests of her children, and awarded custody to the father.

Issue: May a court take judicial notice of a fact (law school will require extended commitment of time away from home) that is well known to the judge but is not common knowledge?

Rule: To be capable of being judicially noticed, a matter must be of common knowledge or capable of certain verification.

Solely v. Star & Herald Co., 390 F.2d 364 (5th Cir. 1968)

Facts: Solely lost his negligence suit against a bus company. A newspaper owned by Star & Herald published an account of the trial that stated that Solely's injuries and lawsuit were fraudulent. Solely then sued Star & Herald for libel. In dismissing the suit, the court made reference to the prior negligence lawsuit, but did not inform the parties of any facts of which the judge had taken judicial notice.

Issue: May a court take judicial notice of information from a prior case?

Rule: A court may take judicial notice of prior cases to support a motion for summary judgment, but the judge must inform the parties as to what was noticed.

Michael M. v. Superior Court of Sonoma County, 450 U.S. 464 (1981)

Facts: Petitioner was charged with having sex with a minor under a California statute that criminalized this conduct by men but not women. Petitioner sought to have the charges dismissed on the ground that the statute was not gender-neutral and thus violated the Equal Protection Clause.

Issue: May a court take judicial notice of the societal need for particular legislation and of the legislative intent in enacting the regulation?

Rule (Rehnquist): The justification offered for the statute is the prevention of illegitimate teenage pregnancies. The court is satisfied that this is one of the "purposes" of the statute, and that the State has a strong interest in preventing such pregnancies. When legislative regulation advances a compelling state interest, a court may take judicial notice of facts that support need for legislation.

Government of the Virgin Islands v. Gereau, 523 F.2d 140 (3d Cir. 1975)

Facts: The defendants were found guilty of murder, assault, and robbery. After the verdict, they filed a motion requesting a new trial on the ground that the verdict had not been freely assented to by all the jurors. Specifically, one juror testified that a verdict was reached primarily so that the jurors would be able to go home. A jury attendant denied that this had occurred, and the trial judge, knowing that the jury attendant appreciated the opportunity to earn income as a jury matron, discredited the juror's statement, and denied the motion for a new trial.

Issue: May a court take judicial notice of a fact merely because the judge has personal knowledge of that fact?

Rule: Facts that can be the subject of judicial notice must be either matters of common knowledge or capable of immediate and accurate determination by resort to easily accessible sources of indisputable accuracy. When a fact does not fall within this definition, judicial notice of it may not be taken, even if the judge personally knows it to be true.

United States v. Gould, 536 F.2d 216 (8th Cir. 1976)

Facts: Defendants were convicted of conspiring to import and importing cocaine into the United States. On appeal, they contended that the District Court erred in taking judicial notice of the fact that cocaine hydrochloride was a Schedule II controlled substance, and instructing the jury that it had to accept this fact as conclusive.

Issue: Is a court precluded by the FRE from instructing the jury that it must accept as conclusive a legislative fact of which it has taken judicial notice?

Rule: Rule 201(g) provides that in a criminal case, the court shall instruct the jury that it may, but is not required to, accept as conclusive any fact judicially noticed. But Rule 201(g) applies only to adjudicative facts, not legislative fact. Thus, under the Federal Rules, a court is not prevented from instructing the jury that it must accept as conclusive a legislative fact of which the court has taken judicial notice. The fact that cocaine hydrochloride is a derivative of coca leaves is a universal, scientific fact that is unrelated to the activities of the parties to the litigation and therefore is a legislative fact.

State v. Finkle, 319 A.2d 733 (N.J. Super. 1974)

Facts: Finkle appealed his conviction for driving 75.3 mph in a 55 mph zone on the ground that the court had erred in not requiring expert testimony to establish the reliability of the VASCAR radar device that had been used by the police officer to measure his speed of travel. The State argued that the scientific reliability of the VASCAR device was a proper subject of judicial notice.

Issue: Is there is sufficient indication of the general scientific reliability of the VASCAR radar device to permit the court to take judicial notice of it?

Rule: VASCAR meets the criteria of the rule for judicial notice because the evidence proves that the device is reliable beyond any reasonable doubt. Neither unanimity of opinion nor universal infallibility is required for judicial notice of generally recognized matters.

De La Cruz v. City of Los Angeles, 2002 WL 358825 (Cal. Ct. App. 2002)

Facts: Mercado and her infant daughter were seriously injured when Wicks, a Los Angeles Police Department officer, struck them with his SUV. Wicks left the scene of the accident without stopping. Later, he was found dead. Mercado brought a suit against Wicks and the City of Los Angeles for negligence. On appeal, the City asked the court to take judicial notice of several geographical facts.

Issue: May an appellate court take judicial notice of geographical facts that were not before the trial court?

Rule: Generally, the reviewing court will decline a request for judicial notice of matters that were not brought to the attention of the trial court or presented to the trier of fact. However, the reviewing court has discretion to grant judicial notice even when the information was not presented to the trial court, if the facts are not reasonably open to dispute and the opposing party does not dispute them. Furthermore, a geographical fact may be deemed to have been brought to the attention of the trial court when it is probable that every person in the courtroom at the trial knew what the character of the location was.

United States v. Amado-Nunez, 357 F.3d 119 (1st Cir. 2004)

Facts: During a random inspection at the San Juan, Puerto Rico airport, customs inspectors found counterfeit tax stamps in Amado's luggage. He was tried and convicted of transporting counterfeit tax stamps in interstate or foreign commerce. On appeal, Amado argued that the evidence against him did not establish the interstate or foreign commerce element of the offense.

Issue: Whether the fact that Amado had arrived from a location outside of Puerto Rico must have been judicially noticed under Rule 201.

Rule: The practice of customs searches for foreign, but not domestic, arrivals is not an adjudicative fact but a "background" or "evaluative" fact. Rule 201(b)'s limitations do not apply to "background" facts. Fact-finders rely on background facts all the time in deciding whether something did or did not happen, and this is possible without having to formally take notice of the facts.

State v. Mann, 39 P.3d 124 (N.M. 2002)

Facts: Mann allegedly killed his son by stabbing him with a screwdriver. However, at trial, Mann argued that it was possible that the victim fell on the screwdriver and impaled himself. He produced a physicist as an expert witness who testified that the probability of the impalement occurring would be "finite" but never zero. After his conviction, Mann filed a motion for a new trial based on the fact that Juror 7 had presented probability calculations to the other members of the jury regarding the chances of the accidental impalement occurring. Juror 7 stated he began with the expert witness's calculations, then used his own "professional judgment" and a five-step probability calculation, and ended with the result of a one in 20 million chance that the event could have occurred.

Issue: Does a juror's statistical analysis during deliberations of the probability that the defendant's version of the facts is true constitute extraneous evidence warranting a new trial?

Rule: Jurors may rely on their background, including professional and educational experience, during deliberations. The use of this knowledge does not constitute extrinsic influence.

State v. Canady, 431 S.E.2d 500 (N.C. 1993)

Facts: Canady was accused of stabbing the victim, who had been involved with Canady's estranged wife. In his statement to the police, Canady claimed it was dark when he arrived at the scene, and that he killed the victim in self-defense. At the trial, the State presented a witness who testified that she had seen the altercation and that it had been light outside. Canady requested that the trial court take judicial notice of the fact that the sunset on the date of the event occurred at 8:19 p.m and that there was a new moon on that date. He submitted verification of those facts in the form of reports published daily in *The Fayetteville Observer*. The trial court refused Canady's request.

Issue: May a trial court take judicial notice of a fact reported in a newspaper excerpt?

Rule: The exact time of sunset and the current phase of the moon on a particular date are not "generally known" facts, but they are facts that are capable of accurate determination by sources "whose accuracy cannot reasonably be questioned." However, *The Fayetteville Observer* is not such a source because it does not identify the source of its data. In the case of these facts, a primary source who had actually gathered the information would most likely be required.

State v. Vejvoda, 438 N.W.2d 461 (Neb. 1989)

Facts: Vejvoda was accused of drunk driving. The sole witness at his bench trial was the officer who had stopped and arrested him. During his testimony, the officer never mentioned the city or county where the events occurred. However, the court took judicial notice of the fact that all the addresses described were within the city limits of the city of Grand Island, which is within Hall County.

Issue: May a trial judge judicially notice the fact that the alleged locations where the offense occurred are within a certain county, thus establishing venue?

Rule: Because the judge is not insulated from the material consulted in deciding whether or not to take judicial notice, as a jury is, it probably makes little difference whether he takes formal judicial notice based on the material or whether he is convinced of the fact as a result of having examined the sources.

Potts v. Coe, 145 F.2d 27 (D.C. Cir. 1944)

Facts: The Commissioner of Patents denied registration of a patent for an automatic stock quotation board. Potts had allegedly invented the board, and had assigned his right to patent it to Teletype Corporation.

The district court dismissed a suit to compel registration. The court of appeals affirmed, based on judicial notice of congressional hearings on the relationship of corporate research in general to the law of patents. The judicial notice indicated that the type of enterprise engaged in by Teletype was a gradual step-by-step development that was not entitled to patent protection.

Issue: May a court take judicial notice of information illustrating the character of a process or event giving rise to a claim?

Rule: The process used by corporations like Teletype of developing devices over long periods of time, then crediting the "invention" to an employee was the subject of congressional hearings. The court properly took judicial notice of these hearings to illustrate what was obvious regarding corporate research and patent law.

CHAPTER 6

Hearsay Evidence

I. HEARSAY

A. General Rule

Person A cannot testify as to a statement made out-of-court by person B if A's testimony is being offered to prove the truth of the matter asserted in B's out-of-court statement.

B. Rationale

The prohibition against the admission of hearsay evidence reflects a general policy concern with the integrity of the adversary system. Specific justifications for the hearsay rules include:

1. Declarant Cannot Be Cross-Examined

An out-of-court declarant cannot be cross-examined. Without cross-examination, the factfinder cannot evaluate the accuracy of the out-of-court statement.

2. Declarant Not Under Oath

The declarant was not under oath when she made the out-of-court statement. Therefore, the statement lacks reliability. (Note: This policy concern is also reflected by the general requirement of oath or affirmation as a condition of witness competence.)

3. Possibility of Faulty Transmittal

The witness might not accurately restate the out-of-court declaration.

4. Futility of Cross-Examination

Cross-examination of the testifying witness will be futile because the testifying witness cannot testify as to declarant's state of mind, intent, bias, or motive.

II. HEARSAY UNDER THE FRE

A. Generally

FRE 801 defines a hearsay statement as "a statement, other than one made by a declarant while testifying in court, that is offered into evidence to prove the truth of the matter asserted in the out-of-court statement." This is substantially the same definition as that used at common law. Hearsay is not admissible in federal court unless the FRE or other laws specifically authorize its admission. (See FRE 802.)

B. Terms Defined
 1. Statement
  a. Definition
   FRE 801 defines a statement as "an oral or written assertion" or as the "nonverbal conduct of a person, if it is intended by the person as an assertion."
  b. Specific Problems
   i. Silence
    Under some circumstances, a person's silence can be understood as a statement, usually one of agreement or contentment. Silence is not a statement in a criminal case in which a person has been provided with *Miranda* warnings. Silence is also not a statement if the person remained silent out of fear.
   ii. Nonverbal Acts
    (1) Under FRE 801(a)(2) a nonverbal act is not a statement unless the person who engaged in the act intended the act to "make a statement."
    (2) Note
     In this regard, the FRE differs significantly from the common law rule. At common law, if an inference could be drawn from a person's nonverbal act, the act was considered as a statement, regardless of the actor's intent.
 2. Declarant
  a. FRE Definition
   FRE 801 defines a declarant as a "person who makes a statement."
  b. Limited to Persons
   Animals (such as drug detection dogs) are not persons or declarants. Therefore, they cannot make statements for purposes of the hearsay rule.
 3. Proof of the Matter Asserted
  a. FRE Definition
   FRE 801 indicates that a declarant's statement is hearsay when the statement was made out-of-court and it is offered to prove the truth of the matter asserted.

       b. Declarant Availability
         i. Generally
           Even if the declarant testifies at the proceeding, the declar-
           ant's out-of-court statement is still hearsay, so long as it is
           offered for the truth of the matter asserted.
   4. Exceptions
      The FRE have several exceptions to the definition of hearsay.

III. STATEMENTS DEFINED AS "NOT HEARSAY"

  A. Prior Statement by a Witness (FRE 801(d)(1) & (2))
     The following statements are not hearsay if: (1) the declarant tes-
     tifies at the trial or hearing and (2) is subject to cross-examination
     about the statement:
    1. Prior Inconsistent Statement
       A prior statement made under oath is not hearsay if it is incon-
       sistent with the declarant's testimony.
    2. Prior Consistent Statement
       A prior consistent statement is not hearsay if it is used to bolster
       the testimony of a witness whose credibility has been attacked,
       directly or by implication, with a charge of fabrication, improper
       motive, or bias.
    3. Prior Identification
       A statement of identification is not hearsay if it was made after
       the witness perceived the identified person.
  B. Admission by a Party-Opponent
    1. Generally
       An admission by a party-opponent is not hearsay. The admis-
       sion may be made by the party, adopted by the party, made by a
       person authorized by the party, made by an agent of the party in
       the scope of agency or employment, or made by a co-conspirator.
       (FRE 801(d)(2).)
    2. Admissions Distinguished from Declarations Against Interest
       Unlike a declaration against interest, an admission by a party-
       opponent need not be against the interest of the declarant at the
       time it was made. Neutral or self-serving statements can consti-
       tute admissions.
    3. Authorized Admissions
       If a person is authorized to speak on behalf of a person or
       corporation, that person's statements are not hearsay; rather
       they are admissions under FRE 801(d)(2).

4. Agents

A statement by a party's agent is an admission, even if the agent was not explicitly authorized to speak for a principal. Admissibility depends, in part, on whether the statement is one made within the scope of the agency, and during the period of agency.

5. Co-Conspirators

Statements made by a co-conspirator during the course of and in furtherance of the conspiracy constitute admissions as to other co-conspirators.

6. As an Exception to Other Rules

An admission by a party-opponent is also an exception to the general rule that a witness must testify from personal knowledge.

7. Specific Examples

a. Opinions and Conclusions of Law

Although opinions and conclusions of law are generally not admissible, they may become admissible if they are part of an admission by a party-opponent.

b. Pleadings

i. Generally

Pleadings are generally judicial admissions and are not hearsay. A party can withdraw a pleading, but the opposing party can still use the original pleading as an evidentiary admission.

ii. Alternative View

Pleadings should not be treated as admissions because the pleadings-as-admissions theory undermines the practice of alternative pleadings.

c. Guilty Pleas

Guilty pleas are generally admissions. However, guilty pleas entered for minor or petty offenses (such as traffic offenses) are generally not treated as admissions, as they may have been made as a matter of convenience rather than as true admissions of guilt. Note: FRE 410 addresses the admissibility of plea negotiations.

d. Admissions by Conduct

Admissions may be inferred from conduct. For example, flight can be understood as an admission of guilt. Note: The admissibility of proof of specific instances of conduct is governed by FRE 404 and 608.

e. Adopted Admissions

Adopted admissions can be express or implied. Thus, silence can be an adopted admission when it is clear that the party heard and understood the statement and, under the circumstances, an ordinary person would have responded or denied the statement.

C. Other Common Issues
  1. Multiple Hearsay (FRE 805)
     Multiple hearsay occurs if an out-of-court statement
     (a) contains or paraphrases one or more out-of-court statements, and
     (b) each of the statements is offered to prove the truth of the matter asserted.

     The multiple hearsay statement is only admissible if all of the included statements independently fall under exceptions to the hearsay rule or are otherwise not hearsay pursuant to the rules of evidence.

IV. EXCEPTIONS TO THE HEARSAY RULE

A. FRE 803
   Hearsay exceptions found in FRE 803 apply regardless of declarant's availability. This section of the outline also mentions any significant distinctions between the common law rule and the rule codified in the FRE.
   1. Present Sense Impression
      a. Generally
         A statement describing or explaining an event or condition that was made while, or immediately after, the declarant was perceiving the event or condition is admissible as a present sense impression.
      b. Reasoning
         Because the statement was made at the time of the event or shortly thereafter the declarant did not have time to develop a false account of the facts, and there is little risk that the declarant forgot what happened.
   2. Excited Utterance
      a. A statement relating to a startling event or condition that was made while the declarant was "under the stress of excitement caused by the event or condition" is admissible.
      b. Reasoning
         The event is so startling that the declarant did not have the capacity to reflect on his statement and fabricate an utterance that concerns the event. The excited utterance must be made while the declarant still feels the shock of the event; if the shock has worn off and the declarant reflected on the statement, the statement does not fall within the exception.

    c. Distinguished from Present Sense Impression
       A statement of present sense impression describes or explains the event or condition. In contrast, an excited utterance relates only to the event or condition.

    d. Note
       An excited utterance can be made after the event and may even be inspired by a "trigger" that causes a flashback to the event.

    e. Independent Evidence of the Event
       Courts are divided over whether the event's existence must be proven by independent evidence.

3. Then Existing Medical, Emotional, or Physical Condition
    a. Rule
       A statement of the declarant's then existing state of mind, emotion, sensation, or physical condition (including intent, plan, or motive) is admissible as an exception to the hearsay rule. Statements of "memory or belief to prove the fact remembered or believed" are not admissible unless they relate to the execution, revocation, identification, or terms of the declarant's will.

    b. Reasoning
       Because the statement was made at the time that the declarant experienced the described sensation, the statement is probably accurate and there is little reason to suspect that it was fabricated.

    c. Who May Testify
       A statement of present bodily condition, generally about pain, could have been made to anyone, but a statement (or part of a statement) that gives an uninformed medical opinion or is not made from firsthand knowledge will not be admitted.

    d. State of Mind
       A statement about the declarant's then existing state of mind may be admitted even if it is used to prove an earlier or later mental state. However, such a statement may not be used to make an independent assertion of fact.

4. Statements for the Purpose of Medical Diagnosis or Treatment
   These statements are admissible if they concern a patient's past or present condition and are made for purposes of diagnosis or treatment.

    a. Statements of Causation
       Statements about the cause of a pain or injury will be admissible if they are related to how the doctor will

administer treatment. Statements that ascribe fault are not admissible.

   b. Doctors Called Just to Testify

      The common law approach only allowed a treating physician to testify, but the FRE allow any examining physician to testify.

5. Recorded Recollection

  A memorandum or record that a witness made before the trial will be admitted if:

   a. The record concerns matters about which the witness once had firsthand knowledge and

   b. The record was made when the matter was fresh in the witness's memory and

   c. The witness testifies that the record was accurate when it was made (or if two people made the record, one making an oral statement and the other transcribing the statement, each will testify that his part was accurate) and

   d. At the time of the witness's testimony, the witness's recollection of the matter is incomplete. (This requirement is intended to guard against parties preparing documents for the specific purpose of their use, at trial, as recorded recollections.)

     i. Common Law Rule

       The common law approach required that the witness have no recollection of the matter recorded.

     ii. FRE

       Under the FRE, the witness must have "insufficient recollection [of the recorded matter] to enable him to testify fully and accurately."

   e. Admissibility as an Exhibit

      The record may be read to the jury, but the FRE limit the admission of the recorded recollection to circumstances in which the adverse party asks for its admission.

6. Distinguished from Present Recollection Refreshed

  A document or object used to refresh a witness's present recollection is used under different evidentiary rules. For example:

   a. The record need not have been made immediately after the event.

   b. The record need not have been made from firsthand knowledge.

   c. The witness need not have been involved in the making of the record.

   d. The witness does not have to vouch for the record's accuracy.

7. Business Records
   a. General Requirements
      Business records are admissible if they are:
      i. Made at or near the time of the matter recorded;
      ii. Made by, or from information received from, a person with personal knowledge of the matter recorded;
      iii. Made in the routine of the business (regular procedure is to make them in the course of business).
   b. Requirements Under the FRE
      i. Definition of Business
         A business is any "business, institution, association, profession, occupation, and calling of any kind," whether or not it operates for profit.
      ii. Opinion
         The records may include opinions, although generally nonexpert opinions are excluded.
      iii. Lack of Trustworthiness
         Notwithstanding the fact that the record may otherwise qualify as a business record, the business record will not be admissible if the "source of information or the method or circumstances of preparation indicate a lack of trustworthiness." Many state statutes make similar provisions for addressing the admissibility of business records.
      iv. Business Duty Requirement
         The person who supplies the information underlying the business record must be supplying that information on behalf of the business.
      v. Regular Course of Business Requirement
         At one time, the Supreme Court had held that records that are not routinely kept under normal operating conditions are not business records. Thus accident reports, which are created as accidents occur, would not be subject to the business records exception. Later jurisprudence and statutory law have changed this requirement. The prevailing modern view is that the business record exception will apply to all records other than those prepared for litigation.
         (1) Computer Printouts
             (a) Generally
                 Computer printouts that are made in the ordinary course of business are admissible if the information was entered into the computer, in the same form as the printout, on or about near the time of the event.

      (b) Trustworthiness

      To show the trustworthiness of a computer printout, the proponent of the evidence may offer testimony about:

- The general acceptance of this type of computer in that field
- The reliability of the computer programming
- Procedures used to detect and correct errors in data entry and computer calculations
- The method and circumstances of the preparation of the computer printout
- The security measures available to prevent tampering with the evidence or calculations.

  c. Absence of Entry in Business Records

The absence of an entry in business records may be used to assert the nonoccurrence or nonexistence of a matter.

8. Public Records and Reports

  a. Common Law

At common law, a written report or record of a public official was only admissible if the official had firsthand knowledge of the facts reported and had a duty to make the record or report.

  b. FRE

Under the FRE, records or reports, in any form, of public agencies are admissible if they set forth:

   i. The activities of the office or agency

  ii. The matters observed under duty of law, excluding matters observed by police officers or other law enforcement personnel in criminal cases.

    (1) The exception that prohibits the admission of public records made by law enforcement applies to other government employees who have law enforcement responsibilities.

    (2) As a general matter, the exclusion in criminal matters only applies to reports from adversarial situations, not routine, objective observations made every day. Factual findings of investigative reports may not be admitted against a criminal defendant.

    (3) Other Considerations

In civil actions and in proceedings against the government in criminal cases, factual findings from investigative reports are admissible unless the circumstances suggest that they lack trustworthiness. Relevant factors might include the timeliness of the investigation, the skill or experience of the investigating official, the opportunity for other persons to add information or test the information, and the possibility of the reporting official's bias or motivation for false statements.

9. Records of Vital Statistics
   Records of births, fetal deaths, deaths (including cause of death), or marriages are admissible if the report was made to a public office in accordance with requirements of law.

10. Absence of a Public Record or Entry
    The absence of a public record is admissible if the record is one that would ordinarily be made and preserved by a public office or agency. Absence can be proved by the testimony of (or an affidavit from) the record keeper stating that the record keeper conducted a diligent search but failed to find the record.

11. Records of Religious Organizations
    Statements of births, marriages, divorces, deaths, legitimacy, ancestry, relationship of blood, or other similar facts of personal or family history in a regularly kept record of a religious organization are admissible even if they are not made by an official in the organization.

12. Marriage, Baptismal, and Similar Certificates
    Statements of fact contained in a certificate that the maker, as a clergy member, performed a religious ceremony are admissible if they claim to have been issued at the time of the act or within a reasonable time thereafter.

13. Family Records
    Statements of fact about personal or family history in family Bibles, and other possible record making devices are admissible.

14. Records of Documents Affecting an Interest in Property
    The record of a document purporting to establish or affect an interest in property is admissible to prove its content and execution and delivery, if the record is one of a public office and an applicable statute authorizes the recording of this type of documents in that office.

15. Statements in Documents Affecting Interests in Property
    A statement in a document purporting to establish or affect an interest in property is admissible if the statement is relevant to the purpose of the document and if subsequent dealings

with the property are not inconsistent with the truth of the statement or the purpose of the document. The document's age is irrelevant.

16. Statements in Ancient Documents

    Statements in a document in existence for 20 years or more are admissible if the document is authenticated.

17. Market Reports and Commercial Publications

    Market quotations, tabulations, lists, directories, or other published compilations, generally used and relied on by the public or by persons in particular occupations are admissible if the proponent of the report shows that it is reliable.

18. Learned Treatises

    To the extent that they are called to the attention of an expert on cross-examination, or are relied on by an expert during direct examination, statements in published treatises, periodicals, or pamphlets on history, medicine, or other science or art may be admitted if the treatise is established as a reliable authority by other expert testimony or by judicial notice. Statements from learned treatises may be read to the jury but may not be received as exhibits.

19. Reputation Concerning Personal or Family History

    Reputation concerning birth, adoption, marriage, divorce, death, legitimacy, relationship by blood, adoption, or marriage, ancestry, or other similar fact of personal or family history is admissible from among members of the person's family, associates, or community.

20. Reputation Concerning Boundaries or General History

    Reputation in a community, arising before a controversy begins, about boundaries of or customs affecting lands in the community, and reputation about events of general history important to the community, state, or nation are admissible.

21. Reputation of Character

    "Reputation of a person's character among his associates or in the community" is generally admissible, subject to the other rules concerning character evidence (see, e.g., FRE 608).

22. Judgment of a Previous Conviction

    Evidence of a prior felony conviction is admissible to prove any fact essential to the previous conviction.

    a. Exception

       This rule does not apply to verdicts entered after a plea of nolo contendere.

        b. Exception

        In a criminal case, the government may not offer evidence of a witness's prior conviction(s) except for purposes of impeachment.

    23. Judgment as to Personal, Family or General History or Boundaries

    Judgments of personal, family or general history, or boundaries may be admitted as proof of matters essential to that judgment, if the same facts would be provable by reputation evidence.

B. **FRE 804**

If an out-of-court statement is one identified in FRE 804 and the declarant is unavailable, the statement is not excluded by the hearsay rule.

    1. Declarant Unavailable (FRE 804)

    A declarant is considered unavailable when, through no fault of the proponent of the statement(s) at issue, the declarant:

        a. Exercises privilege from testifying concerning the subject matter of his statement, including the Fifth Amendment right against self-incrimination; or

        b. Refuses to testify concerning the subject matter of his statement despite a court order to do so; or

        c. Testifies that he has a lack of memory about the subject matter of his statement; or

        d. Is dead or suffers from an incapacitating physical or mental illness; or

        e. Is not present at the proceeding and the proponent of the witness's statement was unable to hale the declarant into court by service of process or other reasonable means.

    2. Former Testimony Not Excluded by Hearsay Rule (FRE 804(b)(1))

    Testimony given by a witness, under oath, at a legal proceeding, offered hearing, is admissible if the party against whom the testimony is now offered, or, in a civil case, a predecessor in interest, had an opportunity and similar motive to develop the testimony by examination.

        a. Opportunity for Cross-Examination

            i. Actual Examination Not Required

            FRE 804(b)(1) does not require that the witness has actually undergone cross-examination; it suffices if the cross-examiner or his predecessor in interest had an opportunity to examine the witness.

            ii. Opportunity and Similar Motive

            For purposes of FRE 804(b)(1), an opportunity to cross-examine means an opportunity at a prior proceeding in which the statement(s) now at issue were of sufficient interest to draw that party's attention and motivate cross-examination.

(1) Note

The modern common law approach requires that the opportunity to examine arose in a prior situation that presented a "substantially" similar "identity of issues" as those issues in play in the current litigation.

(2) Examples of Opportunity and Motive: Preliminary Hearing vs. Trial

Because the issue at a preliminary hearing is whether there is enough evidence to establish probable cause and the issue at trial is whether the prosecution has proven the defendant's guilt beyond a reasonable doubt, the defendant has not had an opportunity to cross-examine with a similar motive.

(3) Examples of Opportunity and Motive: Criminal Trial Followed by Civil Trial

Testimony from a prior criminal trial may be admitted at a later civil trial if the civil trial has a substantial identity of issues with the criminal trial.

iii. Who Must Have Had the Opportunity to Cross- Examine?

(1) Civil Cases

In civil cases, the predecessor in interest requirement has been defined as a party in the prior case with a "like motive" to examine the testimony.

(2) Criminal Cases

In criminal cases, the same party must have had the opportunity to cross-examine in both proceedings.

C. Dying Declarations

1. Common Law

At common law, the exception for dying declarations applied only in homicide cases and only if the victim, believing that death was imminent, made a statement concerning the cause or circumstances of his death.

2. FRE

FRE 804(b)(2) expands the traditional dying declaration rule so that it applies in criminal homicide cases and in civil suits. The rule applies regardless of whether the declarant recovered after making the statement. Moreover, although the declarant must believe that death is imminent, the declarant need not have given up all hope of recovery.

D. Statement Against Interest

This rule applies to statements that are, at the time they are made, so contrary to the declarant's interest that a reasonable person would not have made the statements unless they were true.

1. Common Law

At common law, the exception applied only to statements against pecuniary interest.

2. FRE

FRE 804(b)(3) has expanded the exception to include statements against penal interest. However, a statement that exposes the declarant to liability and is offered to exculpate the accused is not admissible absent corroborating circumstances that demonstrate the trustworthiness of the statement.

a. Self-Serving Statements

If part of a statement against interest is self-serving a court may admit the entire statement, exclude the entire statement, or redact the statement for admission.

E. Forfeiture by Wrongdoing

A hearsay statement is admissible if the statement is offered against a party who has procured, by wrongdoing, the declarant's unavailability.

F. Catch-all Hearsay Exceptions

FRE 807 contains a residual or catch-all hearsay exception. A statement not covered by FRE 803 or 804 that nevertheless has "equivalent circumstantial guarantees of trustworthiness" is not per se excluded as hearsay if:

a. The statement is offered as evidence of a material fact; and

b. The statement is more probative on the point for which it is offered than any other evidence the proponent can reasonably obtain; and

c. The general purposes of the hearsay rules and the interests of justice will best be served by admitting the statement; and

d. The proponent of the evidence gives the adverse party notice sufficient to allow the adverse party to prepare to meet the evidence.

e. Note

Prior to 1997, the FRE codified this single residual hearsay exception at FRE 803(24) and FRE 804(b)(5).

V. CONSTITUTIONAL ISSUES ARISING IN CRIMINAL CASES

A. Confrontation Clause Generally

The Sixth Amendment Confrontation Clause guarantees a criminal defendant the right "to be confronted with the witnesses against him." The Confrontation Clause applies in state and federal prosecutions and operates independently of any hearsay rules. Evidence otherwise admissible under the hearsay rules must nevertheless be excluded if it will violate the defendant's right to confront and cross-examine the declarant.

B. The Confrontation Clause and Hearsay Under the Rule of *Ohio v. Roberts*

Ohio v. Roberts made hearsay evidence admissible in a criminal case if it either fell under a firmly rooted hearsay exception or "particularized guarantees of trustworthiness." Thus, the hearsay rules largely determined whether an out-of-court statement was admissible in a criminal case.

C. The Rule of *Crawford v. Washington*

1. Generally

Crawford divorced Confrontation Clause analysis from hearsay analysis. The *Ohio v. Roberts* "firmly rooted exception" doctrine and the "particularized guarantees of trustworthiness" doctrine no longer apply to testimonial statements (unless the Court adopts the *sui generis* dying declaration doctrine). Thus, in a criminal case, the Confrontation Clause analysis does not depend on either the hearsay rules or on determinations of reliability. Instead, application of the Confrontation Clause depends on whether the statement at issue is testimonial; and, if so, whether the witness (1) testifies at trial or (2) is unavailable and there has been a prior opportunity for cross-examination with the same or similar motives.

2. Rule

If the hearsay declaration offered against the defendant is testimonial, then the Confrontation Clause forbids its admission unless

a. the declarant testifies at the proceeding; or

b. the Government can show

  i. that the declarant is unavailable and

  ii. that the defendant has had a prior opportunity for cross-examination.

3. Declarant Testifies

Once the out-of-court declarant appears for cross-examination at trial, "the Confrontation Clause places no constraints at all on the use of his prior testimonial statements." However, state and federal hearsay rules may still prohibit admission of the statement, notwithstanding the propriety of its admission under the Confrontation Clause.

4. To Evaluate Specific Pieces of Evidence

If the declarant does not testify at the proceeding, the evidence is subject to the answer to three basic questions:

a. Is the evidence *testimonial*?

b. Is the witness *unavailable*?

c. Has the defendant had a prior opportunity for cross-examination?

D. Testimonial Evidence After *Crawford*

1. *Crawford* did not set out a definition of what constitutes testimonial evidence. However, the opinion does provide important insight about how the Court may view testimonial evidence.

2. Evidence is testimonial when it:

a. Resembles the "civil-law mode of criminal procedure" and its "use of *ex parte* examinations as evidence against the accused";

b. Is "given in response to structured police questioning";

c. Was produced with (a) the "involvement of government officers" who (b) had "an eye toward trial"; or

d. Was made "under circumstances which would lead an objective witness to reasonably believe that the statement would be available for use at a later trial."

3. Crawford clearly indicates that testimonial evidence includes:

a. "[e]xtrajudicial statements . . . contained in formalized testimonial materials, such as affidavits, depositions, prior testimony, or confessions."

b. "in-court testimony or its functional equivalent — that is, material such as affidavits, custodial examinations, prior testimony . . . , or similar pretrial statements that declarants would reasonably expect to be used prosecutorially."

c. accusatory documents such as letters to police accusing someone of committing crime.

d. prior testimony from preliminary hearings, grand jury appearances, prior trials, guilty plea allocution, and statements produced at police interrogations, whether formal or informal.

4. Particular Issues

a. Dying Declarations

Historical sources make a clear confrontation exception for dying declarations. The Supreme Court has declined to decide whether testimonial dying declarations warrant exception to the *Crawford* rule. However, the Court did indicate that any such exception would be based on historical grounds and not on the Confrontation Clause analysis adopted in *Crawford*.

E. When Is a Witness Unavailable?
   1. General Rule
   As a general matter, courts have applied the definition of unavailability used under pre-*Crawford* law. However, unavailability is now a necessary, but not sufficient, precondition for the admission of an out-of-court testimonial statement.
   2. Burden
   The Supreme Court places on the government the burden of proving that "the witness is demonstrably unavailable to testify in person."
   3. Does incompetence to testify render a witness unavailable (e.g., a young child)? The *Crawford* Court did not answer this question.
F. When Has a Defendant Had a Prior Opportunity for Cross-Examination?
   1. General Rule
   A majority of courts are employing the pre-*Crawford* test to determine whether a defendant has had prior opportunity for cross-examination. However, a prior opportunity for cross-examination is a necessary, but not sufficient, precondition for the admission of a testimonial statement.
   2. The following are important criteria for determining whether the defendant had a prior opportunity for cross-examination that will satisfy the Confrontation Clause:
   a. Was defendant represented by counsel?
   b. Did counsel have an adequate opportunity to cross-examine the witness at the prior proceedings?
   c. Did counsel have the same or similar motive(s) for cross-examination as she would at trial?
   3. Note
   The prior cross-examination must be conducted by defendant or her counsel to satisfy the Confrontation Clause. Cross-examination by a co-defendant's attorney will not suffice.
G. Nontestimonial Hearsay
   1. The Issue
   What restrictions, if any, does the Constitution impose on the use of nontestimonial evidence? *Crawford* suggests three possibilities but does not decide the issue:
   a. Possibility 1
   All jurisdictions must follow the rule of *Ohio v. Roberts*.
   b. Possibility 2
   Federal courts will continue to be governed by *Ohio v. Roberts* while state courts develop their own framework.
   c. Possibility 3
   Confrontation Clause has no application to the admission of nontestimonial out-of-court statements.

CASE CLIPS

Crawford v. Washington, 541 U.S. 36 (2004)

Facts: Michael and Sylvia Crawford were arrested and charged with assault. Following her arrest, Sylvia Crawford made a tape-recorded statement to police. At Michael's trial, the prosecution subpoenaed Sylvia to the witness stand. However, Michael invoked his spousal privilege and prevented Sylvia from testifying. Over Michael's objection, the prosecution introduced into evidence Sylvia's tape-recorded statement.

Issue: Does the Confrontation Clause prevent the state from introducing against a defendant a tape-recorded statement of a nontestifying witness?

Holding: The admission of a testimonial out-of-court statement, offered against a criminal defendant, is unconstitutional unless the witness testifies at the proceeding and is available for cross-examination, or the witness is unavailable and the defendant has had a prior opportunity for cross-examination. "Testimonial" statements include prior testimony at a preliminary hearing, before a grand jury, or at a former trial, and statements made during a police interrogation.

Note: The *Crawford* opinion does not eliminate the hearsay rules, it simply takes precedence. Thus, if the admission of a statement would violate the Confrontation Clause, the hearsay rules cannot make the statement admissible. However, if the admission of a statement would not violate the Confrontation Clause; the statement may be admitted or excluded, depending on the application of evidentiary rules.

United States v. Owens, 484 U.S. 554 (1988)

Facts: Foster, a correctional counselor at a federal prison, was attacked and beaten. As a result of his injuries, Foster's memory was severely impaired. Before trial, Foster named Owens as his attacker and identified him from a photographic array. At trial, Foster testified that he clearly remembered identifying Owens as his assailant, but on cross-examination, admitted that, because of his memory loss, he could not remember actually seeing his assailant.

Issue: Does either the Confrontation Clause or FRE 802 prohibit a witness in a criminal trial from testifying about a prior out-of-court identification if the witness can no longer testify as to the basis for that identification because of memory loss?

Rule (Scalia): Both the Confrontation Clause and Rule 802 require the declarant to be subjected to cross-examination before a statement is admissible. The Confrontation Clause only guarantees an opportunity for effective cross-examination, not a promise that cross-examination will be effective. The fact that the witness cannot remember the events can be used to demonstrate the unreliability of the witness's testimony.

Dissent (Brennan): The majority has reduced the Confrontation Clause to a procedural right that is satisfied no matter how futile the cross-examination. The Confrontation Clause requires that the cross-examination be sufficiently meaningful to provide the jury with a "satisfactory basis for evaluating the truth of a prior statement." The cross-examination here could not, and did not, elicit any information that would permit a jury to evaluate the trustworthiness or reliability of the identification.

Mahlandt v. Wild Canid Survival & Research Center, Inc., 588 F.2d 626 (8th Cir. 1978)

Facts: Plaintiff's son was injured by a wolf. Although no witnesses saw the occurrence, Defendant's agent admitted that a wolf bit Plaintiff's son.

Issue: Does an admission by a party-opponent require that the person making the admission have personal knowledge of the facts admitted?

Rule: FRE 801(d)(2)(D) allows the admission of statements made by agents acting within the scope of their employment. There is no requirement that the agent have personal knowledge of the facts.

Bourjaily v. United States, 483 U.S. 171 (1987)

Facts: Defendant was charged with conspiring to distribute cocaine and possession of cocaine with intent to distribute. Over Defendant's objection, the government introduced telephone statements of Lonardo, Defendant's co-conspirator, which implicated Defendant in the crime. The trial court held that the out-of-court statements satisfied FRE 801(d)(2)(E) and were not hearsay because the government had established by a preponderance of the evidence that a conspiracy involving Lonardo and Defendant existed, and that Lonardo's statements had been made in the course of, and in furtherance of, the conspiracy.

Issue: To admit the statement of a co-conspirator, must a court use independent evidence to find that a conspiracy existed and that the Defendant and declarant were members of the conspiracy?

Rule (Rehnquist): The old rule requiring independent evidence of a conspiracy before statements of a co-conspirator could be admitted has been superseded by FRE 104(a), which makes the court exempt from the common law rules of evidence (except for those of evidentiary privileges). Therefore the statements of a co-conspirator may be used, in conjunction with other evidence, to establish the existence of a conspiracy.

Note: The Supreme Court's opinion in *Crawford v. Washington* distinguished and refined many of the rulings in *Bourjaily*.

Dissent (Blackmun): Co-conspirator statements are presumptively unreliable. The requirement of independent evidence is an essential safeguard.

United States v. Barrett, 539 F.2d 244 (1st Cir. 1976)

Facts: Defendant was accused of stealing a collection of postage stamps. At trial, pursuant to FRE 804(b)(3), Defendant sought to introduce testimony concerning a conversation, between two other people, which conversation exculpated Defendant.

Issue: Is a third party's statement against interest admissible to exculpate a criminal defendant if that statement tends to expose the declarant to criminal liability?

Rule: A statement tending to expose the declarant to criminal liability and offered to exculpate the accused is admissible under the hearsay exception for statements against interest if corroborating circumstances clearly indicate the trustworthiness of the statement.

Mutual Life Insurance Co. of New York v. Hillmon, 145 U.S. 285 (1892)

Facts: Plaintiff sued to recover on the life insurance policy of her husband. Defendant claimed that there had been a fraud: Another man's body had been passed off as Hillmon's body. In support of this defense, Defendant tried to introduce letters allegedly written by the other man.

Issue: Are out-of-court statements that tend to prove the intention of the declarant at a particular moment in time admissible?

Rule: If the bodily or mental impressions of an individual are material to a case, they may be proven by hearsay evidence. If the intention to be proved is important only to qualify an act, its connection with the act must be shown to make it admissible. When the intention of a party is, of itself, a distinct and material fact in a chain of circumstances, the intention may be proved by the contemporaneous oral or written declarations of the party.

United States v. Pheaster, 544 F.2d 353 (9th Cir. 1976)

Facts: Defendant was charged with kidnapping Adell. Adell's hearsay statements were admitted with a limiting instruction that the jury should consider them only for the purposes of proving Adell's state of mind.

Issue: Whether the *Hillmon* doctrine permits the admission of a hearsay statement by a declarant about his intention to do something for the purpose of permitting the trier of fact to infer that he carried out his intention.

Rule: When the performance of an act is material to a case, a hearsay statement offered to prove state of mind (intent) may be admitted as to the state of mind of the declarant or another person.

Beech Aircraft Corp v. Rainey, 488 U.S. 153 (1988)

Facts: The spouse of a pilot killed during a Navy training mission brought a product liability suit against the aircraft manufacturer. The trial court admitted a statement from a Navy investigative report that, in the opinion of the investigator, "the most probable cause of the accident was the pilot's failure to maintain proper interval." The public records exception to the hearsay rule, FRE 803(8)(C), provided that "factual findings resulting from an investigation made pursuant to authority granted by law" are admissible.

Issue: Does the public records and reports exception to the hearsay rule permit the introduction of opinions and conclusions contained in public records and reports?

Rule (Brennan): Neither the language of FRE 803(8)(C) nor the intent of its framers calls for a distinction between "fact" and "opinion." Evaluative reports are admissible "unless the sources of information or other circumstances indicate lack of trustworthiness." As long as the conclusion is based on factual investigation and satisfies the Rule's trustworthiness requirement, it should be admissible along with other portions of the report.

Note: This case precedes the Supreme Court's ruling in *Crawford v. Washington*; students should remember that, notwithstanding the hearsay rules, the Constitution forbids the admission of statements in violation of the Confrontation Clause.

Idaho v. Wright, 497 U.S. 805 (1990)

Facts: Defendant was charged with two counts of lewd conduct with a minor under 16. The trial court conducted a voir dire examination of the victim, and concluded that she was "not capable of communicating to the jury." At trial, under Idaho's residual hearsay exception, the court allowed the testimony of the examining pediatrician as to statements the victim had made to him during an examination.

Issue: Does the admission under the residual hearsay exception of statements made by a child declarant to an examining pediatrician violate the Confrontation Clause?

Rule (O'Connor): A statement is admissible under the Confrontation Clause if: (1) the witness is unavailable, and (2) his statement bears adequate "indicia of reliability." Reliability can be demonstrated in two ways: (1) if the evidence falls within a firmly rooted hearsay exception, or (2) if there is a showing of particularized guarantees of trustworthiness. The residual hearsay exception is not a firmly rooted hearsay exception for Confrontation Clause purposes. "Particularized guarantees of trustworthiness" must be shown from the totality of the circumstances, but the relevant circumstances include only those that surround the making of the statement and that render the declarant worthy of belief.

Note: This case was decided prior to the Supreme Court's decision in *Crawford v. Washington*. As to testimonial statements, this case is no longer good law.

Dallas County v. Commercial Union Assurance Co., 286 F.2d 388 (5th Cir. 1961)

Facts: The clock tower on a courthouse fell into the courthouse. During a lawsuit related to the accident, the insurance company sought to admit a newspaper article that described a previous fire at the courthouse.

Issue: Does the hearsay rule permit the introduction into evidence of a newspaper article?

Rule: In matters of local interest, when the fact in question is of such a public nature that it would be generally known throughout the community, and when the questioned fact occurred so long ago that the testimony of a witness would probably be less trustworthy than a newspaper account, a federal court, under Fed. R. Civ. P. 43(a), may relax the exclusionary rules to the extent of admitting the newspaper article into evidence. The newspaper article may be admitted as long as the evidence is necessary and trustworthy.

Bill v. Farm Bureau Life Insurance Co., 119 N.W.2d 768 (Iowa 1963)

Facts: Plaintiff sued defendant insurance company to recover on an insurance policy. Insurance company claimed that the death was a suicide and therefore was not covered by the policy. Defendant tried to introduce evidence that a witness nodded his head in response to a question.

Issue: Does a nod of the head constitute an admission against interest admissible as a hearsay exception?

Rule: A gesture that has a universally recognized meaning — such as a nod of the head that is universally understood to be an affirmative or "yes" answer — is admissible to the same extent as the specific words would be admissible. However, it is up to the jury to determine what meaning to assign to the gesture in question.

United States v. McKeon, 738 F.2d 26 (2d Cir. 1984)

Facts: Defendant was charged with several crimes. Defendant's first two trials ended in mistrials. At the third trial, defendant presented a defense that differed from his defense at the prior trials. The prosecution sought to introduce, as an admission, the defense lawyer's prior opening statements.

Issue: Can an attorney's opening statement be admitted against a defendant as an admission against interest?

Rule: An attorney's statements are admissible as prior inconsistent admissions by a defendant. However, prior to admitting such statements into evidence, the trial court must decide that (1) the statements constituted inconsistent assertions of fact, and (2) that the defendant knew of and acquiesced in the statements.

Carpenter v. Davis, 435 S.W.2d 382 (Mo. 1968)

Facts: Plaintiff sued for damages after decedent died in a car accident. Defendant tried to introduce decedent's postaccident statement that the accident was not Defendant's fault.
Issue: Is an opinion as to fault admissible as a declaration against interest when the declarant is no longer available?
Rule: A declaration against interest made by an unavailable declarant is admissible only to the extent that the statement is one of fact and not one of opinion about legal fault.

United States v. DiMaria, 727 F.2d 265 (2d Cir. 1984)

Facts: Defendant was charged with possession of contraband. At trial, the defense tried to elicit testimony from an arresting officer about the defendant's postarrest exculpatory statements. The trial judge excluded the statement.
Issue: Does a statement reflecting a criminal defendant's then-existing state of mind fall under an exception to the hearsay rule?
Rule: A declaration about a witness's state of mind is admissible under FRE 803(3). The fact that the statement appears to have been false does not matter; the jury must decide whether to credit the statement.

Commonwealth v. DiGiacomo, 345 A.2d 605 (Pa. 1975)

Facts: Defendant was charged with murder. At trial, he presented a justification defense, claiming that his actions were justified as an effort to protect a friend's life. In support of his claim, Defendant sought to introduce the friend's hospital records to show the medical opinion and diagnosis of the physician who wrote them.
Issue: To what extent are hospital records admissible as business records?
Rule: Hospital records are admissible as business records for limited purposes, such as to show the fact of hospitalization, the symptoms reported by the patient, and the treatment prescribed. Hospital records that contain expert medical opinions and diagnoses are inadmissible unless the declarant testifies at trial.

Wilson v. State, 468 P.2d 346 (Nev. 1970)

Facts: Defendant was charged with killing Victim with a shotgun blast. Before he died, Victim named Defendant as his killer. The trial court admitted Victim's dying declaration without any showing that Victim believed in God.

Issue: What conditions precedent are necessary to admit a dying declaration as a hearsay exception?

Rule: For a statement to qualify as a dying declaration, the proponent must establish that the declarant was dying and was aware of that fact. The proponent of the dying declaration need not establish that the declarant believed in God. After the dying declaration has been presented to the jury, the other party then has wide latitude to impeach the declarant and discredit his dying statement. However, the weight, credence, and significance of the statement are matters for the jury.

California v. Green, 399 U.S. 149 (1970)

Facts: Witness, who was charged with drug dealing, named Defendant as his supplier. Witness testified at Defendant's preliminary hearing and was cross-examined. Later, at trial, Witness claimed that he could not remember how he obtained the drugs. Prosecution introduced Witness's prior testimony. Defendant argued that Witness's lack of memory rendered him immune to cross-examination, thereby violating Defendant's cross-examination rights.

Issue: Does the Confrontation Clause permit the admission of a witness's prior testimony when the witness, although present in court, cannot be cross-examined about the substance of that statement because the witness does not recall the underlying events in question?

Rule (White): If there was an opportunity for full cross-examination at a preliminary hearing, the testimony of a witness at that hearing can be introduced as evidence against the defendant at trial without violating the Confrontation Clause.

Concurrence (Harlan): The Confrontation Clause extends no further than to require the prosecution to produce available witnesses. The prosecution has no less fulfilled its obligation just because a witness has a memory lapse. The witness is still available.

Dissent (Brennan): The purposes of the Confrontation Clause are not satisfied if the witness cannot be questioned at trial concerning the pertinent facts. When a probability exists that incriminating pretrial testimony is unreliable, its admission — absent confrontation — will prejudicially distort the fact-finding process.

Note: *Crawford v. Washington* now governs resolution of this question.

Ohio v. Roberts, 448 U.S. 56 (1980)

Facts: Defendant was accused of unlawful use of credit cards and forgery of a check. At a preliminary hearing, a witness denied giving Defendant the check and credit cards. At the time of trial, this witness could not be located. The court admitted the witness's prior testimony and Defendant was convicted of forgery of a check and possession of stolen credit cards.
Issue: Is the Confrontation Clause violated by the admission, at a criminal trial, of the prior statements of a witness who was cross-examined by the defendant at a prior proceeding?
Holding: The admission of such a statement does not violate the Confrontation Clause.
Note: *Roberts* held that the admission of a hearsay statement by a non-testifying declarant was consistent with the Confrontation Clause so long as there was independent indicia of the statement's reliability. *Crawford v. Washington* overruled *Roberts* as to testimonial statements made by a witness not available for cross-examination in the current trial. It is unclear whether, and to what extent, *Roberts* continues to govern the admission of nontestimonial hearsay statements.

Banks v. State, 608 A.2d 1249 (1992)

Facts: Defendant was accused of murdering Victim. At trial, the prosecution sought to introduce Victim's out-of-court statements expressing fear of Defendant. Defendant objected, arguing that the statements were both irrelevant and inadmissible hearsay. The prosecution argued that the statements were relevant, nonhearsay declarations about Victim's state of mind. The trial court found the statements to be relevant and admissible nonhearsay and admitted them over Defendant's objection.
Issue: Are statements offered to prove a victim's state of mind inadmissible hearsay?
Rule: Circumstantial evidence of a victim's state of mind is admissible nonhearsay. However, these statements were highly prejudicial and should not, therefore, have been admitted.

United States v. Check, 582 F.2d 668 (2d Cir. 1978)

Facts: Check, a police officer, was indicted for various drug offenses. The key witness against him was an undercover detective who had worked through an informant. At trial, the informant refused to testify, so the State elicited testimony from the detective as to his conversations with the informant. The detective did not directly quote the informant, but he quoted his responses to the informant, which in turn suggested to the jury what the informant had said.

Issue: Whether "framing" testimony that suggests what an unavailable declarant said is admissible under the hearsay rules.

Rule: When testimony is framed to introduce otherwise inadmissible out-of-court statements for the truth of the matter asserted, the hearsay rule applies, even if the statements are not directly quoted. A framing device or narrative cannot convert otherwise inadmissible hearsay into admissible evidence.

United States v. Pacelli, 491 F.2d 1108 (2d Cir. 1974)

Facts: Pacelli was charged with conspiracy to interfere with the constitutional rights of others, stemming from a murder of a government witness. At trial, the government introduced statements that implied, but did not affirmatively allege, the declarant's belief in Pacelli's guilt.

Issue: Do the hearsay rules encompass testimony regarding statements that imply facts presented to prove the truth of the matter implied?

Rule: The statements inquest clearly implied knowledge and belief on the part of third-person declarants as to the source of their knowledge regarding the ultimate fact at issue. Because the third-party declarants were not available, their statements constituted inadmissible hearsay.

Dissent: No declarant actually expressed an opinion that Pacelli committed the murder, so the hearsay rule was not implicated.

Tome v. United States, 513 U.S. 150 (1995)

Facts: Tome was charged with felony sexual abuse of his four-year-old daughter. Tome claimed the allegations were concocted to prevent the child's return to her father. At trial, pursuant to FRE 801(d)(1)(B), and over defendant's objections, the government introduced testimony by witnesses who testified about the child's out-of-court statements. In admitting the statements, the trial court reasoned that the testimony about the child's out-of-court statements rebutted the defense allegation that the child's testimony was motivated by a desire to live with her mother.

Issue: Are prior consistent statements admissible under Rule 801(d)(1)(B) to rebut an allegation of recent fabrication or improper motive?

Rule (Kennedy): A prior consistent statement introduced to rebut a charge of recent fabrication or improper influence or motive is admissible if the statement was made before the alleged fabrication, influence, or motive came into being. If made afterward, the statement is inadmissible.

State v. Motta, 659 P.2d 745 (Haw. 1983)

Facts: Following a robbery, a cashier-witness met with a police artist who, based on the cashier's description, drew a composite sketch of the robbery suspect. The witness later selected Defendant's photograph from a photo array. At trial the court admitted the composite sketch into evidence. On appeal, Defendant argued that the composite sketch was inadmissible hearsay under FRE 802.

Issue: Is a composite sketch admissible under the hearsay rules?

Rule: A composite sketch is hearsay, but it is admissible under the hearsay exception for prior identifications if it complies with Rule 801(d)(1)(C). The sketch will be admissible at trial if the declarant testifies at trial and is subject to cross-examination, and the statement is one of identification of a person made after perceiving him.

Bruton v. U.S., 391 U.S. 123 (1968)

Facts: Co-conspirators Bruton and Evans were jointly tried for armed robbery. At trial, the government introduced evidence of Evans's oral confession saying that he and Bruton had committed the robbery. Bruton objected, arguing that Evans's invocation of his Fifth Amendment privilege against self-incrimination deprived Bruton of Bruton's constitutional right to cross-examination. The trial court admitted the confession against Evans but told the jury that it could not consider the confession as evidence against Bruton.

Issue: Did the trial court's limiting instruction cure any Confrontation Clause violation that might have occurred if the jury used the confession of a co-defendant as substantive evidence against another defendant?

Rule: The confession of a co-defendant is devastating to the defendant and inherently suspect. The unreliability of such evidence is increased when the alleged accomplice does not testify and cannot be tested by cross-examination. Accordingly, it was an error to introduce Evans's statement at Bruton's trial.

United States v. Arnold, 486 F.3d 177 (6th Cir. 2007)

Facts: Witness called 911 and told the operator that Defendant had just threatened her with a gun. When officers arrived at the scene, Witness relayed the story again. Soon after, Defendant returned to the house, and Witness again repeatedly identified Defendant. Witness was subpoenaed to testify at trial but did not appear. Invoking the excited utterance exception, the trial court admitted a redacted recording of the 911 call as well as Witness's on-the-scene statements.

Issue: When is an out-of-court statement by a nontestifying declarant admissible as an excited utterance?

Rule: To satisfy the excited utterances exception under FRE 802, a party must show three things. First, there must be a sufficiently startling event. Second, the statement must be made before there is time to contrive or misrepresent. Third, the statement must be made while the person is under the stress of the excitement caused by the event. Prior cases do not demand a precise showing of the lapse of time between the startling event and the out-of-court statement.

Dissent: The government must provide some proof of the temporal relationship between the startling event and the out-of-court statement.

Ohio v. Scott, 285 N.E.2d 344 (Ohio 1972)

Facts: Scott was charged with attempted murder. At trial, Witness testified that her recollection at the time of making a pretrial statement was better than her recollection at the time of trial. The State then introduced, as a past recollection recorded, Witness's pretrial signed statement.

Issue: Does the past recollection recorded exception to the hearsay rule violate the Confrontation Clause?

Rule: A defendant's Sixth Amendment rights are not violated by admitting into evidence the prior statement of a witness under the past recollection recorded exception to the hearsay rule.

Petrocelli v. Gallison, 679 F.2d 286 (1st Cir. 1982)

Facts: Plaintiffs sued Defendant for medical malpractice. At trial, Plaintiffs attempted to introduce, as a business record, a hospital report of uncertain authorship. Because the source of this information contained in the report was unknown, the trial court excluded the report.

Issue: Is a portion of a business record admissible if the source of the report's contents is unknown?

Rule: FRE 803(6) provides that any report of acts, events, conditions, opinions, or diagnoses, made at or near the time by, or from information transmitted by, a person with knowledge, if kept in the course of a regularly conducted business activity, should be admitted even if the declarant is available as a witness. When a record does not indicate the source of its contents, it is inadmissible as a business record.

Baker v. Elcona Homes Corp., 588 F.2d 551 (6th Cir. 1979)

Facts: Baker sued Elcona after a truck driven by an Elcona employee struck Baker's car. Pursuant to FRE 803(5), the trial court admitted into evidence as a recorded recollection a police accident report that contained notations about relative fault for the accident.

Issue: Are evaluations and opinions in public records and reports admissible as evidence under FRE 803?

Rule: A police report is a public record and report within the meaning of FRE 803(8). The direct observations and recorded data of the officer in the course of his investigation that were placed on the report clearly are "matters observed pursuant to duty imposed by law as to which matters there was a duty to report." The factual findings in the reports are admissible in civil proceedings and against the government in criminal proceedings unless the sources of information or their circumstances indicate lack of trustworthiness. The Advisory Committee Notes list four suggested factors for consideration of trustworthiness: (1) the timeliness of the investigation, (2) the special skill or experience of the official, (3) whether a hearing was held, and (4) possible bias.

United States v. Oates, 560 F.2d 45 (2d Cir. 1977)

Facts: Defendant was convicted of possession with intent to distribute a controlled substance. On appeal, he argued that the trial court incorrectly admitted into evidence the official report and worksheet of the chemist who analyzed the substance in question. On appeal, Defendant argued that the introduction of this evidence was improper because the evidence was inadmissible hearsay, and its introduction into evidence violated his rights under the Confrontation Clause.

Issue: Are reports of police laboratories, which contain investigative findings made pursuant to authority granted by law, admissible against a criminal defendant?

Rule: In criminal cases, public agencies setting forth matters observed by police officers and other law enforcement personnel and reports of public agencies setting forth factual findings resulting from investigations made pursuant to authority granted by law cannot satisfy the standards of any hearsay exception if those reports are sought to be introduced against the accused.

Note: In *Melendez-Diaz*, the Supreme Court explicitly held that forensic laboratory reports prepared by or for the government are testimonial statements subject to the strictures of the Confrontation Clause.

Lloyd v. American Export Lines, Inc., 580 F.2d 1179 (3d Cir. 1978)

Facts: Following a fight between Export crew members Lloyd and Alvarez, Lloyd sued Export, alleging negligence and unseaworthiness. Export impleaded Alvarez as a third-party defendant and Alvarez counterclaimed against Export. At trial, Lloyd was unavailable to testify. After Alvarez testified that Lloyd had attacked him without provocation, Export attempted to rebut this testimony by introducing a transcript of Lloyd's prior sworn testimony before a Coast Guard Examiner. The trial court refused to admit this testimony.

Issue: When is an unavailable witness's prior testimony admissible under FRE 804(b)(1)?

Rule: Under Rule 804(b)(1), the prior testimony of an unavailable witness is admissible when the party against whom it is offered or that party's predecessor in interest has had the opportunity and similar motive to develop the testimony by direct, cross, or redirect examination. To be "predecessors in interest," the parties must have similar motives and interests.

Williamson v. United States, 512 U.S. 594 (1994)

Facts: Defendant was charged with drug offenses. Alleged co-conspirator cooperated with the government and made statements incriminating Defendant; however, co-conspirator refused to testify at trial. Pursuant to FRE 804(b)(3), the trial court permitted a government agent to testify as to the co-conspirator's statements to agent. On appeal, Defendant argued that the admission of the co-conspirator's out-of-court statements violated Rule 804(b)(3) because the statements were not entirely against the co-conspirator's self-interest.

Issue: Does FRE 804(b)(3) allow the admission of non-self-inculpatory statements, even if they are made without a broader narrative that is generally self-inculpatory?

Rule (O'Connor): Rule 804(b)(3) does not allow the admission of non-self-inculpatory statements, even if they are made in the context of a larger set of statements that are self-inculpatory. Whether a statement is self-inculpatory can only be determined by viewing it in context; the proper inquiry is always whether the statement was sufficiently against the declarant's penal interest that a reasonable person would not have made the statement unless that person believed it to be true.

People v. Moreno, 160 P.3d 242 (Colo. 2007)

Facts: Defendant was accused of sexually assaulting a child. The child's therapist testified that requiring her to testify at trial would "retraumatize" her, thereby making her "medically unavailable" to testify under state hearsay statute. State invoked the doctrine of "forfeiture by wrongdoing," and the trial court then permitted the State to introduce a videotaped interview with the child in lieu of her live testimony.

Issue: What constitutes "forfeiture by wrongdoing" such that a defendant forfeits the Sixth Amendment right to confrontation?

Rule: A criminal defendant forfeits the Sixth Amendment right of confrontation by engaging in conduct designed to prevent a witness from testifying. The doctrine requires a showing that the defendant's conduct was intended to keep the declarant from testifying at trial. A defendant does not forfeit the right to confrontation simply because the state accuses the defendant of a criminal act that allegedly resulted in a witness's unavailability.

State v. Weaver, 554 N.W.2d 240 (Iowa 1996)

Facts: Defendant was convicted of the murder of an infant. After her conviction, Defendant moved for a new trial on the basis of affidavits stating that the infant's mother had exculpated Defendant and alleged that the infant had suffered her injuries prior to being placed in Defendant's care. The trial court denied the new trial motion, holding that the affidavits contained inadmissible hearsay. Defendant appealed, arguing that the affidavits were admissible under the catch-all hearsay exception for trustworthiness.

Issue: In making a determination of trustworthiness, what factors must a court consider?

Rule: In making a determination of trustworthiness under the catch-all hearsay exception (now found at FRE 807), a court must consider a wide range of factors including, but not limited to, declarant's propensity to tell the truth, whether the statements were made under oath, the evidence of declarant's personal knowledge, the time span between the events and the statement, the declarant's motivations for making the statement, the existence of evidence corroborating the statement, declarant's efforts to reaffirm or to recant the statement, and the availability of the declarant for cross-examination.

Davis v. Washington, 126 S. Ct. 2266 (2006)

Facts: Assault victim called 911 and identified Defendant as her assailant. At trial, the victim did not testify and the government offered the 911 call into evidence. Defendant objected, arguing that admission of the 911 call violated his rights under the Confrontation Clause.

Issue: Are statements made during a 911 call "testimonial" and thus subject to the requirements of the Sixth Amendment's Confrontation Clause?

Rule (Scalia): Statements to law enforcement are nontestimonial when they are made under circumstances objectively indicating that the primary purpose of the statements was to seek police assistance in resolving an ongoing emergency. The victim's 911 call was nontestimonial hearsay because she made her 911 statements in an effort to help police resolve her emergency.

Dissent (Thomas): The "emergency standard" is too subjective; courts are ill-suited to devise the motives pursuant to which declarants make statements.

Hickey v. Settlemier, 864 P.2d 372 (Or. 1993)

Facts: A news program aired a news video in which Defendant accused Plaintiff of various crimes. In addition, the footage also included a reporter's restatement of Defendant's allegations. Plaintiff then brought a defamation action and offered the videotape of the program as evidence that the statements were made.
Issue: When is multiple hearsay admissible?
Rule: Multiple hearsay is admissible when each level of hearsay is independently admissible as an exception to the hearsay rule.

Wright v. Doe D. Tatham, 5 Clark and Fennelly 670 (House of Lords, 1838)

Facts: Plaintiff challenged validity of Marsden's will because of Marsden's alleged mental incompetence. At trial, in an effort to show that certain business people believed Marsden was sane, Defendant sought to introduce several business letters written to Marsden. The trial court refused to admit the letters.
Issue: Are written statements of nontestifying declarants admissible as illustrations of the belief of the nontestifying declarants?
Rule: The written statements in question were neither made under oath nor subject to cross-examination. Therefore they are inadmissible hearsay.

Headley v. Tilghman, 53 F.3d 472 (2d Cir. 1995)

Facts: Defendant was charged with drug dealing. Shortly after his arrest, Headley received a "beeper" call. When a police officer returned the call, an unidentified man answered, saying "Are you up? Can I come by? Are you ready?" However, when the officer began to speak, the man hung up. Over Defendant's objections, the trial court allowed the police officer to testify at trial about the man's statements, reasoning that the statements were those of a co-conspirator made in furtherance of the conspiracy.
Issue: When, if ever, are out-of-court statements made by an unidentified individual admissible?
Rule: Out-of-court statements by an unknown declarant may be admitted as nonhearsay so long as the statements are not offered to prove the matter asserted. Here, the statements were admissible as circumstantial evidence of the speaker's belief that the defendant used his beeper to deal drugs. The court need not have addressed the co-conspirator exception.

Shepard v. United States, 290 U.S. 96 (1933)

Facts: Dr. Shepard was charged with poisoning his wife (and patient). Under the dying declaration exception to the hearsay rule, the trial court permitted a nurse to testify that, shortly before collapsing, the wife stated, "Dr. Shepard has poisoned me."

Issue: Is the statement in question admissible as a dying declaration? If not, can the appellate court nevertheless deem the statement properly admitted as evidence of state of mind, evidence that the declarant observed the matter asserted, or as another exception to the hearsay rule?

Rule (Cardozo): For a statement to be considered a dying declaration, the declarant must have spoken when the declarant lay in the shadow of death and lacked hope of recovery. Because the record lacked any such evidence, the statement was not admissible as a dying declaration. In addition, the government may not, on appeal, change its theory as to the basis for the admission of the statements.

United States v. Jacoby, 955 F.2d 1527 (11th Cir. 1992)

Facts: Bank officers and borrowers were indicted for violations of federal banking laws. At trial, the court admitted into evidence a memorandum written by an unavailable declarant. The memorandum contained hearsay statements explaining the mechanics of the fraudulent practices. There was evidence that it was the declarant's practice to write such explanatory memos when unusual circumstances arose that might later require clarification.

Issue: Is a business record admissible if it is prepared precisely because it reflects a nonroutine situation or circumstance?

Rule: The business records exception does not turn on the extent to which preparation of a record is routine. Nonroutine records made in the course of a regularly conducted business are admissible as business records so long as they meet the other requirements of the business records rule.

Graham v. Wyeth Laboratories, 906 F.2d 1399 (10th Cir. 1990)

Facts: Plaintiff sued Defendant, alleging that Defendant's defective vaccine caused her injuries. The trial court admitted into evidence a redacted American Medical Association report. The report was admitted into evidence as a learned treatise; the redacted material explained that the report was developed to address compensation for vaccine-related injuries.

Issue: Does FRE 803(18) permit a redacted document to be treated as a learned treatise?

Rule: Where, as here, a redaction prevents the jury from learning *why* a document was created, the redacted document is inadmissible as a learned treatise. An understanding of the document's purpose is essential to the jury's ability to assess the credibility of a purported learned treatise.

Robinson v. Shapiro, 646 F.2d 734 (2d Cir. 1981)

Facts: Plaintiff sued for wrongful death action after her husband died from injuries sustained while working on the roof of Defendant's building. Defendant failed to provide Plaintiff with discovery information necessary to obtain the address of the building superintendent. Therefore, under the residual hearsay exception for unavailable declarants, the trial court allowed decedent's co-worker to testify as to decedent's statements about his (decedent's) conversations with the superintendent.

Issue: When is evidence admissible under the residual hearsay exception of the Federal Rules of Evidence?

Rule: The residual hearsay exception applies whenever (1) the out-of-court statements are offered as evidence of a material fact; (2) the statements are more probative on the point for which they are offered than other reasonably available evidence would be; (3) the general purposes of the rules and the interests of justice are best served by admitting the testimony; and (4) the statements bear circumstantial guarantees of trust-worthiness.

White v. Illinois, 502 U.S. 345 (1992)

Facts: Following his conviction for sexual assault, burglary, and unlawful restraint, White argued that his alleged victim's out-of-court statements were erroneously admitted under the spontaneous declaration and medical examination exceptions to the hearsay rule. White claimed that, because the witness was present but failed to testify, her out-of-court statements should not have been admitted.

Issue: Does the Confrontation Clause require that, before testimony is admissible under the "spontaneous declaration" and "medical examination" exceptions to the hearsay rule, the declarant be unavailable or have testified at trial?

Rule (Rehnquist): If the hearsay testimony in question has sufficient guarantees of reliability such that it falls within a firmly rooted exception to the hearsay rule, the Confrontation Clause is satisfied. A statement that qualifies for admission under a firmly rooted hearsay exception is so trustworthy that adversarial testing can be expected to add little to its reliability.

Note: As to testimonial statements, *Crawford v. Washington* overruled *White v. Illinois*.

United States v. Zenni, 492 F. Supp. 464 (E.D. Ky. 1980)

Facts: Government agents executed a search warrant on Defendant's premises for evidence of illegal gambling activities. During the search, Defendant's phone rang repeatedly and government agents answered the incoming calls; on those calls, unknown callers gave instructions for placing illegal bets. At trial, over Defendant's objections, the government agents testified about the statements of the unknown callers. The trial court permitted this testimony on the theory that the conversations showed the callers' belief that Defendant's premises were used for gambling activities.

Issue: Was the "nonassertive verbal conduct" of the callers offered for its truth and therefore inadmissible under the hearsay rules?

Rule: For purposes of the hearsay rules, "nonassertive verbal conduct" is not the same as a statement. A statement is an oral or written communication — or even a communicative gesture — intended to convey a specific message to another. In contrast, "nonassertive verbal conduct" does not intend to convey a specific message. Here, the government asked the jury to make an inference based on the nonassertive conduct of unknown callers. It did not, however, offer the callers' statements to prove their truth. Therefore the testimony about the phone calls did not violate the hearsay rules.

State v. Moses, 119 P.3d 906 (Wash. Ct. App. 2005)

Facts: Defendant was charged with the murder of his wife. At trial, in regard to prior incidents of domestic violence, the court allowed the prosecution to introduce the victim's out-of-court statements to an emergency room physician and to investigating police officers.

Issue: Are out-of-court statements made by a declarant to a health care provider admissible as a hearsay exception?

Rule: Statements made to a health care provider are admissible when the declarant's apparent motive was receiving treatment, and statements were ones on which a medical provider would reasonably rely for diagnosis or treatment. To the extent that the victim's statements identified the defendant as her abuser, the identity of the abuser may be pertinent and necessary to the victim's treatment. Therefore, those statements are also admissible.

Lewis v. Baker, 526 F.2d 470 (2d Cir. 1975)

Facts: Plaintiff, an employee of the Penn Central Railroad, sued for injuries that were allegedly caused by a faulty brake. At trial, to rebut Plaintiff's allegations, Defendants offered into evidence "accident reports" that stated that the brake had worked properly both before and after Plaintiff's accident.

Issue: Is an accident report a business report and thus admissible under the business records exception to the hearsay rule?

Rule: In this case, the railroad was required by law to make regular monthly reports of accidents involving railroad employees. Moreover, there was evidence adduced at trial indicating that it was routine railroad procedure for a foreman to inspect the equipment involved in any accident and to report the results of the inspection on a printed form. These factors were sufficient indicia of trustworthiness to establish that the reports are admissible as business records.

Commonwealth v. Melendez-Diaz, — U.S. — (2009)

Facts: Melendez-Diaz was charged with drug offenses. At trial, in an effort to prove that the substance in question was illegal, the state offered into evidence a forensic certificate prepared by a state laboratory for the state prosecution. However, relying on a state evidentiary statute, the state did not call the declarant laboratory technician to testify. On appeal, Melendez-Diaz argued that the laboratory report was a testimonial statement and therefore, its admission violated the Confrontation Clause.

Issue: Is a forensic laboratory report testimonial, such that its admission is subject to a defendant's Confrontation Clause rights?

Rule: A forensic laboratory report such as the one at issue here is a classic testimonial statement. It was prepared for use by the prosecution at an impending criminal trial. Accordingly, the statement is testimonial and subject to the ordinary strictures of the Confrontation Clause. The fact that laboratory technicians are highly in demand does not render them unavailable to testify for Confrontation Clause purposes. Accordingly, it was an error to admit the hearsay laboratory report without the declarant's accompanying testimony.

Giles v. California, 128 S. Ct. 2678 (2008)

Facts: Giles was charged with the murder of his girlfriend. At trial, the prosecution introduced evidence of a domestic violence incident three weeks before the murder. Over the defendant's objection, the court admitted into evidence statements that the victim-declarant made to a responding police officer. The statements were admitted under a provision of California law that permitted the admission of an unavailable declarant's out-of-court statements describing infliction or threat of physical injury when the defendant caused the declarant's unavailability and the prior statements are deemed trustworthy.

Issue: When should the out-of-court statements of an unavailable witness be admitted against a criminal defendant pursuant to the "forfeiture by wrongdoing" doctrine's exception to the Confrontation Clause?

Rule (Scalia): The forfeiture by wrongdoing doctrine only applies when the defendant engaged in conduct *intended* to prevent the witness from testifying. In this case, there was evidence that the defendant caused declarant-victim's unavailability but there was no evidence that he did so for the express purpose of preventing her from testifying against him. Therefore, the statements were improperly admitted.

Dissent (Breyer): The defendant here knew that murdering his ex-girlfriend would keep her from testifying. That knowledge is sufficient to show the intent that law ordinarily demands. With a few exceptions, the law holds an individual responsible for consequences known likely to follow just as if that individual had intended to achieve them.

Gray v. Maryland, 523 U.S. 185 (1998)

Facts: Defendant and a co-defendant were jointly charged with beating a victim to death. At trial, the prosecution introduced redacted versions of co-defendant's oral and written confession. Thus, the detective who read the confession into evidence said the word "deleted" or "deletion" whenever Defendant's name appeared. Similarly, the written copy of the confession had a blank space wherever Defendant's name would have appeared. The trial judge specifically instructed the jury to consider the confession as evidence only against the declarant-codefendant and not against the defendant.

Issue: In a joint trial, is a visibly redacted written confession so prejudicial as to moot the curative effect of any limiting instruction?

Rule (Breyer): Incriminating extrajudicial statements of a co-defendant are so prejudicial that limiting instructions are insufficient to guarantee a fair trial. Redaction that replaces a defendant's name with an obvious indication of deletion, such as a blank space, the word "deleted," or a similar symbol, falls within *Bruton*'s protective rule. A reasonable jury will probably realize that the confession refers specifically to the defendant. Indeed, the deletion might only encourage the jury to speculate about the removed name, thereby overemphasizing the importance of the confession's implicit accusation.

Dissent (Scalia): Although the jury may speculate, the statement only implicates the declarant. The word "deleted" does not clearly identify the defendant.

Chambers v. Mississippi, 410 U.S. 284 (1973)

Facts: Defendant Chambers was charged with shooting a police officer. Chambers claimed that another person — McDonald — actually committed the crime. Chambers sought to introduce evidence that McDonald had confessed to the murder, both to his lawyers and to three of his friends.

Relying on Mississippi's hearsay rules, the trial court precluded McDonald's friends from testifying that he had confessed to them. The court also precluded Chambers from calling McDonald as an adverse witness.

Issue: Did the trial court's application of Mississippi's hearsay rules deprive Chambers of his due process right to a fair trial?

Rule (Powell): The exclusion of McDonald's confessions to his three friends, combined with the state's refusal to permit Chambers to cross-examine McDonald, denied Chambers a fair trial that comported with due process. The right of cross-examination is an essential and fundamental requirement for a fair trial. Mississippi's hearsay rules impermissibly interfered with Chambers's right to defend against the state's charges.

Lira v. Albert Einstein Medical Center, 559 A.2d 550 (Pa. 1989)

Facts: Plaintiff sued for medical malpractice based on an injury received from the insertion of a nasogastric tube into her throat. At trial, Plaintiff testified, following the insertion of the tube, she had seen another doctor who, on commencing his examination of her, asked "Who's the butcher who did this?"

Issue: Was the examining physician's out-of-court statement admissible at trial?

Rule: The physician's out-of-court statement was hearsay and did not fall within a recognized exception to the hearsay rule. Medical opinions are generally inadmissible unless the physician-declarant is available for cross-examination.

State v. Jones, 532 A.2d 169 (Md. 1987)

Facts: Defendant was charged with sexual assault. At trial, the state introduced testimony from a state trooper. That trooper did not witness the events, but testified that he heard radio transmissions regarding Jones's flight from the crime scene as Jones's flight was occurring. Jones objected to the admission of these statements.

Issue: When is a statement admissible under the present sense impression exception to the hearsay rule?

Rule: A present sense impression is admissible when its proponent establishes that the statement was made virtually contemporaneously with the event it describes, and that the declarant spoke from personal knowledge.

State v. Carlson, 808 P.2d 1002 (Or. 1991)

Facts: After being dispatched to a domestic dispute, police officers noticed what appeared to be needle marks on Carlson's arms. When asked about them, Carlson said the marks were injuries he received while working on a car. His wife Lisa, who was present, yelled, "You liar, you got them from shooting up in the bathroom with all your stupid friends!" According to the police, Carlson then "hung his head and shook it back and forth." At trial, the court treated Carlson's gesture as an adoptive admission and permitted the police officer to testify about Lisa's accusatory statement and about Carlson's physical reaction to it.

Issue: What are the preconditions to admitting evidence as an adoptive admission?

Rule: Whether a party intended to adopt the statement of another is a preliminary question of fact to be determined by the trial judge. Only after the court has made a preliminary finding of the party's intent to adopt may the factfinder consider the statement.

Big Mack Trucking Co., Inc. v. Dickerson, 497 S.W.2d 283 (Tex. 1973)

Facts: Survivors brought a wrongful death action against employer, Big Mack Trucking, after Dickerson was crushed to death between his own truck and the truck of his co-worker, Leday. A jury found for Dickerson. Leday did not testify at trial. However, the vice president of Big Mack testified that Leday had told him he was having "air pressure troubles" with the truck that day. On appeal, Big Mack argued that there was insufficient evidence to support a judgment against Big Mack because only hearsay evidence linked Leday's negligence to Big Mack.

Issue: Is the hearsay evidence of an employee's negligence and proximate cause admissible against the employer?

Rule: If the trial judge finds, as a preliminary matter, that an employee's statements were authorized, then those statements should be admitted against the employer under the theory of vicarious admissions.

United States v. Doerr, 886 F.2d 944 (7th Cir. 1989)

Facts: Defendants were charged with prostitution conspiracy and related tax crimes. At trial, the court admitted two out-of-court statements that Doerr argued did not satisfy the "in furtherance" requirement of the co-conspirator exception to the hearsay rule.

Issue: When does a statement satisfy the "in furtherance" requirement of the co-conspirator exception to the hearsay rule?

Rule: A co-conspirator's statement satisfies the "in furtherance" requirement when "the statement is part of the information flow between conspirators intended to help each perform his role."

Travelers Fire Insurance Co. v. Wright, 322 P.2d 417 (Okla. 1958)

Facts: Plaintiffs sued Defendant to recover under fire insurance policies. Defendant argued that one of the Plaintiffs had deliberately caused the fire in an effort to defraud Defendant. In support of this theory, Defendant called two witnesses to testify; however, they invoked their Fifth Amendment privilege against self-incrimination. Defendant then offered transcripts of the witness's prior testimony from a criminal trial in which one of the Plaintiffs was charged with arson in connection with the fire involved in the civil insurance case.

Issue: When is prior recorded testimony from a criminal trial admissible at a civil trial?

Rule: Testimony from a criminal case is admissible in a subsequent civil case where (1) it is impossible to otherwise obtain the testimony of the witness; and (2) the party against whom the testimony to be used – or a party with an identical motive and interest in cross-examination – had an opportunity to cross-examine the witness; and, (3) there is an identity of issues. In this case the issue (was there arson?) was the same and the criminal Defendant-Plaintiff had an identical motive to cross-examine as would the other Plaintiffs in the civil case.

Adkins v. Brett, 193 P. 251 (Cal. 1920)

Facts: Adkins sued Brett, charging him with the alienation of the affections of Adkins's wife. The court admitted statements in which Mrs. Adkins declared that her husband was "distasteful" to her and she preferred Mr. Brett.

Issue: Are statements expressing the declarant's state of mind at the time admissible as exceptions to the hearsay rule?

Rule: A woman's declarations that are indicative of her then-state of mind are admissible as a hearsay exception so long as the declarant's intention, feelings, or other state of mind are material to the issues at trial. The evidence is not rendered incompetent by the fact that it also tends to prove other matters besides the declarant's state of mind.

Zippo Manufacturing Co. v. Rogers Imports, Inc., 216 F. Supp. 670 (S.D.N.Y. 1963)

Facts: Zippo sued Rogers for trademark infringement based on Rogers's sale of pocket lighters that closely resembled Zippo's. To establish its case, Zippo conducted a survey to see whether consumers would confuse Rogers's lighters with Zippo's. Zippo then sought to admit the results of this survey into evidence. Rogers objected, arguing that the survey constituted inadmissible hearsay.

Issue: Is a survey prepared in support of a litigation claim admissible evidence as an exception to the hearsay rule?

Rule: Where a survey in support of a consumer confusion claim is conducted with procedural and statistical accuracy, such a survey is admissible as a present sense exception to the hearsay rule. The answers of the survey respondents are hearsay; however, they are also expressions of the respondents' presently existing state of mind, attitude, or belief.

State v. Jensen, Kenosha County (Wis.) Circuit Court, April 7, 2008

Facts: Jensen was charged with murdering his wife, Julie. At trial, the defense claimed that Julie had killed herself and tried to frame her husband. In rebuttal, the prosecution offered into evidence a letter that Julie wrote and delivered to a neighbor with instructions to give it to police officers if anything happened to her (Julie). The letter itself stated that if anything happened to Julie, her husband should be the first suspect. The trial court admitted the letter as a dying declaration.

Issue: Was the letter admissible under the dying declaration exception to the hearsay rule?

Rule: In this case, the letter allowed Mrs. Jensen to "preserve" an utterance until the feared event occurred. At that time, her belief of impending death was made certain. A statement can be delayed and "made" later than the time that it is written.

United States v. Vigneau, 187 F.3d 70 (1st Cir. 1999)

Facts: Vigneau was convicted of money laundering. At trial, the court allowed the government to introduce Western Union "To Send Money" forms that Vigneau allegedly filled out to establish that Vigneau sent the money in question. The forms were admitted as a business records exception to the hearsay rule. On appeal, Vigneau argued the government should not have been allowed to introduce his name, address, and telephone number on the "To Send Money" forms as hearsay evidence of his identity as the sender of money.

Issue: Are routine forms and records completed by individual customers admissible as business records exceptions to the hearsay rule?

Rule: The business records exception does not render admissible statements contained within business records that were made by persons who are not part of the business. Here, the portions of the records that were filled in by the customer (allegedly Vigneau) were not business records and were therefore inadmissible as proof of the matter asserted therein.

Williams v. Alexander, 129 N.E.2d 417 (N.Y. 1955)

Facts: Williams sued Alexander after Alexander's car hit Williams. At trial, Williams introduced portions of a hospital report that related to his injuries and their treatment. Alexander then introduced the rest of the hospital record, including statements that Williams made to a physician concerning the incident itself. Williams objected, characterizing this portion of the report as inadmissible hearsay.

Issue: To what extent are statements in hospital reports admissible under the business records exception to the hearsay rule?

Rule: Statements in a hospital record are only admissible as business records when they are made in the regular course of the business and for the purpose of assisting the hospital in carrying on its "business." The business of a hospital is to diagnose and treat its patients' ailments. Thus, statements that do not relate to treatment or diagnosis do not fall within the business records exception. The portion of the hospital record that described the cause of Williams's injuries should not have been admitted.

Sana v. Hawaiian Cruises, Ltd., 181 F.3d 1041 (9th Cir. 1999)

Facts: Sana sued his employer, Hawaiian Cruises, after he allegedly developed viral encephalitis during his work for Hawaiian Cruises. At trial, Sana attempted to introduce the report of Hawaiian Cruises' now-unavailable insurance investigator who had investigated Sana's condition and filed a report. The trial court held that the report contained inadmissible hearsay and refused to admit it as a business record.

Issue: Is an insurance company's investigative report admissible under the business records exception?

Rule: A ship owner has a legal duty to investigate a crew member's injuries. The investigative report made under obligation of law is admissible as a business record as it was made in the regular course of business. To the extent that the report contained multiple hearsay, it was nevertheless admissible as each layer of hearsay was independently admissible. The "hearsay within hearsay" statements of Sana's co-workers are admissible as admissions by agents concerning a matter within the scope of their employment. In addition, Sana's "hearsay within hearsay" statements are admissible as statements of declarant's then-existing physical condition.

Stroud v. Cook, 931 F. Supp. 733 (D. Nev. 1996)

Facts: Stroud and Cook had a car accident and Stroud sued Cook. At trial, Stroud sought to introduce evidence that, in connection with the accident,

Cook had been convicted of failing to drive with due care, a misdemeanor offense.

Issue: Is a misdemeanor conviction admissible in a civil action that seeks to establish civil liability for the same conduct that resulted in the conviction?

Rule: Judgments of misdemeanor convictions are admissible under the public records exception to the hearsay rule, FRE 803(8). (Under the FRE, felony convictions are automatically nonhearsay.)

Silver v. New York Central Railroad, 105 N.E.2d 923 (Mass. 1952)

Facts: Silver claimed that her illness was exacerbated by the cold temperature in the defendant's railroad car. To prove that the car's temperature was not too cold, Defendant sought to have the railroad employee testify that none of the other passengers had complained. The court refused to permit Defendant to introduce this evidence.

Issue: Is evidence of an absence of complaints admissible to show that the complained of condition did not exist?

Rule: There is no hearsay rule that bars the use of "lack of complaints" as evidence that a defect did not exist. However, "lack of complaint" evidence is only admissible if those who might have complained were in a position substantially similar to the plaintiff's, and they had an adequate opportunity to complain.

United States v. Summers, 414 F.3d 1287 (10th Cir. 2005)

Facts: Summers and two co-defendants were charged with bank robbery. At trial, the government sought to introduce statements made by a co-defendant. In particular, the government sought to introduce testimony that, while being escorted to the patrol car, a codefendant asked the police, "How did you guys find us so fast?" In addition, the government sought to introduce the fact that, in response to police questioning about items in his possession, the co-defendant said, "What do you think? It's bank money." The co-defendant-declarant did not testify and all of his statements were introduced by police officers. On appeal, defendant argued that the admission of his co-defendant's hearsay statements and questions violated his (the defendant's) Sixth Amendment right of confrontation.

Issue: Whether a question asked by a nontestifying witness that could be construed to be an express or implied assertion constitutes hearsay.

Rule: A declaration in the form of a question may constitute an assertion within the meaning of FRE 801(a) and (c). The final determination depends on the declarant's intent to make an assertion. Here, the question implies both guilt and wonderment at the ability of the police to apprehend them so quickly. The assertion thus constitutes hearsay.

Commonwealth v. Daye, 469 N.E.2d 483 (Mass. 1984)

Facts: At a criminal trial, witnesses testified that they could not identify Daye as the gunman. The trial court then permitted the government to introduce those witness's pretrial statements before the grand jury in which they identified Daye as the gunman. On appeal, Daye argued that the trial court erred in admitting evidence of the prior inconsistent statements.

Issue: When is a prior inconsistent grand jury statement admissible for its truth?

Rule: Inconsistent grand jury testimony is admissible when the declarant's prior testimony was under oath and declarant testifies at trial and is thus subject to cross-examination concerning the prior statement.

United States v. Lewis, 565 F.2d 1248 (2d Cir. 1977)

Facts: Defendant was convicted of armed robbery. At trial, a government witness was unable to identify Defendant. However, prior to trial, the witness had picked Defendant's photo from a photographic array. Accordingly, over Defendant's objections, the trial court permitted a government agent to testify that the witness had previously identified Defendant in a photographic arrray.

Issue: May a witness testify about another witness's photographic identification of a defendant?

Rule: The admissibility of testimony about an out-of-court identification does not turn on the witness's ability to make an in-court identification. Moreover, FRE 801(d)(1)(C) now specifically makes a pretrial identification nonhearsay.

United States v. Cornett, 195 F.3d 776 (5th Cir. 1999)

Facts: Defendants were convicted of drug distribution and a related drug conspiracy. At trial, over Defendants' objections, the court permitted the government to introduce the tape-recorded statements of a government informant. The court admitted the statements under FRE 801(d)(2)(e) as statements made during the course and in furtherance of the conspiracy.

Issue: When is a statement admissible under Rule 801(d)(2)(e) as a statement made during the course and in furtherance of the conspiracy?

Rule: Under Rule 801(d)(2)(e), the proponent of the statement must prove, by preponderance of the evidence, that (1) the alleged conspiracy existed; (2) the statement was made by a co-conspirator; (3) the statement was made during the course of the conspiracy; and (4) the statement was made to further the goals of the conspiracy.

United States v. Cain, 587 F.2d 678 (5th Cir. 1979)

Facts: Cain was charged with stealing a truck and taking it across state lines. At trial, under the present sense impression hearsay exception, the court permitted a police officer to testify that a "CB" user told the officer that he had seen Cain walk away from the stolen truck. Shortly thereafter, police found Cain walking on the road nearly six miles from the stolen truck. On appeal, Cain argued that the CBer's statement constituted inadmissible hearsay.

Issue: When is a statement admissible under the present sense impression exception to the hearsay rule?

Rule: To qualify under the present sense impression exception to the hearsay rule, the statement in question must have been made at a time nearly contemporaneous to the events it recounts. In this case, shortly after the statements were made, Cain was found six miles away from the truck; this fact indicates that the CB caller could not have been recounting a present sense impression.

Miller v. Keating, 754 F.2d 507 (3d Cir. 1985)

Facts: Miller sued for injuries sustained when Keating's truck rear-ended Miller's car. At trial, the district court permitted Keating to introduce an unknown bystander's statement to the effect that Miller had "tried to cut in." The statement was admitted as an excited utterance exception to the hearsay rules. Miller appealed.

Issue: Can a statement by an anonymous declarant qualify as an excited utterance exception to the hearsay rule?

Rule: Statements made by unidentified declarants are inadmissible as excited utterances. For a statement to be admitted as an excited utterance, the proponent must demonstrate: (1) a startling event occurred; (2) the statement relates to the startling event; (3) the declarant had an opportunity to observe the startling event; and (4) the statement was made sufficiently close in time to the startling event that the declarant could not have had time to reflect and fabricate. The proponent of an excited utterance by an unknown person bears a heavy burden to demonstrate the statement's admissibility.

United States v. Day, 591 F.2d 861 (D.C. Cir. 1978)

Facts: The government accused Day of murdering Williams. The government sought to introduce testimony that, shortly before his death, Williams gave Mason a slip of paper on which he had written Day's number and told Mason that if he (Williams) did not return home by three o'clock the next day, Mason should call the police and give them Day's number.

The trial court refused to permit Mason to testify as to Williams's statements and the government appealed.

Issue: When does a statement constitute a state of mind exception to the hearsay rule?

Rule: A statement qualifies as an admissible state of mind exception to the hearsay rule when the declarant's state of mind is at issue in the case. In this case, Williams's state of mind was not at issue and the out-of-court statement was highly prejudicial. Accordingly, his out-of-court statement was inadmissible. In contrast, the slip of paper and the words written on it were admissible simply to prove Williams's prior association with Day.

United States v. Iron Shell, 633 F.2d 77 (8th Cir. 1980)

Facts: Iron Shell was tried for assault with intent to rape. On the night of the assault, the victim made statements to the examining doctor about the cause of her injuries. At trial, the victim and the doctor testified about the statements the victim had made that night.

Issue: When are statements made for purposes of medical diagnosis or treatment admissible?

Rule: Pursuant to FRE 803(4), statements made during medical examination are admissible when the statements are those that a doctor would commonly rely on to form a diagnostic or treatment assessment.

United States v. Booz, 451 F.2d 719 (3d Cir. 1971)

Facts: Defendant was convicted of bank robbery. On the day of the robbery, a civilian witness called police to report that he had seen a white pickup truck near the bank that was robbed, and had written down the truck's license plate number. However, at trial, the civilian witness was unable to recall the exact license plate number he had given to the police. The court permitted police to testify about the license plate number the witness had provided to them. The court also permitted the witness to use the police report to refresh his recollection about the license plate number. On appeal, Booz argued that it was an error to allow the witness to refresh his recollection and an error to allow the police to testify as to the conversation with the witness.

Issue: Is a past recollection recorded exception to the hearsay rule available when one witness makes an oral statement and another witness records it?

Rule: There is no limit on what writing a witness may use to refresh recollection. The writing used for refreshing recollection is not itself admissible. Here, if the witness had not had his recollection refreshed, the police would nevertheless have been permitted to testify about the conversation with the witness. The fact that the recorded recollection was the product of two individuals — the reporting witness and the recording officer — is not fatal to its admissibility as a recorded recollection.

United States v. Felix-Jerez, 667 F.2d 1297 (9th Cir. 1982)

Facts: A criminal defendant made pretrial statements to a police interrogator via an interpreter. The police interrogator then wrote a narrative describing the defendant's statements. At trial, the government introduced the statement into evidence. The police interrogator testified about procedure in which the statement was taken, but did not testify that he no longer had any recollection of the statement. On appeal, the defendant argued that the statement was erroneously admitted as it did not satisfy the recorded recollection hearsay exception.

Issue: When is a translated and transcribed statement admissible as a recorded recollection?

Rule: In this case, the translated hearsay statement could only have been admissible as a recorded recollection. However, the witness never testified that his recall of the statement was insufficient to permit him to testify as to its contents. Therefore, the statement was not admissible as a recorded recollection.

United States v. De Georgia, 420 F.2d 889 (9th Cir. 1969)

Facts: De Georgia was charged with stealing a rental car from the Hertz parking lot. At trial, a Hertz employee testified that Hertz computer records indicated that the car in question had been returned to Hertz and that, at the time of the alleged theft, there were no records indicating that the car had subsequently been rented or leased. The Hertz representative testified that all of these records indicated the vehicle had been stolen. The trial court allowed this testimony under the business records exception to the hearsay rule. On appeal, De Georgia argued that the employee's evidence was improperly admitted.

Issue: Does the business records hearsay exception encompass the absence of an entry relating to the type of transaction that is regularly recorded in routinely maintained business records?

Rule: Regularly maintained business records are admissible in evidence as an exception to the hearsay rule because the circumstances under which they are made assure their accuracy. Similarly, if a business record designed to record every transaction of a particular kind contains no notation of such a transaction, the absence of such a notation is admissible under the business records exception.

Potamkin Cadillac Corp. v. BRI Coverage Corp., 38 F.3d 627 (2d Cir. 1994)

Facts: Potamkin retained BRI as its insurance broker. However, the relationship soured and Potamkin sued BRI for fraud. BRI counterclaimed, alleging that Potamkin owed BRI money. In support of its counterclaim, BRI sought to use data compiled from computer printouts. BRI offered the data compilation as a business record exception to the hearsay rule under FRE 803. The court held that the evidence was inadmissible as a business record. **Issue:** What are the requirements for the admissibility of a business record under Rule 803?

Rule: The business records hearsay exception removes from the hearsay rule any memorandum, report, record, or data compilation of acts or events if kept in the course of a regularly conducted business activity, and if it was the regular practice of the business activity to make the record. The principal precondition is that the records have sufficient indicia of trustworthiness to be considered reliable. Here, the proffered evidence was not an actual business record, but data compiled from business records. In addition, the data was compiled for use in litigation, not as a part of a regular recordation of business data. Finally, the evidence showed that the compilation was selective and subject to interpretation, unlike straight-forward business records. For all these reasons, the evidence was properly excluded.

Chesapeake and Delaware Canal Co. v. United States, 250 U.S. 123 (1919)

Facts: United States sued Chesapeake and Delaware Canal Co. for unpaid dividends on stock it held in the company. At trial, the United States called Treasury Department employees to testify about the preparation and authenticity of Treasury Department books and records. The United States then moved the records into evidence under the public records exception to the hearsay rules.

Issue: When are public records admissible as an exception to the hearsay rule?

Rule: When public records are maintained pursuant to constitutional and statutory requirements, they are admissible as official records and reports. The records are deemed to be trustworthy for several reasons: They are public records kept under requirement of law; their contents are of an official nature; their maintenance requires regular and contemporaneous recordation; and, their authors — public officials — have little motive for making false entries or to deleting accurate entries.

United States v. MacCloskey, 682 F.2d 468 (4th Cir. 1982)

Facts: MacCloskey and Edwards were jointly charged in a murder conspiracy. Edwards testified at a pretrial proceeding and charges against her were dismissed. At trial, McCloskey called Edwards to testify. When Edwards invoked her Fifth Amendment privilege against self-incrimination, McCloskey attempted to introduce transcripts of Edwards' prior testimony. The trial court refused to admit these transcripts.

Issue: Is a declarant who asserts the Fifth Amendment privilege against self-incrimination "unavailable" for purposes of the hearsay rule?

Rule: A declarant is unavailable under Rule 804(a) when she "is excepted by ruling of the court" or refuses to testify in defiance of an order to do so. Thus, a witness is unavailable under Rule 804(a)(1) when he invokes his Fifth Amendment privilege and the claim is sustained by the trial court.

United States v. Feldman, 761 F.2d 380 (7th Cir. 1985)

Facts: The defendants were convicted of wire fraud. The government's case relied primarily on the civil deposition of a former business associate. At the time of the deposition, defendants were not facing charges and they did not attend the deposition. On appeal, the defendants argued that the admission of this deposition violated the hearsay rule.

Issue: Whether a civil deposition that precedes the filing of criminal charges is admissible in the subsequent criminal case.

Rule: Under FRE 804(b)(1), prior sworn testimony is admissible only if the party against whom the testimony is offered had "an opportunity and similar motive" to examine the witness. Here, at the time of the civil deposition, the defendants lacked the motive and opportunity to cross-examine the witness. Therefore, the testimony was inadmissible.

Note: As to testimonial statements, *Crawford v. Washington* now governs this question.

Dykes v. Raymark Industries, Co., 801 F.2d 810 (6th Cir. 1986)

Facts: Survivors brought a wrongful death action after Dykes died of asbestos-related cancer caused by exposure to asbestos-containing products at his job. At trial, the survivors sought to introduce the deposition of an expert; however, the deposition was from a similar case — not from Dykes's case. Raymark objected.

Issue: Is a deposition from a prior similar lawsuit admissible?

Rule: Prior testimony from a similar lawsuit is admissible under FRE 804(b)(1) if the testimony is offered against a successor in interest to a party who had, at the time of the prior testimony, an adequate opportunity and motive to examine the testifying witness.

United States v. Dhinsa, 243 F.3d 635 (2d Cir. 2001)

Facts: Dhinsa was convicted of murder and racketeering crimes. At his trial, under FRE 804(b)(6)'s forfeiture by wrongdoing provision, the district court admitted the hearsay statements of two murder victims.

Issue: When are statements are admissible under Rule 804(b)(6) — the forfeiture by wrongdoing doctrine?

Rule: Under Rule 804(b)(6), statements are admissible under the forfeiture by wrongdoing doctrine when their proponent can show that the defendant (1) caused the declarant's unavailability; and (2) was motivated, in whole or in part, by the desire to prevent the declarant from testifying.

Note: The constitutional limitations of the forfeiture by wrongdoing doctrine are set forth in *Giles v. California*.

CHAPTER 7

Evidence in the Courtroom: Presentation, Objections, Mode of Interrogation, and Rulings

I. PRESENTATION OF ORAL TESTIMONY

A. Direct Examination
  1. Generally
     Direct examination typically consists of open-ended questions that invite the witness to respond with a narrative.
  2. Manner of Presentation
     Although narrative presentation is the standard method by which parties offer direct evidence, narrative is not the only means by which to offer direct evidence:
     a. General Rule
        A party may not pose leading questions to his or her own witness.
     b. Exceptions
        i. A party may use leading questions on direct examination if the party has called a hostile witness or adverse party to testify as that party's own witness.
        ii. A party may use leading questions to assist a witness on direct examination who has difficulty responding due to a mental or physical defect or impairment.
        iii. A party may use leading questions on direct examination to establish background facts not in controversy.

3. Preparation

Counsel may prepare a witness for trial and rehearse the witness's testimony provided that preparation does not alter or skew the witness's testimony.

II. CROSS-EXAMINATION

A. Generally

Cross-examination is a mode of interrogation generally accomplished by leading the witness and by posing close-ended or "yes-or-no" questions to the witness.

B. As a Method of Testing Witness Reliability

In the adversary system, cross-examination serves as the primary mode for testing the reliability of evidence provided through oral testimony.

C. In Criminal Cases

In a criminal case, the Confrontation Clause entitles a defendant to confront and cross-examine the witnesses against him.

1. Generally

The Confrontation Clause bestows upon a criminal defendant the right to confront and cross-examine all witnesses against him.

2. Conflicts with the Hearsay Rules

As discussed in Chapter 6, the hearsay rules often authorize the admission into evidence of an out-of-court statement.

3. *Crawford* Case

a. Generally

In the *Crawford* case, the Supreme Court held that the Confrontation Clause forbids the introduction of any out-of-court testimonial statement, offered against the defendant, to prove a fact at issue in the case.

b. Testimonial

The Court did not provide a definition of what constitutes "testimonial" evidence. However, the Court provided an illustrative list of statements that are clearly testimonial:

i. Prior sworn statements

ii. Prior testimony

iii. Letters of accusation

iv. Statements during formal or informal police interrogation

c. Exceptions

An out-of-court testimonial statement may be offered into evidence against a defendant if the declarant testifies at trial or if:

i. The witness is unavailable; and

       ii. The defendant has had a prior opportunity to cross-examine the declarant; and

      iii. The defendant had the same motive for cross-examination on that occasion as he would at trial.

III. MATTERS AVAILABLE FOR INQUIRY ON CROSS-EXAMINATION

A. Matters Within Scope of Direct Examination
The majority rule in this country is that cross-examination is limited by the scope of the direct examination. This rule does not limit the cross-examiner to questions about the witness's specific testimony. Once the "door has been opened" for questioning about a specific subject, the cross-examiner may inquire further about that subject.

B. Credibility
A cross-examiner may ask questions on almost any subject designed to attack a witness's credibility, regardless of its relevance to the facts in dispute in the underlying case.

C. Collateral Matters
Although the cross-examiner may question a witness regarding collateral matters, the cross-examiner is bound by the answer the witness gives. As a general matter, the cross-examiner may not introduce extrinsic evidence to impeach or contradict the witness on that point. As noted in the discussion of impeachment, the cross-examiner may introduce extrinsic evidence that bears on the witness's credibility.

D. Re-Cross-Examination
The right to re-cross-examination arises only if there has been redirect examination. The re-cross-examination is limited to the scope of the redirect examination.

E. Proper Decorum
Although the scope of cross-examination is wide, the cross-examiner is expected to observe proper courtroom decorum.

IV. REFRESHING A WITNESS'S RECOLLECTION

A. Writing to Refresh the Witness's Memory
A writing may be used in two ways to refresh the memory of a witness:

1. Present Recollection Refreshed
When a writing is used to refresh the witness's present recollection:

    a. the examining party provides the witness with a writing

      b. the witness reviews the writing

      c. the witness testifies as to her present recollection, as refreshed by a review of the writing.

      d. Note: The writing is not introduced into evidence, but must be made available to the opposing side for use during cross-examination.

  2. Past Recollection Recorded

      a. Generally

      The "Past Recollection Record" method is used to substitute for witness testimony when a witness has no present recollection of the matters at issue. To use a writing in this manner, the proponent of the evidence must establish that

        i. the witness remembers producing the writing;

        ii. the witness does not remember the contents of the writing; and

        iii. the witness's recollection is not refreshed by reviewing the writing.

      b. Limitations

      The hearsay rules may prevent admission of a past recollection recorded. However, if the witness who made the writing testifies at the trial, the Confrontation Clause places no limits on the use of that witness's prior out-of-court statements.

V. OFFERING EVIDENCE

  A. Offering Evidence

  When a party anticipates a significant objection to evidence it plans to offer, the offering party may file an in limine motion seeking an advance ruling on the admissibility and use of the evidence in question. If a party plans to offer evidence of a type generally prohibited by the FRE, that party almost always files an in limine motion.

  B. Objecting to the Admission or Use of Evidence

    1. To challenge the admission of evidence or to challenge the purpose for which it is offered, a party must

      a. raise a timely objection with the court and

      b. state the basis for the objection.

    2. To assess an objection, the court may require more information about the evidence. The court may obtain that information by

      a. Attorney Proffer

      The lawyer represents to the court the nature and content of the evidence at issue. This is also called an offer of proof.

      b. Witness Proffer

      The court takes witness testimony out of the jury's presence.

      c. Tangible Offer of Proof
         When the evidence in question is a tangible item, the offering party may present the item to the judge.
    3. Note
      The trial court need not wait for a party to object to evidence; the court can, sua sponte,
      a. exclude evidence; or
      b. direct that evidence be admitted for a limited purpose.

C. Evidence with Limited Admissibility
    1. Generally
      If a court admits the evidence for a restricted or limited purpose, the evidence has "limited admissibility." Evidence may be limited to proof of a particular fact or to use against a particular party.
    2. Procedure
      If a party objects to the admissibility of evidence, the proponent of the evidence is responsible for reoffering the evidence for a limited and permissible purpose. If the offering party fails to do so, the evidence is excluded.

D. Ruling on the Objection
    1. To make an informed ruling, a trial court may
      a. Allow the parties to proceed by proffer — either attorney or witness proffer — about what the controverted evidence will show; or
      b. Allow the parties to conduct the controverted examination outside the presence of the jury.
    2. If the ruling is made without allowing the parties an opportunity to argue the issue, the court may permit a party to supplement the record with a full explanation of the basis for the party's objection.

E. Appellate Issues
    1. Making the Objection
      Under the FRE, and in almost all jurisdictions, if a party fails to make a timely objection, that party will be deemed to have waived the objection.
    2. Preserving the Objection for Appellate Review
      a. Federal Rule
         Once the court rules on the objection, FRE 103(a) deems the objection preserved, even if the court's ruling occurs pretrial. A party need not renew the objection, following the presentation or exclusion of the evidence.
      b. Other Jurisdictions
         Many states require that an objecting party renew an objection after the use or preclusion of the controverted evidence.

In those jurisdictions, an unrenewed objection will be deemed waived.

3. A party whose proposed evidence has been excluded may seek to supplement the trial record by making an "offer of proof" that preserves, for appellate review, the evidence that would have been introduced, but for the trial court's ruling.

CASE CLIPS

United States v. Riccardi, 174 F.2d 883 (3d Cir. 1949)

Facts: Riccardi was charged with felonious transportation of stolen property in interstate commerce. To prove the specific property involved, the government relied on the testimony of the complaining witness and her antiques dealer. The complaining witness testified that as she entrusted items to Riccardi, she made handwritten notes that she later copied on her typewriter. At trial, the government used the typewritten list to refresh the complainant's recollection. After looking at the list, complainant testified that her recollection was refreshed and that she presently recognized and could identify each item that Riccardi allegedly stole. Additionally, the government used the same typewritten list to refresh the recollection of an antiques expert. He was shown the list, and with its aid testified that he could recall the items individually.

Issue: May a witness refresh her recollection by looking at a writing that was not created on or shortly after the time of the transaction about which she is testifying?

Rule: A trial witness may refresh her recollection by examining a document created well after the transaction about which she is testifying. However, if the writing does not refresh the witness's recollection and the witness instead testifies about the contents of the writing, the writing is then subject to the ordinary rules governing the admission of a witness's out-of-court statements. Here, the list was used to revive the witness's memory; she then presently recollected the facts and testified to them. The primary evidence was not the writing, but the testimony of the witness. (This is distinguishable from "past recollection recorded," where the witness has no present recollection of the matter contained in the writing and must ask the court to accept a writing for the truth of its contents because she is willing to swear that the contents are true.)

Straub v. Reading Company, 220 F.2d 177 (3d Cir. 1955)

Facts: Plaintiff Straub injured his back while working for Defendant Reading Co. Straub brought a claim under the Federal Employers' Liability Act for his on-site injury. At trial, Plaintiff's attorney proved his claim, to a large extent, through leading questions. Although Defendant's counsel objected, the conduct continued throughout the trial. On appeal, Defendant argued that it was deprived of a fair trial by the conduct of Plaintiff's attorney throughout the trial.

Issue: Does the repeated use of leading questions during direct examination of witnesses justify a new trial?

Rule: Generally, the problem of leading questions is within the control of the trial court. However, where the court loses control or is ignored and the offending conduct continues throughout the trial, a warped version of the issues has been presented to the jury, and the judgment must be set aside.

United States v. Segal, 534 F.2d 578 (3d Cir. 1976)

Facts: Defendant Segal was a CPA who represented Hurst during an audit of his tax returns by an Internal Revenue Service (IRS) agent. Defendant allegedly offered to bribe the IRS agent in connection with the IRS audit. At trial, the prosecution offered into evidence excerpts of tape recordings of conversations between the agent and Hurst. On cross-examination of the agent, Defendant's counsel sought to play for the jury the parts of the tapes that had not been presented on direct examination. However, the court prohibited Defendant's attorney from using transcripts or playing parts of a recording that had not been heard during direct examination.

Issue: May a party cross-examine a witness about issues not specifically covered during direct examination?

Rule: On cross-examination, a witness may be examined regarding evidence and issues not specifically addressed during direct examination, so long as the subject of the cross-examination is sufficiently related to the subject matter of the direct examination. Here, the tapes were inter-related and the defendant had the right to cross-examine the agent about the rest of the recorded conversations. The fact that some of the points that the defendant sought to explore could have been introduced in the defense case does not preclude their development on cross-examination, as long as the prosecution made the subject matter part of its direct testimony.

United States v. Brown, 603 F.2d 1022 (1st Cir. 1979)

Facts: Defendant was accused of stealing 16 birds worth more than $100 from an air freight terminal. At trial, the prosecution called Defendant's friend to testify about how Defendant had learned about the birds' presence at the airport. With the trial judge's consent, the prosecution treated Defendant's friend as a hostile witness and therefore used leading questions on direct examination.

Issue: May a party conduct direct examination by using leading questions?

Rule: FRE 611(c) permits the use of leading questions on direct examination when necessary to develop the witness's testimony. When a party calls a hostile witness, an adverse party, or a person identified with an adverse party, at the discretion of the trial judge, the interrogation may be by leading questions.

United States v. Beaty, 722 F.2d 1090 (8th Cir. 1983)

Facts: Defendant was convicted of a number of drug-related offenses. At trial, the trial judge questioned three of the Defendant's four alibi witnesses at length in a manner the Defendant labeled "cross-examination." On appeal, Defendant argued that the trial judge's conduct deprived him of a fair trial.

Issue: May a judge cross-examine defense witnesses?

Rule: A trial judge's isolated questioning to clarify ambiguities may be permissible, but a trial judge may not assume the role of an advocate and take over cross-examination for the government. Here, the court's vigorous participation in examining Defendant's witnesses must have conveyed the judge's skepticism about Defendant's alibi to the jury.

Commonwealth v. O'Brien, 645 N.E.2d 1170 (Mass. 1995)

Facts: Defendant O'Brien was on trial for the murder of an infant. On direct examination, victim's mother testified about two statements she made to the police. On redirect, the victim's mother testified about her state of mind at the time of her first statement. On re-cross-examination, defense counsel attempted to ask the victim's mother about the second statement. The judge sustained objections to that testimony as beyond the scope of redirect examination.

Issue: Does a defendant have an automatic right to re-cross-examination?

Rule: As opposed to cross-examination, which is an essential part of the right to a fair trial, a defendant has no right to re-cross-examination unless the examination addresses a new matter brought out for the first time on redirect examination. Here, Defendant's counsel could have examined the victim's mother about the second statement during cross-examination. Because the proposed re-cross-examination raised issues not raised on redirect, the trial judge did not abuse his discretion in refusing to allow such examination.

Baker v. State, 371 A.2d 699 (Md. App. 1977)

Facts: Defendant Baker was convicted of murder and robbery. On appeal, she argued that the trial judge erroneously denied her the opportunity to refresh the present recollection of a police witness by showing him a report written by a fellow police officer.

Issue: May a witness's recollection be refreshed by reviewing a document created by someone other than the witness?

Rule: There is no limit to what materials may be used to refresh a witness's recollection. It does not have to be a writing, and the witness need not ever have seen the refreshing item before; all that is required is that it refreshes the witness's recollection of the event. Thus, a witness's recollection may properly be refreshed by a writing created by someone other than the witness.

James Julian, Inc. v. Raytheon Co., 93 F.R.D. 138 (D. Del. 1982)

Facts: Plaintiff James Julian, Inc. sought injunctive relief and damages under the Sherman Act and the National Labor Relations Act. Defendant requested that Plaintiff produce a binder of materials prepared by Defendant's counsel for Defendant's officers to review in preparation for their deposition testimony.

Issue: Is the work-product privilege waived if such product is used to prepare a witness to testify?

Rule: The use of protected documents to refresh a witness's memory prior to testifying constitutes a waiver of the work-product privilege.

Resolution Trust Corp. v. H.R. "Bum" Bright, 6 F.3d 336 (5th Cir. 1993)

Facts: In investigating a case, Plaintiff's attorneys interviewed a witness and asked her to review and sign an affidavit summarizing what she had told them. Attorneys warned the witness to read it carefully because it contained material they hadn't discussed in their interviews. The witness refused to sign the affidavit, and a session of editing and discussion followed. Eventually, the witness signed a draft that was acceptable to her. Defendants moved for sanctions against Plaintiff's attorneys based on their presentation of the initial affidavit and their subsequent aggressive questioning of the witness.

Issue: Whether placing statements in a draft affidavit that have not been previously discussed with a witness automatically constitutes bad-faith conduct by an attorney.

Rule: Placing statements in a draft affidavit that have not been previously discussed with a witness doesn't automatically constitute bad-faith conduct. Here, there is no indication that the plaintiff's attorneys lacked a factual basis for the additional statements included in the draft affidavit. Moreover, the plaintiff's attorneys brought the new statements to the witness's attention and warned her to read them carefully.

United States v. Rhynes, 218 F.3d 310 (4th Cir. 2000)

Facts: Defendants were tried on a number of drug-related charges. Pursuant to FRE 615, at the commencement of the trial, the court ordered sequestration of the witnesses. Before calling a defense witness to the stand, defense counsel discussed with that witness the prior testimony of a prosecution witness.

Issue: Did counsel violate FRE 615 by discussing the opposing party's witness testimony with his own witness?

Rule: FRE 615 does not address counsel participating in the trial at hand; the Rule relates only to "witnesses" and serves only to exclude witnesses from the courtroom. Moreover, an attorney is required to thoroughly interview and prepare witnesses before they testify.

CHAPTER 8

Authentication of Evidence and the Best Evidence Rule

I. AUTHENTICATION

A. Generally

Before evidence may be admitted, the proponent must show that it is authentic, that is, that the evidence is what the proponent claims it is. Authentication rules apply to writings, documents, photographs, recordings, and other similar instruments.

B. FRE 901

FRE 901 requires that evidence be authenticated prior to its admission. Under FRE 901 evidence is authenticated when its proponent produces evidence "sufficient to support a finding" that the evidence is genuine inasmuch as it is "what its proponent claims."

C. Methods of Authentication

Evidence may be authenticated by either direct evidence or circumstantial evidence. Generally, any evidence that tends to establish genuineness may be used to authenticate a writing. Examples of evidence sufficient to support the authenticity of evidence are included in FRE 901(b).

D. Authenticating Documents

A party may authenticate a document by presenting a wide range of evidence, including evidence relating to:

1. Admission

One party may admit the authenticity of a writing offered by the opposing party. In addition, a party who acts upon a document as authentic will be deemed to have admitted its authenticity.

2. Testimony

A witness may testify, from personal knowledge, that the document is what its proponent claims it to be.

3. Handwriting Comparison
   a. Lay Opinion
      A lay witness, who is familiar with the handwriting of the purported author of the document, may testify as to the document's authorship. See FRE 901(b)(2).
   b. Comparison by Expert Witness
      An expert witness may testify as to the document's authorship based on the expert's comparison of handwriting in the document and authenticated handwriting samples. (These samples may include samples generated for the purpose of expert comparison.) See FRE 901(b)(3).
4. Characteristics
   A document may be authenticated by evidence of its distinctive appearance, contents, substance, or pattern. See FRE 901(b)(4).
5. Process or System
   A document may be authenticated by evidence about the system or process that produced the document. (This is often how parties authenticate computer-generated documents.) See FRE 901(b)(9).
6. Reply Letters
   A writing that responds to another writing may be authenticated if the content of the responsive writing clearly demonstrates that it is a reply to a previously authenticated writing.
7. Public Records or Reports
   A document may be authenticated by evidence it was (1) recorded or filed in a public office, and (2) was supplied to the party by a public office. See FRE 901(b)(7).
8. Ancient Documents
   Under the FRE, as at common law, special rules apply to the authentication of ancient documents.
   a. Requirements (See FRE 901(8))
      i. A party may authenticate an ancient document with evidence that
         (1) The document has been in existence 20 years or more; and
         (2) The document's condition raises no suspicion concerning its authenticity and
         (3) The document was found in a place where an authentic version of the document would be.
      ii. Note: Distinction Between Federal Rules v. Common Law
         (1) Common law restricted the ancient documents rule
            (a) Dispositive instruments, such as wills and deeds
            (b) That are at least 30 years old.
         (2) Under the Federal Rules, the ancient document rule applies to all writings.
9. Self-Authenticating Documents

a. Generally

Certain "self-authenticating" documents carry a presumption of authenticity.

b. Self-Authenticating Documents Under the FRE

Pursuant to FRE 902, the following documents are presumptively genuine:

    i. Public documents under seal or having an official signature, either foreign or domestic, see FRE 901(1) and (3);

    ii. Certified copies of public records, see FRE 901(2) and (4);

    iii. Official publications: books, pamphlets or other publications purporting to be issued by public authority, see FRE 902(5);

    iv. Newspapers and periodicals, see FRE 902(6);

    v. Trade inscriptions and the like: inscriptions, signs, tags, or labels

(1) purportedly affixed in the course of business, and

(2) indicating ownership, control, or origin, see FRE 902(7);

    vi. Acknowledged Documents

Documents accompanied by a certificate of acknowledgment executed by a notary public or other officer authorized by law to take acknowledgments, see FRE 902(8);

    vii. Commercial paper and related documents (to the extent provided by the general, applicable, commercial law), see FRE 902(9).

E. Authenticating Voices

1. Generally

A voice may be authenticated by a witness who is familiar with the voice of the purported speaker. A witness may authenticate a familiar voice, regardless of whether the witness heard a "live" voice or a recording of the voice, see FRE 901(b)(5).

2. Identification of Voices on the Telephone

A witness may authenticate a voice heard on the telephone if:

a. the call is made to a specific person; and

    i. the caller recognizes the voice of the person speaking, or

    ii. the circumstances, such as self-identification, authenticate the identity of the person who answers as the person who was called, see FRE 901(b)(6).

II. BYPASSING AUTHENTICATION

If the parties may agree to the authenticity of a document or instrument, the court need not make any further inquiry.

A. Admission

A party may admit the genuineness of a document offered by the opposing party.

B. Stipulation

The parties may stipulate that a particular document is genuine.

III. BEST EVIDENCE RULE

A. Generally

The best evidence rule expresses a preference for the use of original documents, rather than reproductions. Thus some commentators refer to the "best evidence" rule as the "original document" rule.

B. Definitions (See FRE 1001)

1. Writings and Recordings

Letters, words, or numbers, or their equivalent, set down by handwriting or various mechanical devices, or electronic data compilation, see FRE 1001(1).

2. Photographs

Still photographs, X-rays, videotapes, and motion pictures, see FRE 1001(2).

3. Original

The writing or recording itself, or any duplicate intended to have the same effect by a person executing or issuing it, see FRE 1001(3). Note: An original of a photograph may be a print or the negative from which the print was produced.

4. Duplicate

A counterpart produced by the same impression as the original or by a mechanical device that accurately reproduces the original, see FRE 1001(4).

C. General Application

The best evidence rule only applies if:

1. Offered to Prove Contents

The proponent of the writing seeks to prove its contents; and

2. The writing is closely related to a material issue.

D. Requirements

To satisfy the best evidence rule, the proponent of the evidence must

a. Produce the original document; or

b. Demonstrate that

   i. the original writing is unavailable; and

   ii. the offering party is not responsible for the unavailability.

E. Use of Secondary Evidence in Lieu of Best Evidence

1. Minority Rule/FRE 1004

When the offering party presents a satisfactory explanation for not producing an original document, FRE 1004 authorizes a party to use secondary evidence to prove the contents of a writing. The FRE do not distinguish between degrees of secondary evidence. Once the court excuses the proponent of the evidence from production of the original, the proponent may use any available secondary evidence. Secondary evidence may be used when the original is

a. lost or destroyed; or

b. not obtainable by judicial process or procedure; or

c. in the possession of the opposing party; or

d. addressed to a collateral issue.

2. Majority Rule

Most courts recognize degrees of secondary evidence and require that the proponent of the evidence use the best available secondary evidence.

F. Rules Concerning Duplicates

A duplicate that is an exact copy of the original is admissible to the same extent as the original, unless a genuine question is raised as to the authenticity of the original, or under the circumstances it would be unfair to admit the duplicate in lieu of the original.

1. Independent Basis of Fact Exception

The best evidence rule does not apply to the use of facts that have, by happenstance, been recorded. If the facts contained in the writing have an existence independent of the writing, a party may prove those facts with secondary evidence. For example:

a. Goods received may be proven without a receipt.

b. Birth, age, marriage, and death may all be proven by secondary evidence.

c. Admissions or confessions may be proven by oral testimony even if the admission or confession was subsequently written down.

2. Collateral Issues

The best evidence rule does not apply if the writing, recording, or photograph concerns a collateral issue. See FRE 1004(4).

3. Public Records

Under FRE 1005, the contents of an official record may be authenticated by a certified copy, or a copy that is testified to be correct by a witness who has compared it with the original.

4. Summaries

Under FRE 1006, the contents of voluminous writings, recordings, or photographs may be presented as part of a chart, summary, or calculation. However, the court may order the offering party to produce, for examinations, the original documents that have been summarized.

CASE CLIPS

Amoco Production Co. v. United States (1980)

Facts: Parties disputed the contents of a deed. Because an authenticated copy of the deed was readily available from the recorder's office, the trial court excluded secondary evidence of the deed.

Issue: Does the availability of a properly recorded version of a document prevent the admission of any other evidence of the contents of the document?

Rule: This problem illustrates the nexus between authentication and the best evidence rule. Under the FRE, the deed can be authenticated by its storage in, and retrieval from, the appropriate public office. However, notwithstanding the authentication of the deed, the dispute as to its contents mitigates in favor of the production of the original document.

Seiler v. Lucasfilm, Ltd., 808 F.2d 1316 (9th Cir. 1987)

Facts: Seiler sued Lucasfilm for an alleged copyright infringement. Seiler sought to introduce reconstructed drawings of his original work. The trial court made a finding that Seiler had lost or destroyed the originals in bad faith. Accordingly, the trial court refused to authorize the admission of secondary evidence. Seiler argued that the best evidence rules did not apply because the documents in question were drawings, not writings.

Issue: Does the best evidence rule apply to drawings and other nonverbal facsimile writings?

Rule: The best evidence rule applies to writings "and their equivalent." The drawings were "writings" within the meaning of Rule 1001(1), which defines writings and records as "letters, words, or numbers, or their equivalent." The policy considerations underlying the best evidence rule are best served by application of the rule to drawings such as those in Seiler's case. Accordingly, the trial court properly excluded the secondary evidence.

Zenith Radio Corp v. Matsushita Electric Industrial Co. Ltd., 505 F. Supp. 1190 (E.D. Pa. 1980)

Facts: Plaintiff alleged that Defendant had violated antitrust laws and had conspired to monopolize the American consumer electronics industry. Both parties challenged the authenticity of several documents, including diaries kept by Defendant's employees; testimony recorded by the Japanese Fair Trade Commission; minutes from meetings held by Defendant's executive offices; and various public records from Japan.

Issue: Does a finding of authenticity endorse the genuineness of the instrument, or does a finding of authenticity endorse the instrument as accurate and reliable?

Rule: Authenticity addresses itself to the genuineness of an instrument, not to the reliability or accuracy of the contents of the instrument. Moreover, authenticity does not serve as a proxy for admissibility.

Keegan v. Green Giant Co., 110 A.2d 599 (Me. 1954)

Facts: Plaintiff brought a suit for damages alleging that the Defendant negligently prepared, manufactured, packed, and distributed a can of peas that contained a concealed sharp piece of metal, which Plaintiff swallowed while she was eating the peas. The can bore the label "Green Giant Brand Great Big Tender Sweet Peas. Distributed by Green Giant Company." At trial, Plaintiff attempted to introduce the can and label into evidence to show that Green Giant Company was the distributor and packer of that particular can of peas. The trial judge refused to admit the can and label into evidence.

Issue: May the authorship of a printed matter be determined solely by its contents?

Rule: Printed matter in general bears no mark of authorship other than as implied by content. Therefore, the content of a document alone is not sufficient to determine authorship. As such, the writing cannot go to the jury without extrinsic evidence of genuineness to authenticate it.

Dissent: Every day consumers accept the label on canned food products as sufficient proof of the brand and the producer or distributor. That is how we identify types and brands of food products.

Meyers v. United States, 171 F.2d 800 (D.C. Cir. 1949)

Facts: Defendant was indicted for perjury and suborning perjury. At trial, the court permitted a government witness to testify about Defendant's allegedly perjurious testimony. Later in the trial, the court permitted the government to introduce into evidence a transcript of Defendant's testimony. On appeal, Defendant argued that the best evidence rule should have prevented the government from introducing testimony about the alleged perjury because the transcript was the best evidence of Defendant's statements.

Issue: Does the best evidence rule apply to a transcript of oral testimony?

Rule: If the transcript is being offered to prove its contents, then the best evidence rule applies. Here, there was no attempt to prove the contents of a writing. The issue was what Defendant said, not what the transcript contained.

Dissent: The transcript speaks for itself; thus, it is the best evidence.

People v. Lynes, 401 N.E.2d 405 (N.Y. 1980)

Facts: Victim identified Defendant as her attacker and a detective left a message with Defendant's brother. A few hours later, the detective received a phone call from a man who identified himself as Defendant. Although the officer was unfamiliar with Defendant's voice, the trial court found that other circumstances provided sufficient corroboration of the identity of the caller and permitted the recorded conversation to be introduced at trial.

Issue: May a phone conversation be authenticated when the witness cannot independently verify the other participant's voice?

Rule: Authentication of a phone conversation may be achieved if the surrounding circumstances indicate to the court it is improbable that the caller's voice belongs to anyone other than the purported caller.

Wilson v. State, 348 N.E.2d 90 (Ind. Ct. App. 1976)

Facts: In a trial for robbery, a copy of the stolen check, rather than the original, was introduced as evidence. On appeal, Defendant argued that it was an error to introduce a copy of the paycheck into evidence because no proper foundation had been laid to excuse the requirement for the government to produce the original.

Issue: Is a photocopy of a document admissible as evidence?

Rule: A duplicate of a document or other writing is admissible in evidence to the same extent as an original unless a genuine issue is raised as to the authenticity of the original, or under the existing circumstances it would be unfair to admit the duplicate as an original.

United States v. Carbone, 798 F.2d 21 (1st Cir. 1986)

Facts: Defendant was convicted of several drug offenses. On appeal, he challenged the admission of tape recordings on the grounds that none were authenticated properly, some were inaudible, and one was enhanced. He also challenged the use of transcripts of the recordings. On appeal, Defendant challenged the accuracy and audibility of tape recordings and their transcripts, both of which were used as evidence against him.

Issue: Must tape recordings and transcripts be authenticated before being admitted as evidence?

Rule: The government had the duty of laying a foundation that the tape recordings accurately reproduced the conversations that took place. When a tape recording is challenged on the ground of audibility, the test is whether "the inaudible parts are so substantial as to make the rest more misleading than helpful." When transcripts are offered for use they should be authenticated in the same manner as the tape recordings that are offered in evidence.

United States v. Duffy, 454 F.2d 809 (5th Cir. 1972)

Facts: Duffy was convicted of transporting a stolen car in interstate commerce. On appeal, he alleged that the court erred in permitting two witnesses to testify about a t-shirt with the laundry mark "D-U-F." Duffy argued that, under the best evidence rule, the government should have been required to produce the shirt itself rather than testimony about the shirt.

Issue: Does the best evidence rule apply to a shirt with a laundry mark?

Rule: The best evidence rule is applicable only to the proof of the contents of a writing. The rule does not apply to the shirt with the laundry mark. Because the writing involved was simple, there was little danger that the witnesses' memory of the writing would be inaccurate.

Sylvania Electric Products v. Flanagan, 352 F.2d 1005 (1st Cir. 1965)

Facts: Flanagan alleges that he made an oral agreement with Sylvania to haul away certain materials from a parking lot Sylvania was constructing for a certain amount per hour per truck. Flanagan performed the necessary tasks, but Sylvania refused to pay the bill. Flanagan then brought suit for breach of contract. At trial, Flanagan introduced an exhibit that was a summary of data contained in invoices and tally sheets. Sylvania objected on the ground that the summary was barred by the best evidence rule. When asked by the court where the originals were, Flanagan replied he had some of them at home. He never produced the originals but the summary was admitted anyway.

Issue: May summaries of records be introduced if the records themselves are not shown to be unavailable?

Rule: In proving the terms of a material writing, the original writing must be produced unless it is shown to be unavailable for some reason other than the fault of its proponent. Upon a proper showing of the unavailability of the original, secondary evidence of its contents may be admitted.

United States v. Branch, 970 F.2d 1368 (4th Cir. 1992)

Facts: Branch was convicted of conspiracy to distribute and distribution of heroin and cocaine and conspiracy to evade or defeat income taxes. On appeal, he argued that the district court erred by not requiring the government to offer sufficient evidence before the jury to support a finding of authenticity.

Issue: What showing is required to properly authenticate evidence?

Rule: The requirement of authenticity is satisfied by evidence sufficient to support a finding that the matter in question is what its proponent claims.

Before admitting evidence for consideration by the jury, the court must determine whether its proponent has offered a satisfactory foundation from which the jury could reasonably find that the evidence is authentic. The district court must make the preliminary determination; however, the jury ultimately determines whether the evidence admitted is that which the proponent claims. An in camera determination of authenticity was appropriate because it guaranteed that the jury would not be tainted by hearing prejudicial evidence until the proponent had demonstrated an adequate foundation for the admission of that evidence.

Buckingham Corp v. Ewing Liquors Co., 305 N.E.2d 278 (Ill. App. Ct. 1973)

Facts: The trial court found that Buckingham's whiskey is sold pursuant to a valid fair trade agreement, and that Ewing knowingly sold that whiskey at a price below the fair trade price. Ewing contends that Buckingham failed to adequately prove an essential element of its cause of action — the existence of a fair trade agreement. At trial, Buckingham's marketing director testified that he recognized the signature of Ewing's vice president because he had received correspondence from him in the past; however, he had never actually seen the vice president sign his name.

Issue: May a handwriting be authenticated by a witness's showing of familiarity with it?

Rule: A handwritten document may be authenticated by a witness's showing of familiarity with it. This familiarity may be gained from having seen the party actually write, or from having been acquainted with the handwriting in the course of business dealings. The extent of the knowledge of the witness goes to the weight to be given to his opinion.

United States v. American Radiator & Standard Sanitary Corp., 433 F.2d 174 (3d Cir. 1970)

Facts: Appellants were convicted of various violations of the Sherman Act. On appeal, they argued that they were prejudiced by certain rulings on government evidence. Specifically, they challenged the admissibility of six pages of undated and unsigned handwritten notes on hotel stationary that related to figures and statements on an American Standard price worksheet. They argued that, because there was insufficient evidence concerning the authorship of the notes, the notes should not have been admitted into evidence.

Issue: Must author's identity be established before documents may be admitted into evidence?

Rule: Only a prima facie case of the alleged author's identity must be established for documents to be admitted into evidence. The ultimate issue of their authorship and the probative weight to be given to them are for the jury to decide.

United States v. Sutton, 426 F.2d 1202 (D.C. Cir. 1969)

Facts: Sutton was indicted for the shooting death of Matilda Glass. An envelope was found beside Mrs. Glass's body, which stated that it was "From Alexander Sutton" to his wife and daughter. Inside the envelope were three notes that were introduced into evidence. The prosecution also introduced a note that was removed from Sutton's pocket. On appeal, Sutton argued that none of the notes had been properly authenticated as being written by him.

Issue: May authorship of writings be established by circumstantial evidence?

Rule: Authorship of writings may be shown by circumstantial evidence. The contents of a writing, considered with the circumstances surrounding its discovery, may provide an adequate basis for its admission into evidence.

United States v. Siddiqui, 235 F.3d 1318 (11th Cir. 2000)

Facts: Siddiqui appealed his convictions for fraud and false statements, challenging the trial court's admission of several e-mails into evidence.

Issue: Was the e-mail properly authenticated for admission into evidence?

Rule: A number of factors support the authenticity of the e-mail. The e-mail sent bore Siddiqui's e-mail address, which was the same as the e-mail introduced by Siddiqui's counsel in his cross-examination of a witness. The context of the e-mail shows the author of the e-mail to have been someone who would have known details of Siddiqui's conduct. The e-mail sent referred to the author as "Mo," which is Siddiqui's nickname. Additionally, the witnesses who received the e-mail testified that they spoke with Siddiqui soon after the receipt of the e-mail and that Siddiqui made the same requests that had been made in the e-mail.

State v. Nano, 543 P.2d 660 (Or. 1975)

Facts: Nano was convicted of the theft of a box of calculators. During trial, the state called the manager of the department from which the calculators were missing. The manager testified that, based on a lack of entries in their sales records, the calculators had not been sold. Nano alleged this testimony violated the best evidence rule.

Issue: Does testimony concerning an absence of entries in a writing violate the best evidence rule?

Rule: The best evidence rule only applies when the material issue in a case is the precise wording of a document. Here, the witness testified to what the document did not contain. Literally, this is not proof of the terms of a document. Nor was the precise language of a writing the prima facie issue in the case. Thus, the production of the original records was not necessary.

CHAPTER 9

Real and Demonstrative Evidence

I. GENERAL PRINCIPLES

A. Definitions

Tangible evidence is evidence directly addressed to the senses of the factfinder. Although the use of the term "tangible" implies an object or item that can be touched or held, as used in this outline, the term "tangible" evidence refers to any evidence addressed to the senses, regardless of whether it is corporeal. Thus a series of musical notes can be considered tangible evidence.

B. Demonstrative Evidence Distinguished from Real Evidence

1. Real Evidence

Real evidence is evidence that played an actual role in the matter in dispute, such as a murder weapon.

2. Demonstrative Evidence

Demonstrative evidence is evidence that illustrates a matter of importance in the dispute, such as a diagram of the crime scene.

3. Laying the Foundation for Real and Demonstrative Evidence

When a party offers either real or demonstrative evidence, that party must lay a foundation for the evidence.

a. Real Evidence

A proper foundation for real evidence is a foundation that would, if credited, prove that the offered evidence was present at, or the object of, the disputed event or matter.

b. Demonstrative Evidence

A proper foundation for demonstrative evidence is a foundation that would, if credited, prove that the object is a fair and accurate representation of the materials or matters it purports to illustrate.

II. RULES RELATED TO THE ADMISSION AND USE OF TANGIBLE EVIDENCE

A. Special Considerations

Tangible evidence is presented directly to the trier of fact. Thus, the rules of evidence place special limitations on the admissibility of tangible evidence. These limits are analogous to the authenticity and best evidence rules that govern the admission of writings and similar instruments.

1. Authenticity

Tangible evidence is not admissible until the proponent of that evidence has established that the evidence is genuine or authentic.

2. Applicability of Other Evidentiary Principles

Even authenticated tangible evidence must still survive scrutiny under ordinary evidentiary principles and rules.

3. Specific Rules

As already noted, the proponent of real or demonstrative evidence must authenticate that evidence. Authentication requirements vary depending on whether the tangible evidence is offered as real evidence or as demonstrative evidence.

a. Rules for Admission of Real Evidence

i. Chain of Custody

(a) Explained

If real evidence is of a type or quality that does not establish the evidence as unique or inherently capable of identification, the proponent of such evidence must prove its authenticity by establishing an unbroken chain of custody.

(b) Example

Imagine, for example, a criminal drug case, in which the prosecution wants to introduce into evidence the white powdery substance seized from the defendant. To do so, the prosecution must prove that the white powdery substance it is offering is, in fact, the white powdery substance seized from the defendant.

ii. Break in Chain of Custody

A break in the chain of custody does not, per se, render the evidence inadmissible. Rather, when confronted with a break in the chain of evidence, a trial court generally will require that the proponent of the evidence offer some proof of the integrity of the offered evidence.

iii. Unchanged Condition

Real evidence is generally irrelevant unless it is in an unchanged or substantially similar condition as it was at the time of the disputed events.

    b. Rules for Admission of Demonstrative Evidence
      i. Fair Representation
        Because demonstrative evidence illustrates a factual allegation or proposition, the evidence must fairly represent that which it is intended to illustrate.
      ii. Useful
        Demonstrative evidence must be useful to the factfinder; that is, it must aid the factfinder in understanding or assessing the evidence. Demonstrative evidence need not be "essential" to be admissible.
      iii. Unfair Prejudice
        Although all admissible evidence must be more probative than prejudicial, courts typically scrutinize demonstrative evidence with particular care, to insure that it neither prejudices nor confuses the jury.

B. Considerations Applicable to Particular Types of Real and Demonstrative Evidence
  1. Photographs, Videotapes, and Related Materials
    Parties typically offer photographic evidence either as "pictorial testimony" illustrating witness testimony, or as "silent witness" evidence offered as independent proof of facts.
    a. Pictorial Testimony
      Photographic evidence that illustrates witness testimony is admissible as pictorial testimony. Pictorial testimony is admissible if, and only if, the relevant witness testifies that the photographic material fairly and accurately represents its subject matter.
    b. Silent Witness Theory
      When a party offers photographic evidence as direct proof of facts, rather than as an illustration of witness testimony, the photographic evidence serves as a "silent witness" to the facts depicted in the photographic material. Silent witness photographic evidence is not admissible unless the proponent of that evidence demonstrates the reliability of the process that produced the evidence. Digital images and X-rays are frequently offered into evidence to serve as "silent witnesses" to the facts depicted in the images.
  2. Maps, Charts, and Diagrams
    A trial court enjoys wide discretion in determining the admissibility of maps, charts, and diagrams. However, factors mitigating in favor of the admissibility of a map, chart, or diagram include the extent to which the evidence is:
    a. Helpful to the jury's understanding of the evidence; and
    b. Accurately representative of the fact(s) for which it is offered.

3. Child in Paternity Suits
   a. At common law, courts struggled to determine whether parties to a paternity suit should be permitted to "exhibit" a child to the jury for assessment of the child's physical resemblance to that of the alleged father. Scientific advances in the area of DNA testing have mooted this question.
4. Demonstrations
   Courts generally permit parties to conduct demonstrations for the jury. Like all other types of evidence, demonstrations must be more probative than prejudicial. Courts scrutinize with care certain demonstrations that have a tendency to prejudice or mislead a jury. Such demonstrations include:
   a. Displays of Injury
      Although a party can generally exhibit an injury to the jury, a party may not conduct the exhibition in a manner that unduly emphasizes the injury or upsets and inflames the jury.
   b. Demonstrations Within the Sole Control of the Witness
      As noted elsewhere in this outline, the availability of meaningful cross-examination is a prerequisite to witness competence. For similar reasons, courts also prohibit the use of demonstrations that are so exclusively controlled by the witness as to inhibit meaningful cross-examination.
5. Viewings
   a. If otherwise relevant and admissible evidence cannot be adequately presented to the jury or explained by witness testimony, a judge may permit the jury to travel, as a jury, outside the courtroom to view the evidence. Jury visits to the scene of the disputed event or occurrence are the most common forms of viewings.
6. In deciding whether to permit a viewing, a court considers, among others factors:
   a. The importance of the scene or evidence to the issue in dispute;
   b. The adequacy of evidence that can be presented in the courtroom (for example, maps of a crime scene, diagrams of a building, or photographs of a cruise vessel);
   c. The extent to which the scene or evidence is in the same condition as it was during the disputed events.
7. Other Rules Relevant to Viewings
   a. All viewings must be authorized by the trial court and must be conducted under the supervision of the court or its designated representative. If a juror engages in an unauthorized viewing, the court will declare a mistrial.

    b. In most cases, a court will direct that a court-appointed chaperon accompany the jury to the viewing. There is no requirement that the court or counsel attend the viewing.

    c. If the parties attend the viewing, they may not comment on the evidence. Usually the parties are also prohibited from conducting demonstrations during the viewing.

8. Viewings and Their Status as Evidence

    a. A majority of courts do not treat a viewing as trial evidence because the viewing is not available for evaluation and consideration by an appellate court.

    b. A minority of courts treat a viewing as evidence because, as a practical matter, jurors are unlikely to be able to separate their impressions from the viewing from their perception of the evidence presented in court.

    c. Note: The dilemma of insuring adequate appellate review of cases involving viewings has been partially solved by the increasing availability of high-quality videotape and digital recording devices.

9. Experiments

    a. General Rule

    Courts typically permit parties to offer evidence about the outcome of experiments conducted prior to trial. In addition, a court may permit the parties to conduct experiments in the jury's presence.

    b. Limitation

    Experiments are not admissible unless the conditions under which the experiment occurs are substantially similar to the conditions that existed during the disputed event.

    c. Prohibition on Juror Experiments

    Although jurors are generally prohibited from conducting their own experiments, jurors can experiment with (but not destroy, damage, or alter) real evidence that the trial court has admitted into evidence at the trial.

C. Judge and Jury Determinations

Most of the factual issues underlying the best evidence rule are decided by the judge as part of pretrial rulings on in limine matters. However, the value or weight to be assigned to documentary evidence is a matter for the trier of fact. For example, a jury may be required to decide:

1. Whether the asserted writing ever existed;

2. Whether the writing, recording, or photograph produced at trial is the original of that instrument;

3. Whether any secondary evidence admitted at trial correctly reflects the contents of the original evidence.

CASE CLIPS

McAndrews v. Leonard, 134 A. 710 (Vt. 1926)

Facts: Plaintiff, who suffered from a skull injury, sought damages on the basis that, during surgery, her skull fissures had been erroneously filled in with soft fibrous tissue instead of bone. At Plaintiff's request, the court permitted the jurors to touch Plaintiff's skull and compare original skull hardness with repaired skull hardness.

Issue: Is a jury permitted to examine for itself the extent of an injury?

Rule: As long as the particular examination is not technical in nature, nor one requiring special knowledge or skill, a jury should be permitted to examine for itself the extent of an injury. A jury cannot base its verdict exclusively on the knowledge so acquired, but it has a right to base its verdict on such examination together with all the evidence in a case.

Watson v. State, 140 N.E.2d 109 (Ind. 1957)

Facts: In a trial for armed robbery, the jury based its verdict in part on the basis that Defendant was over the age of 16, as required by statute. Defendant did not testify and no evidence of his age was introduced. However, the court gave the jury the instruction that it could observe Watson and draw on their observations of him in determining whether or not he was over 16 years of age at the time of the commission of the alleged offense. The jury determined that Defendant was over 16.

Issue: May the jury base its verdict on its own observations rather than evidence presented at trial?

Rule: A jury has no right to draw inferences from, or base its verdict on, objects seen in the courtroom that have not been properly introduced as evidence.

State v. Scarlett, 395 A.2d 1244 (N.H. 1978)

Facts: Defendant was charged with aggravated sexual assault. At trial, the state displayed a blood-stained bedspread without testimony from a chemist that the stains were actually blood.

Issue: May evidence be displayed to the jury without laying a proper foundation for its admissibility?

Rule: Evidence cannot be presented to the jury without first establishing a proper foundation. Without this foundation the evidence is inadmissible and displaying it to a jury causes prejudicial error.

Anderson v. Berg, 451 P.2d 248 (Kan. 1969)

Facts: Plaintiff sued Defendant after she slipped on Defendant's waxed floor. At trial, Defendant sought to introduce a sample bottle of floor wax.
Issue: What is the proper foundation for the admission of a sample?
Rule: At the time a sample is offered in evidence, it must be shown that it is in the same or substantially the same condition it was in at the time such condition became material to the issues involved. However, the fact that the offered sample has undergone some change in condition might not itself afford sufficient grounds for excluding it. The determination of whether a change preventing admission rests in the discretion of the trial court.

State v. Murphy, 355 P.2d 323 (Wash. 1960)

Facts: In a murder trial, Defendant was given tranquilizers before testifying. Defendant, who pleaded insanity, contended that the tranquilizers changed his demeanor sufficiently to prejudice the jury, which sentenced him to death.
Issue: Does it constitute prejudicial error if the Defendant's demeanor is affected by circumstances beyond his control?
Rule: Where there is a reasonable possibility that Defendant's attitude, appearance, or demeanor, as observed by a jury, is substantially influenced or affected by circumstances over which he had no control, grounds for a new trial exist where the projected image might have influenced the jury in sentencing.

United States v. Wanoskia, 800 F.2d 235 (10th Cir. 1986)

Facts: Defendant, charged with murder, contended that the victim shot herself. Expert testimony revealed that the gun was 18 inches from the victim's face when fired. Prosecution used a demonstration to prove that it was physically impossible for the victim to have fired the gun.
Issue: Must demonstrative evidence precisely replicate the situation the evidence seeks to clarify?
Rule: If a demonstration purports to simulate actual events and to show the jury what presumably occurred at the scene of the incident, the party introducing the evidence has the burden of demonstrating substantial similarity of conditions. Conditions do not have to be identical, but they must be sufficiently similar as to provide a fair comparison. The court must take special care to ensure that the demonstration fairly depicts the events at issue.

Hall v. General Motors Corp., 647 F.2d 175 (D.C. Cir. 1980)

Facts: Plaintiff sought damages when her vehicle suddenly crashed as the result of an allegedly defective drive shaft. Defendant attempted to introduce simulated tests that showed that a defective drive shaft could not have caused the accident.

Issue: When is a test admissible as demonstrative evidence?

Rule: A test is inadmissible unless the test conditions are "so nearly the same in substantial particulars as those involved in the episode in litigation as to afford a fair comparison in respect to the particular issue to which the test is directed."

Knihal v. State, 36 N.W.2d 109 (Neb. 1949)

Facts: In a trial for murder, Defendant objected to the admission of pictures of the scene of the crime. The photographer testified that the pictures were taken at the tavern an hour after the shooting, they were true reflections of the objects intended to be photographed, and that one of the pictures included Defendant.

Issue: May photographs be admitted into evidence without testimony describing or authenticating the events portrayed in the photographs?

Rule: As a general rule, photographs are admissible in evidence only when they are verified or authenticated by some other evidence. Photographs are generally inadmissible as original or substantive evidence. They must be sponsored by a witness or witnesses whose testimony they serve to explain and illustrate. The witness must have competent knowledge of the facts portrayed in the picture, and must be able to describe them to give them some meaning.

Bannister v. Town of Noble, Oklahoma, 812 F.2d 1265 (10th Cir. 1987)

Facts: In a personal injury suit, Defendant objected to films that showed Plaintiff's daily life after he sustained his injury. On appeal, Defendant claimed that the "day in the life" video was unduly prejudicial.

Issue: May "day in the life" films be admitted into evidence to demonstrate the effect of injuries on a plaintiff?

Rule: The prejudicial effect of a videotape must be decided on a case-by-case basis. The court must determine whether the probative value of a particular film outweighs the possibility of prejudice in light of the identified concerns. The lower court examined the film, concluded it accurately portrayed the daily routine of the victim and held that it was not unduly prejudicial. This was not an abuse of the court's discretion.

United States v. Sliker, 751 F.2d 477 (2d Cir. 1984)

Facts: Defendant was charged with passing bad checks. A tape recording of a phone conversation, allegedly between Defendant and a co-conspirator, was admitted into evidence with the condition that the jury would decide for itself whether the voice on the tape was actually Defendant's.

Issue: May the authenticity of a tape recording be determined by the jury?

Rule: A jury may authenticate a tape recording by comparing it with specimens that have been authenticated, such as oral testimony. However, the judge must make a preliminary determination whether there is sufficient evidence of authenticity to let the question go to the jury.

Turnage v. State, 708 N.W.2d 535 (Minn. 2006)

Facts: Defendant was convicted of murder. When the victim's body was discovered, Defendant was in the County Workhouse. While in the workhouse, he made several phone calls; recordings of these calls were admitted at trial. Defendant argued the prosecution failed to establish that the recorded copies of the tapes of his calls were the same as the originals.

Issue: Whether copies of tape recordings have an adequate foundation for admission into evidence if the person who made the copies did not compare the copies to the original recordings.

Rule: Under Rule 1003, a duplicate recording is admissible to the same extent as the original tape unless there is a genuine question regarding the authenticity of the original or it would be unfair to admit the duplicate in lieu of the original.

Smith v. Ohio Oil Co., 134 N.E.2d 526 (Ill. App. Ct. 1956)

Facts: In a personal injury case, Plaintiff's medical witness was permitted to use a plastic model of a human skeleton to assist in his explanations. Defendant appealed, arguing that the model was unnecessary to an understanding of the issues and tended only to unnecessarily arouse the jury's emotions.

Issue: When does the use of demonstrative evidence constitute reversible error?

Rule: Demonstrative evidence is distinguished from real evidence in that it has no intrinsic probative value; rather, it serves as a visual aid to help the jury understand the witness's testimony. The demonstrative evidence must be relevant and explanatory. Relevance and explanatory value are determined by the trial court. If the demonstrative exhibit was used for dramatic effect or emotional appeal rather than factual explanation, there is reversible error.

Gallagher v. Pequot Spring Water Co., 199 A.2d 172 (Conn. Cir. Ct. 1963)

Facts: Plaintiff sued Defendant for injuries sustained after she consumed a soda that had a foreign substance inside it. Defendant argues that the admission of a soda bottle containing an unidentified substance was in error.

Issue: What foundational showing is required for the admission as evidence of an item alleged to have caused an injury?

Rule: Plaintiff sought to admit the bottle as the alleged item to have caused her injury. Therefore, Plaintiff had to prove that the substance in the bottle at the time of trial was the same substance, without any material change, as the substance allegedly contained in the bottle when she first opened it.

Clark v. St. Thomas Hospital, 676 S.W.2d 347 (Tenn. Ct. App. 1984)

Facts: Plaintiff sued for personal injuries sustained in a fall in Defendant's hospital. On appeal, he argued that it was an error to admit a videotaped reenactment of Defendant's version of the accident.

Issue: Are videotaped reenactments admissible as evidence?

Rule: Reenactments are illustrative evidence, and are admissible only to the extent that they illustrate facts otherwise shown by sworn testimony. Thus as long as the videotape reasonably reflects the testimony, it is admissible.

Commonwealth v. Serge, 896 A.2d 1170 (Pa. 2006)

Facts: Defendant was indicted for the murder of his wife. Prior to trial, the Commonwealth filed a motion in limine seeking to present the prosecution's theory of the shooting through a computer-generated animation (CGA) based on forensic and physical evidence. Following an evidentiary hearing, the trial court granted the motion, provided that certain evidentiary foundations were established at trial. It required the Commonwealth to authenticate the animation as both a fair and accurate depiction of expert reconstructive testimony and exclude any inflammatory features that might cause unfair prejudice. Defendant was convicted, and on appeal challenged the admission of the CGA.

Issue: Is a computer-generated animation illustrating a theory of homicide admissible evidence?

Rule: A CGA should be deemed admissible as demonstrative evidence if it is properly authenticated, is relevant, its probative value outweighs the danger of unfair prejudice or confusion, and the court gives a limiting instruction to the jury explaining the nature of the specific CGA as demonstrative evidence.

Fisher v. State, 643 S.W.2d 571 (Ark. Ct. App. 1982)

Facts: Fisher was convicted of theft. On appeal, she argued that the trial court erred in ruling that certain portions of a videotape recording were properly admitted into evidence.

Issue: When is a videotape admissible as evidence?

Rule: Videotape evidence is admissible when the trial court finds sufficient foundational evidence to indicate the evidence is what its proponent says it is.

Evansville School Corp v. Price, 208 N.E.2d 689 (Ind. Ct. App. 1965)

Facts: Decedent was killed when he was hit by a ball at a baseball game. His father brought a wrongful death action and, at trial, offered into evidence a color photograph of Decedent lying in his casket. On appeal, Defendant argued that, because there was no triable issue as to the fact or cause of death, the introduction of the photograph was improper; the photograph was inflammatory, and it was not material to any issue involved in the case.

Issue: When is a photograph admissible?

Rule: For a photograph to be admissible, it must first be accepted by the trial court as material and relevant, and must tend to prove or disprove some material fact in issue. The photograph in this case should not have been admitted into evidence. It was immaterial and irrelevant to any of the material facts in issue, and was prejudicial to the Defendant.

Ensor v. Wilson, 519 So. 2d 1244 (Ala. 1987)

Facts: Plaintiff sued Defendant-doctor for medical malpractice after premature child suffered from brain damage and retardation. At trial, the court allowed an in-court demonstration between child and a special educational therapist, showing child's physical and mental abilities and limitations. On appeal, Defendant argued that the trial court erred in permitting the in-court demonstration.

Issue: Is an in-court demonstration of an injured plaintiff permissible?

Rule: A demonstration is impermissible when its capacity for prejudice exceeds its probative worth. Under the control of the trial judge, this demonstration was not different in theory and practice from the relevant exhibition of wound or movement whether by the witness himself or through the use of photographs. The therapist who conducted the demonstration was sworn as a witness and subject to cross-examination. It is also clear that the child's cognitive and physical abilities were in issue on the matter of damages.

McDowell v. Schuette, 610 S.W.2d 29 (Mo. Ct. App. 1980)

Facts: Defendants hired Plaintiff to construct a house. Plaintiff sued to recover payment for their work, and Defendants countersued, claiming the house was not constructed properly or in a timely manner. On appeal, Defendants argued that the court erred when it allowed the jury to inspect the home in question because the viewing constituted evidence of a lay opinion.

Issue: Does a jury viewing constitute evidence?

Rule: A jury viewing is not evidence. It allows the jury to secure a better understanding of the evidence and enables it to determine the relative weight of conflicting testimony. However, the jury's observations are no substitute for testimony.

CHAPTER 10

Privileges

I. INTRODUCTION

A. Overview

A privilege is a rule that excludes otherwise relevant and admissible evidence to protect certain relationships and further public policy goals.

B. Rationale

Most evidentiary rules are intended to assist the factfinder in the search for the truth. Thus, the rules exclude evidence that is immaterial, has little probative value, or is likely to prejudice and confuse the factfinder. In contrast, evidentiary privileges promote public policies by excluding evidence that may advance the search for truth to advance public policies such as protection of constitutional interests (the constitutional privilege against self-incrimination) advancement of marital relationships (the spousal privilege), and the professional relationship of trust between an attorney and client (the attorney–client privilege).

C. Sources of Privilege Law

Evidentiary privileges arise from common law as well as from state and federal statutes.

1. Common Law

Historically, common law recognized many of the evidentiary privileges that exist today. However, modern courts have expanded the scope of some common law privileges (such as the attorney–client privilege) and have narrowed the scope of other common law privileges (such as the spousal privilege).

2. Statutes

State and federal legislators have codified many common law privileges. Legislators' privileges have also created new evidentiary privileges that did not exist at common law.

    a. State

State statutory evidentiary privileges are not constitutionally mandated; states are free to create, expand, or eliminate evidentiary privileges. State-created evidentiary privileges are only restricted by the Due Process Clause.

    b. Federal

Congress has never enacted specific federal evidentiary privileges. Accordingly, FRE 501 governs the application of privilege law in federal court.

      i. Federal courts sitting on federal question cases and on federal criminal cases apply the federal common law of privileges.

      ii. Federal courts sitting in diversity cases apply the privilege laws of the applicable state law.

3. The United States Constitution creates a privilege against self-incrimination. This is the only evidentiary privilege that has its origins in the Constitution.

II. PRIVILEGE AGAINST SELF-INCRIMINATION

A. Overview

The Fifth Amendment to the United States Constitution states that no person shall be compelled, in any criminal case, to be a witness against himself. The Fourteenth Amendment Due Process Clause makes this privilege applicable to criminal proceedings in state courts.

B. Rationale

    1. Historical Rationale

At common law, a criminal defendant's interest in the case rendered the defendant incompetent to testify as a witness on his own behalf.

    2. Modern

Modern courts have abandoned the common law rule that made a criminal defendant incompetent to testify on his own behalf. In an adversary system the burden of proof in a criminal case is on the prosecution; the defendant need not assist the prosecution in any way. Thus the modern rationale for the privilege against self-incrimination arises from the burden of proof borne by the prosecution.

C. Application

    1. Generally

An individual may invoke privilege against self-incrimination if she is a criminal defendant or a witness who is called on to give testimonial evidence that might tend to incriminate her in a current or future criminal proceeding.

2. Process

An individual may invoke the privilege in any official proceeding. The means of invocation is circumstance-dependent.

a. Invocation by Criminal Defendant

    i. A suspect in police custody may invoke the privilege by refusing to answer questions or make a statement.

    ii. A criminal defendant may invoke the privilege by choosing not to testify at a pretrial or post-trial hearing.

    iii. A criminal defendant may invoke the privilege by choosing not to testify at his criminal trial.

b. Invocation by Witness

    i. No General Refusal

    A witness who is called to testify at a trial, grand jury proceeding, pretrial, or sentencing hearing may not invoke the privilege with a general refusal to testify.

    ii. Question-Specific Invocation

    To properly invoke the privilege, a witness must claim the Fifth Amendment privilege after she has been asked a specific question, the answer to which may tend to incriminate the witness. Upon hearing the question, the witness may decline to answer in reliance on her Fifth Amendment privilege. Thereafter, any effort to compel the witness's testimony will be subject to judicial review, including a judicial determination of whether the witness properly invoked the privilege.

c. Matters Protected by the Privilege

The privilege against self-incrimination protects an individual from being compelled to give incriminating testimony. The key terms are explored below:

    i. Testimony

    The privilege against self-incrimination applies only to compelled testimonial statements. Thus the testimony sought must be testimony that would be communicative of the witness's thoughts, recollections, intentions, or actions. Testimonial evidence may be oral, written, or physical (for example, evidence of a communicative gesture).

    (1) Exemplars and Physical Samples

    Blood samples, fingerprints, and voice and handwriting exemplars are not testimonial; therefore a witness or defendant may be compelled to produce such samples.

    (2) Documents, Writings, or Similar Instruments

      (a) General Rule

      Personal documents and business records are not considered to be testimonial. Therefore, neither a witness nor a defendant may avoid document production by invoking the privilege.

(b) Exception

If the act of producing physical evidence would itself be a testimonial or communicative act, the privilege shields a witness or defendant from the act of production.

ii. Compelled

The privilege only applies to testimony that is compelled by official processes.

iii. Incriminating

Evidence is incriminating when it provides a link in a chain of evidence that might lead to criminal prosecution or conviction. If there is no possibility of prosecution, the privilege does not apply.

iv. Individual

(1) As Applied to Individual Persons

(a) Personal Privilege

The privilege against self-incrimination is a personal privilege. It must be invoked by the individual who seeks its protections.

(b) Third-Party Invocation

A third party cannot invoke the privilege on behalf of the protected individual unless the individual directs the third party to do so.

(2) As Applied to Businesses

(a) Business Documents

The custodian of business documents may be required to produce and identify those documents, even if they tend to incriminate the custodian.

(b) Sole Proprietorships

Because a sole proprietorship has no existence independent of its owner, a business that is a sole proprietorship may properly invoke the privilege. Similarly, the records of a sole proprietorship are personal to its owner.

D. Waiver

1. Criminal Defendants

a. Generally

When a criminal defendant testifies at trial, the defendant's trial testimony constitutes a waiver of the privilege regarding the crime at issue. The defendant may not both testify on direct examination and then assert the privilege on cross-examination.

    b. Guilty Pleas

    A defendant's guilty plea is not a complete waiver of the privilege. Notwithstanding the guilty plea, a defendant may still invoke the privilege at any post-plea proceeding, such as a sentencing hearing.

  2. Witness

    A witness does not waive the privilege by taking the stand or by answering nonincriminating questions. However, when a witness answers an incriminating statement, the witness waives the right to invoke the privilege with respect to further questions about that topic. However, if the answer(s) to related questions tend to incriminate the witness in connection with new or previously undiscussed crimes, the witness may invoke the privilege as to the newly raised matters.

E. Effect of Privilege

  Invocation of the Fifth Amendment privilege may have various effects, depending on the context in which the privilege is invoked.

  1. Civil Trial

    In a civil trial, parties may comment on the silence of a witness or defendant. Moreover, the jury is free to draw adverse inferences from silence.

  2. Criminal Trials

    a. No Comment on Silence

      Neither the judge nor the prosecution may comment on the silence of the defendant in a criminal trial.

    b. Inferences Prohibited

      The jury may not be permitted to draw inferences from the silence of a defendant.

    c. Jury Instruction

      Upon the defendant's request, the trial court must instruct the jury that they may not draw any inference from the defendant's silence.

F. Exclusionary Rule

  In a criminal case, the exclusionary rule prohibits the use of testimony obtained in violation of the Constitution.

G. Immunity

  Prosecutors may agree not to prosecute an individual. Once an individual is no longer at risk of prosecution, the individual has no recourse to the privilege. Thus immunity operates to blunt or eliminate the privilege.

  1. Co-Extensivity of Immunity and Privilege

    A court may not compel a witness to offer self-incriminating testimony. However, if the prosecution offers immunity co-extensive with the privilege, the privilege is unavailable.

2. Use and Derivative Use Immunity
   Use and derivative use immunity are immunity protections that guarantee that evidence provided by an individual will not be used against that individual in later criminal proceedings.
3. Transactional Immunity
   Transactional immunity is immunity from prosecution for any transaction about which the witness testifies.

III. ATTORNEY–CLIENT PRIVILEGE

The attorney–client privilege is the oldest common law privilege, and has been recognized by every state. Most states have codified the attorney–client privilege.

A. General Rule
   A client may refuse to disclose, or may prohibit disclosure by another, of any confidential communication between the client and attorney.
B. Who Can Assert the Attorney-Client Privilege?
   1. Client or Representative
      The privilege belongs to the client and may be invoked by the client or by her representative.
   2. Attorney or Agent
      An attorney or the attorney's agent may invoke the privilege on the client's behalf, if the client so directs.
C. Scope of the Attorney-Client Privilege
   1. Generally
      The attorney–client privilege only applies to confidential statements made in the context of the professional attorney–client relationship. Key terminology is explored below:
      a. Professional Relationship
         i. General Rule
            For the privilege to apply, the attorney and client must have a professional relationship. A professional relationship exists when the client has reason to believe that the person she consulted
            (1) is a practicing member of the bar, and
            (2) that her communications to this person will be confidential.
         ii. Fees Not Required to Establish Relationship
            The client need not pay a fee to establish the requisite attorney–client relationship. Communications made during an initial consultation may also be privileged.

       iii. Legal Advice

The privilege applies only to statements in a relationship that has, as its purpose, the giving and receiving of professional legal advice.

  b. Confidential Communications

The privilege only applies to confidential communications. These communications may include nonverbal communications such as gestures or nonverbal acts.

  c. Statements Made by Client to Attorney

The attorney–client privilege protects statements made by a client to his lawyer for the purpose of obtaining legal advice.

  d. Statement Made by Attorney to Client

     i. General Rule

An attorney's statements to her client are privileged to the extent that they reflect and convey confidential information that the client provided to the attorney.

     ii. Note

When an attorney makes statements as a messenger of the court, for example by informing a client of the time and place of a trial, the privilege does not apply.

     iii. Eavesdropping

When an attorney and client have taken reasonable precautions to maintain the confidentiality of their communications, those communications are privileged, even if a third party overhears the communications.

     iv. Third-Party Agents

When an attorney retains the assistance of a third-party agent, such as a doctor or investigator, the privilege extends to confidential communications made by, to, or through that agent.

  e. Common Problems

     i. Client's Identity or Decision to Retain Counsel

Normally, the privilege does not shield against the disclosure of a client's identity, a client's retention of counsel, or the details of the attorney's fee. If, however, disclosure of this information would itself reveal a confidential communication, the privilege may apply.

     ii. Physical Evidence

An attorney may not knowingly conceal evidence from the prosecution or court. If an attorney receives such evidence, the attorney may retain the evidence for a reasonable period of time before returning the evidence to its source, or disclosing the evidence to the prosecution.

     f. Documents
       i. Prepared by the Defendant
        When a client provides her counsel with nontestimonial documents, those documents are privileged only to the extent that they would be protected from disclosure if in the client's possession.
       ii. Prepared by Third Party
        Documents prepared by a third party and possessed by attorney are usually not privileged.
     g. Ongoing Crime or Fraud
       If the client seeks legal advice to perpetuate an ongoing crime or fraud, communications regarding that crime or fraud are not privileged.
     h. Advice in Contravention of Law
       The privilege does not cover advice offered to further the destruction of evidence or evasion of the law.
     i. Death of Client
       The attorney–client privilege survives the death of the client.
     j. Joint Clients
       i. When a dispute arises among multiple parties who jointly consulted an attorney, the discussions between those clients and the attorney may not be privileged.
       ii. Joint clients who meet with their counsel pursuant to a joint defense agreement may enjoy the privilege as to communications during the joint defense meeting.
     k. Perjury
       The privilege does not apply to client statements that show the attorney that the client has committed, or will commit, perjury.

IV. THE ATTORNEY WORK-PRODUCT DOCTRINE

    A. Generally
      The privilege that protects attorney work-product is separate and distinct from the attorney–client privilege. The work-product doctrine is a common law doctrine that has no constitutional underpinnings.
    B. Scope
      The work-product doctrine protects the attorney from forced disclosure of her mental impressions, thought processes, and conclusions.
    C. Exception
      The work-product privilege is limited by the "substantial need" exception that applies to tangible materials and documents.

V. SPOUSAL PRIVILEGE

A. Generally

The modern spousal privilege reflects the common law rule that rendered spouses incompetent to testify against each other. Few jurisdictions categorically prohibit one spouse from testifying against the other spouse. Most jurisdictions, however, recognize at least one of the two modern spousal privileges.

1. Adverse Spousal Testimony

This privilege shields one spouse from adverse testimony offered by the other spouse. The adverse spousal privilege is only applicable if the couple is married at the time of the proceeding in which the testimony is sought. Either the witness spouse or the defendant spouse may invoke the privilege.

2. Confidential Marital Communications

This privilege protects confidential marital communications.

   a. Features

      i. Covered Communications

The marital communications privilege applies to all confidential communications made during the marriage.

      ii. Marital Status Irrelevant

It is irrelevant whether the couple is still married at the time of the court proceedings.

      iii. Invocation

         (1) Majority Rule

Either spouse may invoke the privilege.

         (2) Minority Rule

Only the spouse who made the confidential communication may invoke the privilege.

VI. PHYSICIAN/PSYCHOTHERAPIST–PATIENT PRIVILEGE

A. Generally

The physician–patient privilege is a statutory privilege that did not exist at common law. Almost every state has enacted a physician–patient privilege. Some states have extended the privilege to cover the psychiatrist–patient relationship, and other states have recognized a separate but co-extensive privilege that covers the psychotherapist–patient relationship.

B. Rationale

This privilege promotes free and full communication between patient and physician. The privilege also protects individual privacy.

C. Applicability

The privilege only applies to confidential communications between patient and physician, when the patient has consulted the physician for purposes of diagnosis and treatment. Key terms are discussed below:

1. Confidential

   The privilege only applies to those communications or aspects of treatment that

   a. the patient reasonably expects to be kept confidential; and,

   b. that the patient herself has maintained as confidential.

2. For Diagnosis and Treatment

   The privilege only applies to communications made for diagnosis and treatment purposes. The privilege will not apply:

   a. If a patient consults a physician solely to prepare for litigation, or

   b. If the court appoints the physician to make an examination and testify about a diagnosis to assist the trier of fact.

3. Invocation

   The privilege belongs to the patient, not the physician; therefore, the patient may invoke the privilege or the doctor may invoke the privilege on the patient's behalf and at the patient's instruction.

D. Exceptions

1. Patient-Litigant

   When a patient acts affirmatively to put his mental or physical health in issue in litigation, the patient waives the physician-patient privilege, as to the communications related to the disputed matters in the litigation.

2. Public Safety

   When a physician or psychiatrist has reason to believe or knows that a patient may be dangerous to others, that physician has a duty to warn the intended victim or appropriate authorities.

VII. GOVERNMENTAL PRIVILEGE

A. Generally

As to the application of privileges, the law treats the government as an individual. Therefore the government can assert privileges when it is either (a) a party to a judicial proceeding or (b) subpoenaed as a witness whose testimony is sought for a judicial proceeding. For example, government attorneys may claim the protections of the work-product privilege and the government may invoke the attorney–client privilege to prevent a government attorney from testifying about information acquired in the course of representing the government.

B. Common Problems
1. Military, Diplomatic, or National Security Secrets
When the government properly asserts a privilege based on military, diplomatic, or national security secrets, the privilege is absolute. To determine whether the privilege applies to the requested information, a court will either proceed by attorney proffer, or will review the evidence in camera.
2. Assertion of General Need for Secrecy
When the government asserts a privilege based on a generalized need for secrecy in government operations or communications, the court generally balances the public's interest in confidential government communications against the requesting party's need for the disclosure.
3. Note: Freedom of Information Act
The Freedom of Information Act (FOIA) requires that most government documents be made available to the public. Exceptions to FOIA reflect the policy concerns raised by governmental privileges.
4. Informant Identity
The government enjoys a limited privilege not to disclose the identity of informants. If disclosure of the informant's identity is necessary to allow a criminal defendant to prepare and present a trial defense, the court may order the government to disclose the informant's identity. In the alternative, the government may choose to dismiss the charges against the defendant, rather than reveal the informant's identity.
5. Probable Cause
When an application for a search or arrest warrant rests on information provided by an anonymous government informant, the court may decide not to issue the warrant unless:
a. the totality of circumstances corroborate the informant's tip; or
b. the application itself demonstrates a basis for the informant's knowledge, and the affiant avers a reasonable basis for crediting the informant.

VIII. MISCELLANEOUS PRIVILEGES

A. Other Privileges
Aside from these privileges, some states and some federal courts have created or acknowledged other privileges that reflect a consensus about the need for the promotion and protection of other confidential relationships.

B. Accountant–Client Privilege
   1. Generally
      An accountant–client privilege is slowly developing in many states.
   2. Federal Privilege for Auditor Work Papers
      Acting under FRE 501, federal courts have recognized a limited privilege for the work papers of certain auditors. For example, the Securities Exchange Act requires corporations to maintain an independent auditing system and federal courts recognize the extension of a privilege between the corporation and the auditor.
C. Journalist Privilege
   The Supreme Court has held that the press enjoys no special evidentiary privileges under the First Amendment. However, several states have developed statutory shields to provide the press with a privilege not to divulge confidential sources of information.
D. Insured–Insurer Privilege
   Certain states recognize a privilege for communication between an insured and insurer regarding incidents that (1) the insured is obligated to report; and (2) for which the insurer is obligated to indemnify the insured.
E. Priest–Penitent Privilege
   The priest–penitent privilege recognizes that priests and other religious counselors have religious obligations to maintain the confidentiality of confessional information.
F. Parent–Child Privilege
   Some states recognize a limited parent–child privilege analogous to the marital communication privilege. Most such privileges cover statements made by a minor child to a parent.

IX. PRIVILEGING THE JUDICIAL PROCESSES: CERTAIN RULES, ANALOGOUS TO PRIVILEGES, PROTECTING THE CONFIDENTIALITY OF JUDICIAL PROCESSES

A. Jury Deliberations
   FRE 606(b) prohibits a juror from testifying about the jury's deliberations, except that a juror may testify about (1) extraneous and prejudicial information improperly brought to any juror's attention; and (2) any outside influence brought to bear upon any juror.
B. Grand Jury Proceedings
   1. General Rule
      Federal grand jury proceedings, and most state grand jury proceedings, are confidential. Transcripts of grand jury testimony and deliberations are available only when

a. A litigant makes a substantial showing of need (for example, in a challenge claiming racial discrimination in the grand jury); or

b. When the grand jury testimony is either exculpatory material, or witness impeachment material that must be disclosed to a criminal defendant to guarantee his right to a fair trial.

CASE CLIPS

Clark v. State, 261 S.W.2d 339 (Tex. Crim. App. 1953)

Facts: Defendant murdered his wife and then called his attorney. In that call, Defendant confessed to the murder and the attorney advised him to dispose of the gun. A telephone operator eavesdropped on the conversation. At trial, she testified about the call, describing Defendant's confession and his attorney's advice that Defendant get rid of the gun. Defendant appealed, arguing that admission of the operator's testimony was error as the testimony related to a privileged attorney–client communication.

Issue: Does the attorney–client privilege apply to communications that are in furtherance of criminal activity?

Rule: The crime/fraud exception to the attorney–client privilege renders such communications unprotected. Defendant was not seeking advice from his attorney about preparing his legal defense. The shield of the attorney–client privilege does not extend to one who, having committed a crime, seeks advice from counsel as to how to evade arrest and punishment.

United States v. Zolin, 491 U.S. 554 (1989)

Facts: The IRS sought access to tape recordings of meetings between the Church of Scientology and its legal counsel, claiming that the communications fell within the crime/fraud exception to the attorney–client privilege. The IRS urged the District Court to consider the testimony of an undercover agent and partial transcripts of the recordings in camera. The district court ruled, based on independent evidence, that the tapes contained privileged information and the crime/fraud exception did not apply.

Issue: May a court hold an in camera review to determine whether privileged attorney–client communications fall within the crime/fraud exception?

Rule (Blackmun): A district court may conduct an in camera review of the materials in question to determine whether allegedly privileged attorney–client communications fall within the crime/fraud exception. The party opposing the privilege may use any nonprivileged, relevant evidence in support of its request for an in camera review, even if the evidence is not independent of the contested communication. The judge should require a showing of a factual basis adequate to support a good faith belief by a reasonable person that in camera review of the materials might reveal evidence to establish the claim that the crime/fraud exception applies.

Carter v. Kentucky, 450 U.S. 288 (1981)

Facts: Defendant was indicted for burglary. At his trial, he decided not to testify because he did not want evidence of his prior convictions to be introduced. Defense counsel requested that an instruction be given to the jury stating, "The defendant is not compelled to testify and the fact that he does not cannot be used as an inference of guilt and should not prejudice him in any way." The trial court refused the request.

Issue: Does the Fifth Amendment require a judge, on a defendant's request, to give an instruction to the jury that a defendant's decision not to testify cannot be used as an inference of guilt?

Rule (Stewart): The Fifth Amendment requires that, when requested by a defendant to do so, a criminal trial judge must give a "no-adverse-inference" jury instruction. The Fifth Amendment is an absolute constitutional guarantee against compulsory self-incrimination, and a defendant must pay no court-imposed price for the exercise of his constitutional privilege not to testify.

Dissent (Rehnquist): Neither the Fifth Amendment nor precedent requires that state courts give this requested instruction. The defendant is taking away from the trial judge virtually any control over the instructions to be given to the jury.

Braswell v. United States, 487 U.S. 99 (1988)

Facts: Braswell was the sole shareholder and president of two corporations: Worldwide Machinery Sales and Worldwide Purchasing. A federal grand jury issued a subpoena to Braswell, requiring him to produce the books and records of the two companies. Braswell moved to quash the subpoena on the ground that the act of producing the records would incriminate him in violation of his Fifth Amendment privilege against self-incrimination. The District Court denied the motion to quash.

Issue: May the custodian of corporate records resist a subpoena for such records on the ground that the act of production would incriminate him in violation of the Fifth Amendment?

Rule (Rehnquist): A custodian may not resist a subpoena for corporate records on Fifth Amendment grounds. For purposes of the Fifth Amendment, corporations and other collective entities are treated differently from individuals. The custodian's act of production is not a personal act, but an act of the corporation because the corporation can only act through its agents. A custodian of corporate records holds those documents in this representative capacity. Any claim of Fifth Amendment privilege asserted by the agent is tantamount to a claim of privilege by the corporation, which possesses no Fifth Amendment privilege.

Dissent (Kennedy): Although a custodian has no necessary relation to the contents of documents within his control, the act of production is his own. In some cases, production might require the custodian's own testimonial assertions (e.g., the assertion that the documents satisfy the description in the subpoena), in which case the potential for self-incrimination is great."

United States v. Doe, 465 U.S. 605 (1984)

Facts: Doe owned several sole proprietorships. During an investigation of corruption, a grand jury served five subpoenas on Doe. Two demanded the production of telephone records, one demanded the production of bank statements, and two demanded the production of various business records. Doe filed a motion to quash the subpoenas, claiming the privilege against self-incrimination. The District Court granted the motion, except in respect to documents and records required by law to be disclosed to a public agency, on the ground that the materials sought might be incriminating and the act of production would violate Doe's Fifth Amendment privilege.

Issue: Does the Fifth Amendment privilege against self-incrimination apply to the business records of a sole proprietorship?

Rule (Powell): The contents of a business record are not privileged, but the act of producing the records might be. The act of producing the documents would involve testimonial self-incrimination. Responding to the subpoena forces Doe to admit the records exist, they are in his possession, and they are authentic. These compelled communications would violate his Fifth Amendment rights. Thus, the act of producing the documents at issue here is privileged and cannot be compelled without a statutory grant of use immunity.

In re Farber, 394 A.2d 330 (N.J. 1978)

Facts: Farber was a reporter for the New York Times whose investigative reporting led to a murder prosecution. Defendant subpoenaed from Farber the documents and materials he gathered during the course of the investigation, including the names of Farber's sources. Farber refused to comply, citing the New Jersey News Media Privilege Act and the Free Speech and Free Press clauses of the First Amendment of the United States Constitution.

Issue: Does a journalist possess a constitutional privilege to withhold subpoenaed documents?

Rule: The New Jersey Shield Law grants newspeople and other media representatives the privilege of declining to reveal confidential sources of information. The Sixth Amendment right to compulsory process prevails over the Shield Law. When a defendant makes a preliminary showing that the privileged material is necessary, relevant, and unobtainable in a less intrusive manner, then the material sought should be submitted to the court for an in camera inspection.

Dissent: Although the Supreme Court has ruled that the First Amendment grants no special privilege to the media, it has also ruled that states are free to provide such a privilege. The state legislature, in passing this shield law, has weighed the varying interests of defendants and the press and decided on an absolute privilege, not one to be determined on a case-by-case basis.

Fisher v. United States, 425 U.S. 391 (1976)

Facts: Fisher, an attorney, received an IRS summons to produce documents that had been prepared by the client's accountant and delivered to him by the client. Fisher claimed that the documents were protected both by the attorney–client privilege and the client's privilege against self-incrimination.

Issue: If the self-incrimination clause of the Fifth Amendment prohibits the compelled production of documents within the possession of a defendant, does the attorney–client privilege forbid their compelled production once the documents have been delivered to the defendant's attorney?

Rule (White): The documents in question were prepared by accountants. They were not prepared by the client, and thus contain no testimonial declarations by the client. Furthermore, the preparation of the documents was entirely voluntary, and so the documents do not contain any compelled testimonial evidence. The act of producing the documents does not involve testimonial self-incrimination.

Upjohn Co. v. United States, 449 U.S. 383 (1981)

Facts: Defendant learned that some of its foreign subsidiaries might have made illegal payments to foreign officials. It began its own internal investigation and reported the matter to the SEC and the IRS. General counsel sent questionnaires to employees and conducted interviews with those employees. The government sought to discover these documents and the general counsel's memoranda regarding oral interviews. Defendant declined to produce the documents on the grounds that they were protected from disclosure by the attorney–client privilege.

Issue: In the corporate context, when does the attorney–client privilege apply?

Rule (Rehnquist): In the case of a corporation, the "control group test" no longer governs. Whether a particular communication is privileged must be determined on a case-by-case basis. Here, the communications at issue were made by Defendant's employees to Defendant's counsel, at the direction of corporate superiors to secure legal advice. The information concerned matters within the scope of the employees' corporate duties, and was considered confidential. The communications, questionnaires, and notes reflecting responses to interviews must be protected against compelled disclosure.

Concurrence (Burger): The majority should articulate a new rule: A communication is privileged when an employee or former employee speaks at the direction of the management with an attorney regarding conduct or proposed conduct within the scope of employment.

Trammel v. United States (S. Ct. 1980)

Facts: Trammel and his wife were arrested for importing and conspiring to import heroin. Mrs. Trammel agreed to testify against her husband in exchange for immunity. Mr. Trammel sought to invoke the spousal privilege and prevent her testimony.

Issue: Does a spousal privilege exist under which a criminal defendant-spouse may prevent his or her other spouse from testifying for the prosecution?

Rule (Burger): Under the modern spousal privilege, the decision to testify or invoke privilege lies with the witness spouse and not the defendant. There is also a separate privilege that protects confidential marital communications, which may be invoked by either spouse.

Kastigar v. United States, 406 U.S. 441 (1972)

Facts: Kastigar was subpoenaed to appear before a grand jury but refused to testify, asserting the privilege against compulsory self-incrimination. The government agreed to grant Kastigar use and derivative use immunity; that is, Kastigar's grand jury could not be used directly against him nor could it be used to derive evidence against him. Kastigar claimed that this immunity was not co-extensive with the Fifth Amendment privilege, and therefore was insufficient to compel his testimony.

Issue: Is use and derivative use immunity sufficient to compel testimony over a Fifth Amendment claim of privilege, or must the compelling authority grant transactional immunity, which prevents any prosecution for the transaction about which a witness will testify?

Rule (Powell): The privilege against compulsory self-incrimination is not a privilege against prosecution. Transactional immunity grants a witness broader protection than is provided by the privilege; use and derivative use immunity are coextensive with the privilege and are sufficient protection to require a witness to testify over Fifth Amendment objections.

People v. Meredith, 631 P.2d 46 (Cal. 1981)

Facts: Defendant told his attorney that an important piece of evidence was in Defendant's trash can. The attorney sent an investigator to retrieve the item. At trial, over Defendant's objection, the investigator and the attorney testified that the item had been found in Defendant's trash can.

Issue: Is an observation by defense counsel that is the product of a privileged communication admissible at trial?

Rule: An observation by defense counsel or his investigator that is the product of a privileged communication is privileged and inadmissible unless the defense, by altering or removing physical evidence, has precluded the prosecution from making the same observation.

Commonwealth v. Hughes, 404 N.E.2d 1239 (Mass. 1980)

Facts: Hughes was indicted on two counts of assault by means of a dangerous weapon, to wit, a pistol. The police obtained and executed a search warrant for Hughes's car, but failed to recover a weapon. The Commonwealth then filed a "Motion to Order Defendant to Produce Weapon" for ballistics examination. An accompanying affidavit stated that Hughes had registered the revolver with the firearms identification division of the Department of Public Safety. After a hearing, Hughes was ordered to produce the described revolver. Hughes did not do so, and he was held in contempt by the court.

Issue: May a defendant be compelled to produce the instrumentality of a crime?

Rule: The production of the gun is testimonial. If Hughes produced the revolver, he would be implicitly making a statement about its existence, location, and control, which the Commonwealth says it would reference at trial to show he had possession and control at some point after the crime. This information is incriminating, thus the compelled production of the gun would violate Hughes's Fifth Amendment self-incrimination privilege.

People v. Lines, 531 P.2d 793 (Cal. 1975)

Facts: Defendant informed the court that he was likely to plead insanity. The court appointed two psychiatrists to examine Defendant and assist in his defense. At trial, Defendant pled not guilty by reason of insanity, and the court reappointed the two psychiatrists, and appointed a third to examine him and testify before the court. Defendant objected to the testimony of one of the earlier psychiatrists as protected by attorney–client privilege.

Issue: Are the communications a defendant makes to a psychiatrist who is appointed to assist counsel in representing him protected by the attorney–client privilege?

Rule: The confidentiality of the attorney–client privilege is not destroyed by the disclosure of communications to third persons to whom disclosure is reasonably necessary for the accomplishment of the purpose for which the lawyer is consulted. All information obtained by doctors and transmitted to attorneys to assist them in the legal matter for which they have been retained constitutes protected communications within the attorney–client privilege.

United States v. McPartlin, 595 F.2d 1321 (7th Cir. 1979)

Facts: Defendant and a co-defendant in a trial for fraud sought to discredit the testimony of the major prosecution witness. With the consent of Defendant's counsel, an investigator acting for co-defendant interviewed Defendant to determine whether there was a basis for challenging a prosecution witness. Defendant made statements that tended to support co-defendant's defense. At trial, co-defendant offered evidence of those statements and Defendant's counsel objected on the ground of attorney–client privilege.

Issue: Does the attorney–client privilege protect statements made by a defendant in confidence to a co-defendant's attorney?

Rule: A defendant is entitled to the protection of the attorney–client privilege for statements made in confidence to a co-defendant's attorney for a common purpose related to both defenses.

In the Matter of the Grand Jury Subpoena of Ford, 756 F.2d 249 (2d Cir. 1985)

Facts: Ford's wife was one of the targets of a grand jury investigation. Ford moved to quash the subpoena compelling his appearance because of his claim of privilege against adverse spousal testimony. The government filed an affidavit setting forth a procedure to insulate Ford's wife from any inculpatory effect from Ford's testimony. The affidavit stated the government's promise not to use any of Ford's testimony, either directly or indirectly, in the investigation or prosecution of his wife. Ford still refused to comply. The district judge held Ford in civil contempt for his refusal to appear and testify.

Issue: Whether a witness who is relying on a claim of privilege against adverse spousal testimony may be compelled to testify if he receives government assurances that his testimony would not be used against his wife.

Rule: The government's promise not to use any of the witness-spouse's testimony before the grand jury, either directly or indirectly, against the nonwitness spouse, is sufficient to meet the claim of privilege by the testifying spouse. If the testimony or its fruits cannot be used in the prosecution of the spouse, then the dangers sought to be avoided by the privilege are avoided. The "use-fruits" immunity is fully co-extensive with the scope of the privilege against adverse spousal testimony.

Ghana Supply Commission v. New England Power Co., 83 F.R.D. 586 (D. Mass. 1979)

Facts: Ghana Supply Commission (GSC) filed a complaint against New England Power Co. (NEPCO) to recover the unpaid portion of the sales price of fuel oil allegedly converted by NEPCO to its own use. A governmental agency in Ghana created a Committee of Inquiry to investigate the underlying situation in an in camera proceeding. NEPCO sought to obtain the content of certain documents, memoranda, reports, and correspondence, and the substance of testimony introduced before the Committee of Inquiry. Ghana withheld documents created solely for the Committee and all oral testimony before the Committee pursuant to a claim of executive privilege.

Issues:

1. Whether a state's rule of decision as to privileges applies in a federal case.
2. Whether, if a sovereign state institutes a civil action, that state waives executive privilege.

Rule 1: Under FRE 501, in civil actions and proceedings, privileges are to "be determined in accordance with state law."

Rule 2: Authority in Massachusetts holds that fairness to the defendant requires the government instituting a civil suit to make available all information relevant to the defense as long as that information does not contain military or diplomatic secrets or involve the informant privilege.

Jaffee v. Redmond, 518 U.S. 1 (1996)

Facts: Allen was killed by Redmond, an on-duty police officer. After the shooting, Redmond underwent counseling with a licensed clinical social worker. The plaintiff, as administrator of Allen's estate, sued Redmond and his government employer, alleging that Redmond had used excessive force. Plaintiff sought to discover the social worker's notes of her conversations with Redmond. Redmond and his attorney refused to turn the materials over, arguing that a psychotherapist–patient privilege protected the communications. The trial court gave an adverse inference charge and Redmond appealed.

Issue: Should confidential communications between a licensed social worker and a patient be protected from compelled disclosure under the "psychotherapist privilege" of FRE 501?

Rule (Stevens): Confidential communications between a licensed psychotherapist and her patients in the course of diagnosis and treatment are protected from compelled disclosure under Rule 501. The privilege should extend to confidential communications made to licensed social workers in the course of psychotherapy. The proposed privilege promotes interests that outweigh the need for probative evidence. The psychotherapist privilege serves the public interest by facilitating the provision of appropriate treatment for individuals who suffer from a mental or emotional problem. Moreover, all 50 states and the District of Columbia have enacted into law some form of the privilege.

Dissent (Scalia): Adoption of a social-worker psychotherapist privilege is a job for Congress. The fact that all 50 states have legislated a psychotherapist-patient privilege argues against judicial adoption of the privilege.

Baltimore City Department of Social Services v. Bouknight, 493 U.S. 549 (1990)

Facts: The Baltimore City Department of Social Services (BCDSS) accused a mother of abusing her infant son. Although the child was initially removed from the mother, she sought and received conditional custody of her son. The mother later allegedly violated conditions of order permitting her to keep her son. BCDSS sought a court ruling directing the mother to produce the child so that he could be removed from his mother's control. She refused to produce the child, arguing that order unconstitutionally compelled her to admit, through the act of production, a measure of continuing control over the child, in circumstances in which she had a reasonable apprehension that she would be prosecuted.

Issue: Does the "act of production" doctrine protect a mother from producing a minor child in child welfare proceedings, when the mother has custody of the child pursuant to a court order that conditions mother's custody on continued compliance with conditions set by a government social services agency?

Rule: A mother who is the custodian of her child pursuant to a court order may not invoke the Fifth Amendment privilege against self-incrimination to resist a subsequent court order to produce the child. Although the Fifth Amendment privilege may, on occasion, protect against the act of production, the mother consented to production of the child, at the state's request, when she accepted the terms of conditional custody. Moreover, the right to invoke the privilege diminishes when (1) invocation would disrupt a regulatory regime that serves the state's public purposes unrelated to the enforcement of its criminal laws; and (2) and when a person assumes control over items that are the legitimate object of the state's noncriminal regulatory powers. Here, the state had formally determined that the child was in need of state's assistance. State's interest in the child was asserted as part of a wide-ranging, noncriminal regulatory scheme and the state sought production of the child to ensure his well-being rather than to justify or assist in proving criminal conduct. Accordingly, the mother could not invoke her Fifth Amendment privilege to avoid producing the child. However, if the state subsequently pursues criminal action against the mother, the trial court may limit the state's ability to use, either directly or indirectly, the testimonial aspects of the mother's act of producing her son.

University of Pennsylvania v. Equal Employment Opportunity Commission, 493 U.S. 182 (1990)

Facts: Petitioner filed a claim with the EEOC, alleging that the University denied her tenure based on her race and sex. The EEOC issued a subpoena seeking Petitioner's tenure-review file and the tenure files of five male faculty members as to whom Petitioner claimed her qualifications were equal or better. University refused to produce the tenure-review documents and urged the court to recognize a privilege against disclosure of "confidential peer review information."

Issue: Does a university enjoys a special privilege, grounded in either the common law or the First Amendment, against disclosure of peer review materials that are relevant to charges of racial or sexual discrimination in tenure decisions?

Rule (Blackmun): There is no federal common law basis for granting academic institutions a qualified privilege for confidential peer review materials. Moreover, First Amendment academic freedom privilege acts to protect academic speech against content-based restrictions. The university seeks to maintain confidentiality of records because it believes that their disclosure will lead to a decline in the candor of peer reviews and the eventual decline in the quality of faculty scholarship. Under this circumstance, disclosure of the materials will not create a risk of content-based discrimination in employment decisions.

United States v. Goldberger & Dubin, P.C., 935 F.2d 501 (2d Cir. 1991)

Facts: Internal Revenue Code Section 6050-I requires a person who, in the course of his trade or business, receives more than $10,000 cash in one transaction to file a Form 8300. This form contains the cash payer's name and other identifying information. Respondents are attorneys who have received cash fees in excess of $10,000 from various clients. All filed a Form 8300 disclosing the cash fee payment, but did not identify the payer. The IRS issued summonses directing them to appear and produce information identifying the payers. The district court required Respondents to comply with the summonses and provide the payer information.

Issue: Does an attorney's disclosure to the IRS of clients who paid cash fees in excess of a certain amount violate the attorney–client privilege?

Rule: The attorney–client privilege only protects those disclosures that are necessary to obtain informed legal advice, and that would not be made without the privilege. The identification of the payers here is not a disclosure of privileged information. The direct consequence of the disclosure isn't the incrimination of the payer.

Izazaga v. Superior Court, 815 P.2d 304 (1991)

Facts: California's evidence code required criminal defendant to disclose, in advance of trial, the names, addresses, and prior statements of any trial witnesses. Izazaga objected, arguing that these pretrial disclosures violated his Fifth Amendment privilege against self-incrimination, and Sixth Amendment right to confidentiality of attorney work-product.

Issue: Does a state statute requiring criminal defendants to disclose to the prosecution the names, addresses, and statements of all witnesses they intend to call at trial violate the self-incrimination clause?

Ruling: A rule requiring pretrial discovery of the names and addresses of a defendant's alibi witnesses does not constitute compelled self-incrimination in violation of the Fifth Amendment. As to the disclosure of witness statements, the Fifth Amendment privilege is personal to the defendant. Because the compelled disclosure is not a statement of the defendant, there is no Fifth Amendment violation.

Ralls v. United States, 52 F.3d 223 (1995)

Facts: A grand jury subpoenaed Ralls, a criminal defense attorney, seeking to obtain information from Ralls about a person who paid the fees for Ralls's client. In particular, the grand jury sought the person's name, the amount of money paid, the method of payment, the existence of any retainer agreement, and the substance of any conversations Ralls had with the fee-payer. Ralls invoked the attorney–client privilege, moved to quash the subpoena, and refused to disclose the information. In support of the claim of privilege, Ralls submitted a sealed affidavit for in camera review. The district court ordered Ralls to testify regarding the fee-payer's identity and the fee arrangements, but concluded that all conversations between Ralls and the fee-payer were privileged.

Issue: Does the attorney–client privilege protect against disclosure of information about fee payers and fee arrangements?

Rule: Generally, the attorney–client privilege does not protect the disclosure of either the identity of the fee-payer or the fee arrangement because the privilege applies only to confidential professional communications, and the payment of a fee is usually incidental to the attorney–client relationship. However, the privilege may be invoked when disclosure of the fee-payer or client identity and the fee information would infringe on a privileged communication. The test to be applied is whether the fee-payer's identity and fee arrangements are so intertwined with confidential communications that revealing either the identity or the arrangements would be tantamount to revealing a privileged communication.

In re Sealed Case, 737 F.2d 94 (1984)

Facts: Attorney formerly served as sole in-house counsel to corporation. A grand jury subpoenaed Attorney and requested him to testify, in a bid-rigging investigation, about matters that the corporation viewed as privileged. The company instructed Attorney to raise the attorney–client privilege.
Issue: When, if ever, does the attorney–client privilege apply to communications made by the attorney to the client?
Rule: Attorney–client privilege generally protects only communications made by a client to his or her lawyer. However, when an attorney's communication to his or her client is based in part "upon a confidential communication from the client to the lawyer," the privilege extends to that communication as well.

Suburban Sew'n Sweep v. Swiss-Bernina, 91 F.R.D. 254 (N.D. Ill. 1981)

Facts: Suburban sued Swiss-Bernina alleging antitrust violations. During its investigation, Suburban searched a dumpster in the parking lot of an office building occupied by Swiss-Bernina. It found hundreds of relevant documents, including drafts of confidential letters from the president of Swiss-Bernina to a lawyer for the corporation.
Issue: Is the attorney–client privilege waived when adequate safeguards to disclosure are not utilized?
Rule: The relevant consideration here is the intent of the defendants to maintain the confidentiality of the documents as manifested in the precautions they took as the client has the duty to take all possible precautions to ensure confidentiality. Placing the documents in the garbage indicated a lack of concern about disclosure, which precludes application of the attorney–client privilege.

United States v. Montgomery, 384 F.3d 1050 (9th Cir. 2004)

Facts: Defendant and his spouse were charged with conspiracy and mail fraud. Wife discussed conspiracy with Defendant and expressed concerns in a letter to him. At Defendant's trial, Wife testified about her communications with Defendant and the government introduced the letter she wrote to him.

Issue: Can either spouse invoke the marital communications privilege?
Rule: Either spouse may assert the marital communications privilege to prevent testimony regarding communications that were privately made between the spouses.

United States v. Marashi, 913 F.2d 724 (9th Cir. 1990)

Facts: Marashi was charged with attempted tax evasion and willful subscription to a false tax return. Marashi and his ex-wife, Smith, had divorced after Smith learned that Marashi was having an affair with his secretary. Smith contacted the IRS and gave detailed statements as to how, during their marriage, Marashi had enlisted her aid in evading federal income taxes. At trial, Marashi moved to suppress Smith's testimony on the basis of the marital communications privilege. The district court denied the motion.
Issue: Does the marital communications privilege apply to statements made in furtherance of joint criminal activity?
Rule: The marital communications privilege does not apply to private communications having to do with present or future crimes in which both spouses are participants. This exception applies even if both spouses are not charged with criminal activity.

Menendez v. Superior Court of Los Angeles County, 834 P.2d 786 (Cal. 1992)

Facts: The parents of Erik and Lyle Menendez were killed at home. The police obtained a search warrant for the office of the Menendez brothers' psychotherapist, Dr. Oziel, and seized audiotape recordings and notes of meetings. Oziel and the Menendez brothers filed a motion to claim the psychotherapist–patient privilege and prevent disclosure of the audiotapes. The government argued that the dangerous-patient exception applied to the privilege claim.
Issue: When does the dangerous-patient exception to the psychotherapist–patient privilege apply?
Rule: The dangerous-patient exception to the psychotherapist–patient privilege applies if there is reasonable cause for the psychotherapist to believe that the patient is dangerous to either the psychotherapist or to others and that disclosure is necessary. In this situation, confidential communications can be disclosed.

Swidler & Berlin v. United States, 524 U.S. 399 (1998)

Facts: Foster, the Deputy White House Counsel, met with Hamilton, an attorney at Swidler & Berlin, to seek legal representation concerning possible investigations of firings from the White House Travel Office. During the meeting, Hamilton took three pages of notes. Several days later, Foster committed suicide. A federal grand jury issued a subpoena for Hamilton's notes of his meeting with Foster. Petitioners filed a motion to quash, arguing that the notes were protected by the attorney–client privilege.

Issue: To what extent does the attorney–client privilege survive the death of the client?

Rule (Rehnquist): The attorney–client privilege survives the death of the client. Knowing that communications will remain confidential even after death encourages the client to communicate fully and honestly with counsel. Posthumous disclosure may be as feared as disclosure during the client's lifetime.

In re Von Bulow, 828 F.2d 94 (2d Cir. 1987)

Facts: Von Bulow had been tried and acquitted of murdering his wife. Afterward, his attorney, Alan Dershowitz, published a book called *Reversal of Fortune — Inside the Von Bulow Case*. Mrs. Von Bulow's children then sued Von Bulow, alleging common law assault, negligence, fraud, and RICO violations. The children moved to compel discovery of certain discussions between Von Bulow and his attorneys, arguing that publication of the book constituted a waiver of the attorney–client privilege.

Issue: When does the extrajudicial disclosure of attorney–client communications waive the attorney–client privilege?

Rule: Attorney–client privilege belongs solely to the client and may only be waived by him. However, a client may impliedly waive the privilege or consent to disclosure. Additionally, an attorney may in certain circumstances possess an "implied authority" to waive the privilege on behalf of his client. It is the client's responsibility to insure continued confidentiality of his communications. The extrajudicial disclosure of an attorney–client communication does not waive the privilege as to the undisclosed portions of the communication.

In re Grand Jury, 103 F.3d 1140 (3d Cir. 1997)

Facts: Three appeals presenting the same issue were consolidated into one hearing. In all three, a son or daughter of the target of a grand jury investigation had been subpoenaed to testify against his or her parent.

Issue: Should federal courts recognize a parent–child testimonial privilege?

Rule: A privilege should be recognized only where it would be indispensable to the survival of a relationship that society deems should be fostered. The fact that the majority of states have chosen not to create a parent–child privilege supports the view that "reason and experience" dictate that federal courts should refuse to recognize the privilege. Confidentiality is not essential to a successful parent–child relationship, and it's not clear whether children would be more likely to discuss private matters with their parents if a parent–child privilege were recognized than if one were not. Furthermore, any injury to the parent–child relationship resulting from nonrecognition of a privilege would be insignificant.

United States v. Woodruff, 383 F. Supp. 696 (E.D. Pa. 1974)

Facts: Defendant, who was free on bail pending trial, did not appear for trial. The government requested that the court ask defense counsel whether he had advised Defendant of the time and place of the trial and whether Defendant responded and acknowledged that he understood the time and place of the trial.

Issue: Does the disclosure of communications concerning the time, date, and place of trial violate the attorney–client privilege?

Rule: The transmission from the attorney to the defendant of the fact of the date and time of trial is not privileged. Communications between counsel and defendant as to the trial date do not involve the subject matter of the defendant's legal problem, and the facts involved in the communication were obtained by the attorney from a source other than his client.

City and County of San Francisco v. Superior Court, 231 P.2d 26 (Cal. 1951)

Facts: Hession sued San Francisco and the Western Pacific Railroad. At the request of Hession's attorneys, Dr. Catton gave Hession two neurological and psychiatric examinations. In his deposition, Dr. Catton testified there was no prelitigation physician–patient relationship, that the only purpose of the examination was to aid Hession's attorneys in the preparation of the lawsuit, and that he was the agent of the attorneys. He refused to answer questions about Hession's condition on the grounds that the information was privileged.

Issue: May a person who acts as an intermediary between an attorney and a client invoke the attorney–client privilege?

Rule: A person who is an intermediate agent for communication between a client and an attorney may invoke the attorney–client privilege. The same policies aimed at promoting full disclosure between clients and attorneys apply where there is an intermediate agent.

Prink v. Rockefeller Center Inc., 398 N.E.2d 517 (N.Y. 1979)

Facts: Surviving spouse brought a wrongful death action against the defendant, alleging that her husband fell from an office window because he was forced to kneel on his desk to open a jammed window. The defendant argued that decedent had committed suicide. Decedent had been seeing a psychiatrist. The defendant sought to introduce testimony from the psychiatrist.

Issue: Does the psychotherapist–patient privilege prevent disclosure in a wrongful death action?

Rule: The physician–patient privilege is not terminated by death alone. The privilege applies unless it is waived. The circumstances of decedent's death put his mental condition in issue because they are consistent with both accidental death and suicide. Because the decedent's mental condition was put at issue, the psychotherapist–patient privilege must be deemed to be waived.

United States v. Reynolds, 345 U.S. 1 (1953)

Facts: The widows of three civilian bystanders killed in the crash of a B-29 aircraft sued under the Federal Tort Claims Act. In the pretrial stages, Plaintiffs moved under Fed. R. Civ. P. 34 for production of the Air Force's official accident investigation report and the statements of the three surviving crew members in connection with the official investigation. The government moved to quash the motion, claiming these matters were classified and therefore privileged.

Issue: Is the U.S. Government required to produce classified information, based on a showing of need for discovery by the adverse party?

Rule (Vinson): A privilege may exist when the court finds, based on all the circumstances of the case, that there is a reasonable danger that compulsion of the evidence will expose military matters that, in the interest of national security, should not be divulged.

United States v. Nixon, 418 U.S. 683 (1974)

Facts: A grand jury returned an indictment charging seven named individuals with various offenses, including conspiracy to defraud the United States and to obstruct justice. The grand jury named the President as an unindicted co-conspirator. A subpoena duces tecum was issued to the President, which required the production of certain tapes and other writings pertaining to specific meetings between the President and others. The President's counsel responded with a motion to quash the subpoena on the grounds of executive privilege.

Issue: Whether the President of the United States must honor a subpoena for documents relating to private presidential communications.

Rule (Burger): Absent a claim of a need to protect military, diplomatic, or sensitive national security secrets, there is no absolute, unqualified, presidential privilege of immunity from judicial process under all circumstances.

When the ground for asserting privilege as to subpoenaed materials sought for use in a criminal trial is based only on the generalized interest in confidentiality, it cannot prevail over the fundamental demands of due process of law in the fair administration of criminal justice.

United States v. Estes, 793 F.2d 465 (2d Cir. 1986)

Facts: Estes was convicted of testifying falsely before a grand jury concerning his involvement in a robbery. On appeal, he argued that the testimony of his former wife, Lydia, concerning confidential communications between them was introduced erroneously at trial.

Issue: Are statements about past crimes made to a spouse protected by the spousal privilege?

Rule: Although statements made in the course of an ongoing criminal enterprise are not protected by the spousal privilege, statements made regarding past crimes are privileged.

State v. Pratt, 398 A.2d 421 (Md. 1979)

Facts: Defendant, who shot and killed her husband, offered an insanity defense. At trial, each side presented psychiatric testimony. The government called, as a prosecution witness, a psychiatrist who had examined Defendant after her attorney retained him to aid in preparing the insanity plea.

Issue: Is the attorney–client privilege violated when a psychiatrist who was retained by defense counsel to examine his client in preparing an insanity defense is permitted to testify as a witness for the prosecution?

Rule: The scope of the attorney–client privilege includes those agents whose services are required by the attorney to properly prepare his client's case. A client does not waive this privilege by claiming an insanity defense.

Henke v. Iowa Home Mutual Casualty Co., 87 N.W.2d (Iowa 1958)

Facts: Two suits were brought against Henke, the insured. The insurer, Iowa Home, failed to settle the cases and judgment was rendered against Henke in an amount that greatly exceeded the limits of his policy. Henke sued Iowa Home for bad faith and negligence and requested that Iowa Home produce all communications concerning the two previously tried cases. Iowa Home refused to comply, claiming the communications were privileged. The trial court ruled that because the communications in question had been made to a law firm that had represented both Henke and Iowa Home in the earlier actions, no privilege existed.

Issue: Are communications between joint clients and their attorney privileged in a later action between those clients and their representatives?

Rule: When two or more parties consult an attorney for their mutual benefit, the testimony as to the communications between the parties or the attorney as to that transaction is not privileged in a later action between such parties or their representatives.

In re Sealed Case, 107 F.3d 46 (D.C. Cir. 1997)

Facts: In connection with a grand jury investigation of violations of federal election laws, the government sued to compel the production of two documents from a corporation whose vice president allegedly used corporate funds to reimburse donors who contributed to a candidate. The court held that the crime/fraud exception applied to the documents and ordered the vice president to testify at the grand jury proceeding.

Issue: When does the crime/fraud exception to the attorney–client privilege apply?

Rule: For the crime/fraud exception to apply, two conditions must be met: (1) the client must have made or received the otherwise privileged communication with the intent to further an unlawful or fraudulent act, and (2) the client must have carried out the crime or fraud.

TABLE OF CASES

217